T0306018

Managing Customer Value

Second Edition

One Step at a Time

Managing
Customer
Value Second Edition

One Step at a Time

Dilip Soman
University of Toronto, Canada

Sara N-Marandi
Google

World Scientific

JERSEY · LONDON · SINGAPORE · BEIJING · SHANGHAI · HONG KONG · TAIPEI · CHENNAI · TOKYO

Published by

World Scientific Publishing Co. Pte. Ltd.

5 Toh Tuck Link, Singapore 596224

USA office: 27 Warren Street, Suite 401-402, Hackensack, NJ 07601

UK office: 57 Shelton Street, Covent Garden, London WC2H 9HE

Library of Congress Cataloging-in-Publication Data
Names: Soman, Dilip, author. | N-Marandi, Sara, author.
Title: Managing customer value : one step at a time / Dilip Soman,
    University of Toronto, Canada, Sara N-Marandi, Google.
Description: Second edition. | New Jersey : World Scientific, [2022] |
    Includes bibliographical references and index.
Identifiers: LCCN 2021062816 | ISBN 9789811240799 (hardcover) |
    ISBN 9789811247408 (ebook) | ISBN 9789811247415 (ebook other)
Subjects: LCSH: Customer relations--Management. | Marketing--Management. |
    Customer loyalty.
Classification: LCC HF5415.5 .S67 2022 | DDC 658.8/12--dc23/eng/20220111
LC record available at https://lccn.loc.gov/2021062816

British Library Cataloguing-in-Publication Data
A catalogue record for this book is available from the British Library.

For any available supplementary material, please visit
https://www.worldscientific.com/worldscibooks/10.1142/12382#t=suppl

Desk Editors: Balasubramanian Shanmugam/Pui Yee Lum

Typeset by Stallion Press
Email: enquiries@stallionpress.com

Printed in Singapore

DS: To Meera, Neel, and Teesta
SN: To Ian

Preface

How do you take individuals that have never interacted with your organization and work on them till they eventually become your best possible stakeholders, customers, or advocates? How do you decide how much to spend on various marketing interventions? How do you think about the pricing decision with a view to optimizing the value of your customers as an asset? Where do you start, what tools do you use, what heuristics are helpful in making these decisions? How do things change if, rather than being a for-profit organization, you are not-for-profit or welfare organization? This book attempts to answer questions such as these. The one-sentence summary, though, is simple — Hold the individuals hands and walk them up a value ladder, one step at a time.

This is the second edition of the *Managing Customer Value* book. The first edition was written at a time which was dramatically different from the one we live in today — the first iPhone had only recently been released then, the sharing economy did not exist, tablet computers were non-existent, and newspapers and magazines were still the primary source of news. While much has changed in the world around us, and technology, connectivity, and the ability to process vast amounts of data have given us new tools and new capabilities, the basics of how an organization should deal with their various stakeholders has remained the same. In particular, not only should the organization seek to create value for its stakeholders (be the customers, consumers, or other external agents, like donors or supporters), but they should also try and develop stakeholders who are valuable to the organization.

The past few years since the first edition of this book has also seen advances in academic disciplines that give us better insight into how to add value to customers. First, we have seen the emergence of a discipline popularly called behavioral economics, or more generally behavioral science. This discipline borrows from tools in cognitive psychology, social psychology, economics, and judgment and decision-making research to help us understand what factors drive actors in a marketplace (organizations and customers) to make decisions, and how those decisions can be influenced. Likewise, we now have the ability to analyze data and make predictions by using machine learning techniques. As a recent book by three University of Toronto professors argues, machines can make incredibly better predictions than humans can. As a result, machine learning has the potential to revolutionize how we think about the propensity with which stakeholders may make decisions — Be they decisions to make purchases, upgrade to higher-quality products, create positive word of mouth, or to increase the volume of engagement with the organization. The second edition of the *Managing Customer Value* book dives into both these new sciences in order to help us amplify how we can create and manage customer value. It has two completely new chapters (one on behavior change, and another on digital and social marketing), extensively rewritten materials in a few other chapters, as well as a new final chapter that brings together a number of tools, templates, and flowcharts as a practitioners guide.

This book had its roots over twenty years ago when one of us (Soman) was asked to develop a new course in marketing to be taught to executive and EMBA students. These students had already taken classes on the principles of marketing, market research, branding, and sales and distribution. As Soman pondered about what he would cover, he went back to his own experiences as a student and as a sales and advertising executive. During this period, he had read a lot of books, and in particular books about marketing and customer-facing activities of the organization.

In our discussions about these classics, we realize that three things about these books bothered us. First, while we love the content and examples presented in them, we felt that the materials did a better job of helping the manager understand what worked, but only in hindsight. There was a lot of discussion on value, but there was very little by way of prescriptive advice and frameworks that guided the manager on how to go about creating and managing value. Second, most of the writings claimed that marketing is customer focused. However, all of the popular frameworks in marketing are based on what marketers do and not on what they want customers to do. In particular, the consequences of marketers' actions on customer behaviors are not studied as deeply as we would like. For instance, the classic 4P framework organizes and marketing along functional lines. What about organizing along customer outcome lines? For instance, why do we not have different sets of activities that increase acquisition versus increase loyalty? Or, activities that increase purchasing versus increase advocacy? Third, we would have loved to see marketing materials that have more rigor. Rigor does not necessarily mean horribly complicated equations to express ideas that could be written more elegantly, but rigor does call for more systematic frameworks for thinking through customer-related situations.

As we were debating these issues, we were asked a rather unusual question; "Why do marketers get very little respect in organizations?" Without blinking, one of us responded, "Because they don't do a very good job at marketing themselves within the organization." That is indeed the impression we had formed in our own interactions. As a group, people in marketing did not speak the language of finance and accounting. They made their own trade seem excessively complicated, and they were very secretive about the processes that they used to arrive at conclusions. In sum, the general belief was that good marketing is an art, and while we don't disagree, we also believe that there is a great deal of science to it.

Between the two of us, we have accumulated over two decades of teaching, and over two decades as consultants, executives in consumer packaged goods, advertising, and in the tech sector. This book covers all of the materials that we have developed in our own work over the years. Since the first edition of this book has been used extensively by students in many universities and departments, we also have received a lot of feedback and suggestions from various people for whom we are extremely grateful.

We would like to thank all of our students, our classmates, and our colleagues for feedback and suggestions. In particular, a number of colleagues and students pushed our thinking through intriguing yet challenging conversations, questions, and collaborations. These include Charles Brian-Boys, Honnus Chung, Delaine Hampton, Joy Lee, Jocelyn Phi, Craig Smith, Rajesh Subramaniam, Malcolm Sullivan, Avi Goldfarb, Spike Lee, Lisa Brenneman, and Rory Sutherland. In addition, the materials in this book draw on extensive research done both by others (cited appropriately) and by us, with the able assistance of Vivian Lam, Stewart Lawrence, Kim Ly, Margie Moscow, Minah Kim, Liz Kang, Melanie Kim, and Bing Feng. Thanks are also due to the EMBA and MBA office teams at the University of Toronto's Rotman School of Management and at the Hong Kong University of Science and Technology, as well as to Bell Canada's support of the first edition of this book through its Bell University Laboratories R&D Program at the University of Toronto. Soman also thanks the Social Sciences and Humanities Research Council of Canada for supporting a lot of the research that has found its way into many chapters of this book, and for funding the Behaviourally Informed Organizations Partnership that supported this book project.

We are also grateful to Angela Li and Cindy Luo who served as project managers for the second edition. Their organization and management skills were invaluable in keeping us on track and on getting the revised manuscript done.

Whether they are from a for-profit or a not-for-profit, from business or other organizations, or from any part of the globe and from any sector, we hope that the reader finds value in the frameworks proposed here as they go about creating value for their own customers and organizations.

Dilip Soman
Toronto
Sara N-Marandi
San Francisco

About the Authors

Dilip Soman is a Canada Research Chair in Behavioural Science and Economics at the Rotman School of Management, University of Toronto, and a professor of marketing. He has degrees in behavioral science, marketing, and engineering, and is interested in the applications of behavioral science to business, welfare, and policy. He is the co-author of *Managing Customer Value: One Stage at a Time* (2008), author of *The Last Mile* (2015), and co-editor of *The Behaviorally Informed Organization* (2021) and *Behavioral Science in the Wild* (in press). He has taught in the U.S.A, Hong Kong, and Canada, and has worked with several corporations, governments, and start-ups. His non-academic interests include procrastination, cricket, travel, and taking weekends seriously.

Sara N-Marandi is a Product Lead on Android Privacy with over nine years of experience at Google working alongside product and sales leaders in Canada and the United States. She earned her Masters of Business Administration from the Rotman School of Management at the University of Toronto and is the co-author of *Managing Customer Value: One Stage at a Time.* Prior to Google, she led corporate strategy for multi-million dollar brands across various industries including media, government, pharmaceutical, airline, and many others.

Contents

PART 1

Chapter 1

Managing Customer Value

> How do you take individuals who have never done business with your organization and develop them until some of them eventually become your highest quality customers?

This is the question that this book sets off to address. We do so by proposing a framework that includes both the value that the organization creates for a customer and the value of a customer to the organization. Our framework is prescriptive — it gives the reader specific guidelines on how to develop their customers. By developing a customer, we mean the act of acquiring a customer for the first purchase, and over time gradually adding to the customer's basket of products that not only create value for the customer, but also create profitable customers for the organization. The framework is intuitive yet rigorous. It uses a language familiar to most readers, but is also backed up with the language of mathematics and statistics. The framework suggests that the discipline of creating value is based on customer activities, and not on organization activities. We organize our discussion (and indeed call upon organizations to organize themselves) along the activities that we would like customers to engage in — for example, the activity of visiting a website or a store, converting a visit to a purchase, or increasing loyalty rates.

The essence of our framework can be summarized as follows:

(1) Customers progress from being a prospect to a highly valued customer in a stepwise fashion, akin to climbing a ladder one step at a time. Each rung (step) in the ladder is associated with a particular set of customer behaviors.

(2) The organization can estimate the dollar value of their customers at each step (e.g., what is a customer at a given step worth to the organization) of the ladder, as well as the costs involved in moving customers up by a step.

(3) The organization aims to move those customers up the ladder for whom the extra value gained from the move is greater than the cost to move the customer. If the cost exceeds the gains in value, the customer is likely not worth pursuing.

(4) The organization can use a number of different interventions (marketing activities) to move people up by a step.[1] These might include incentives (discounts, promotions, and rewards), information and persuasion (advertising, highlighting benefits), or choice architecture (framing and presenting information differently, changing contexts to steer choice).

(5) The goal of managing customer value (MCV) is twofold — to create value to the customer (through superior products and services) and to create valuable customers for the organization (through appropriate customer selection and development).

1.1 A Changing Landscape

The first draft of the first edition of this book was written in 2008. Much has changed in the world since then. Many of the products, technologies, and services that we take for granted today did not exist back then. The iPhone had only recently been introduced, and humankind had yet to experience the iPad or other tablet computers. Driverless cars were still a thing of the future, as were many

---

[1] Soman, D. (2015). *The Last Mile: Creating Social and Economic Value from Behavioral Insights.* Toronto, Canada: University of Toronto Press.

other products and services that dominate our perceptual landscape today. The gig economy had not yet been developed — Uber came online after our book was published, Airbnb came later, as did restaurant delivery services like DoorDash and Uber Eats.[2] Internet penetration has more than doubled and retail e-commerce sales have increased fivefold. Smartphone penetration has increased more than threefold, content consumption on mobile devices has increased 11-fold, while the consumption of television has marginally decreased.[3] Back then, a cloud was only a phenomenon of nature; a tablet primarily a carrier of medication; the term "smart" was rarely used to describe phones, homes, and domestic appliances. Microblogging was nowhere as widespread and diverse as it is today; music artists still recorded albums; and while personal assistants might have been named Siri or Alexa, they were almost always human.

Among the many changes that we outlined in the earlier paragraph, a few stand out as changes that will have impact on the way businesses interact with their customers. The first significant change has to do with the increasing volumes of data that flow through mobile devices, and the vastly large reach of Wi-Fi networks all over the world. This, along with the development of mobile smartphone technology has meant that consumers are more interconnected to each other than ever before. Furthermore, customers are much more likely to be able to rely on each other to help them make choices and decisions, and their choices and experiences are easily shared and visible to others.

A second development relates to advances in the field of data science and machine learning. Given that the costs of recording, storing, organizing, and analyzing data have plummeted in the recent past, companies now have the resources to use data to make

[2]Stanford, J. (2017). The Resurgence of Gig Work: Historical and Theoretical Perspectives. *The Economic and Labour Relations Review, 28*(3), 382–401. doi:10.1177/1035304617724303.
[3]Internet Trends. (2019). *BOND*. Retrieved April 21, 2021, from https://www.bondcap.com/report/itr19/.

more accurate predictions.[4] This capability along with the ability to reach customers in real time and in specific geographies has created massive opportunities for just-in-time advertising, sales promotions, and product-related marketing opportunities. These dual trends of greater interconnectedness and lower costs of data collection, storage and analysis have resulted in the growth of new business models. For instance, the gig economy (and peer-to-peer platforms more generally) arises from the ability of organizations to match demand and supply in certain areas in real time and as a function of geography. It has also created an important role for an omnichannel approach. Thanks to technological advances, consumers can seamlessly move between the internet, a mobile channel (or app), a telephone call center, and an in-person service provider and receive the same exact experience.

A third development is related to improvements in payment technology and the ease of making payments, more generally. Unencumbered by the need to carry cash or write cheques, the individual customer can make, schedule, and manage payments easily. This has had important implications for spending, customer experience, and for the financial services industry more generally.

The greater interconnectedness has also created new units of analysis for marketers. We have seen a shift away from the customer as an individual or the customer as a family, toward the customer as a member of a larger peer group or social network. Influencers are now easier to identify and harness, and they play an increasingly significant role in the marketing landscape.

Yet, despite all of these changes in the landscape, the fundamental goals of organizations remain unchanged. Organizations are still in the business of creating value for the customers, and conversely, creating a portfolio of valuable customers for the organization. Our capabilities for how to achieve this are different today than when the first edition of this book was written, but the fundamentals

---

[4]Agrawal, A., Gans, J., & Goldfarb, A. (2018). *Prediction Machines: The Simple Economics of Artificial Intelligence.* Boston, MA: Harvard Business Review Press.

underlying the framework remain unchanged. The easy access to data creates new opportunities to create value through customized solutions, but also places a greater responsibility on organizations to respect the privacy of their customers and to use the new tools ethically and respectfully.

1.2 This Book Is Not about "Marketing"

This is not the first book to address this important question of how to create and manage value over the life of a customer, nor will it be the last. Indeed, the field of marketing ranging from the early work of Theodore Levitt and Philip Kotler to the more modern concepts of customer relationship management and one-to-one marketing addresses similar questions, albeit from different perspectives.[5] Marketing identifies four tools in the arsenal of the organization — its products, prices, promotion, and places of distribution (the 4P's of marketing) — and develops a framework for how each could be used to enhance the organization's market performance. It calls for an analysis of the 3C's — the company, customers, and competitors — to support the 4P's in developing strategies and tactics to go to market with products and services.

This book is not about the 3C's and the 4P's. We are by no means challenging or disagreeing with the traditional approach. Instead, we are proposing an orthogonal approach to the 4P's of marketing. Our aim is not to provide an answer to the question, "What can marketers do?" Rather, we aim to answer the complementary question, "What do we want our customer to do?" Developing our framework on the building blocks of customer behaviors, actions, and

---

[5]Levitt, T. (1960). *Marketing Myopia*. Cambridge, MA: Harvard Business Review Press; Kotler, P. (2002). *Marketing Management*. Hoboken, NJ: Prentice Hall; Peppers, D. & Rogers, M. (2004). *Managing Customer Relationships*. Hoboken, NJ: John Wiley & Sons; Buttle, F. (2008). *Customer Relationship Management*. Burlington, MA: Butterworth-Heinemann.

associated outcomes allows us to prescribe approaches that are customized and hence more cost effective.

In fact, this is not a book about marketing — as the term is used by marketing departments in organizations all over the world — at all. We make a distinction between *marketing as a discipline* and *marketing as a department*, and contend that marketing department activities only occupy a small portion of the spectrum of activities that fall under the umbrella of MCV. Our framework will embrace all activities that are involved in the creation or management of customer value — these might include product design and testing, behavioral change interventions, research, communications, logistics and distribution, sales, pricing, and after-sales service. Going forward we will refer to this framework as MCV.

> **Insight Box 1.1**
>
> **MCV Insight**
> We make a distinction between *marketing as a discipline* and *marketing as a department*. A marketing department's activities only occupy a small portion of the spectrum of activities that fall under the umbrella of MCV.

The fundamental idea underlying our approach is that it is highly unlikely to succeed with a strategy that asks a customer to make significant changes in behavior. It is unreasonable to expect an individual that has never exercised to now have a well-structured exercise regimen overnight; or for a tourist who has never been on a cruise ship to go on a two-week cruise across the Pacific Ocean. Similarly, it is unreasonable to expect a potential customer who has never purchased from an organization to become their best customer overnight. Instead, a better approach is to break down the transition into a number of discrete steps.

Imagine a ladder that starts at the floor (next to a prospective customer) and ends at a height (a highly valuable customer). Each step in the ladder might represent an incremental and gradual increase in customer activity, resulting in both greater value to the customer and to the organization (Figure 1.1). The response to the

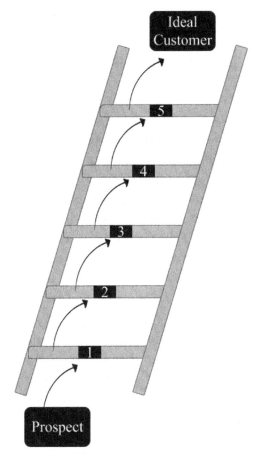

Figure 1.1 The value ladder.

question of how to create the best customer from a prospect is simple — hold their hand and walk them up the ladder, one step at a time, till the time that their upward movement adds value.

The process of MCV entails the following steps:

(1) Understand the metrics of success (often referred to as KPI's; key performance indicators) that the organization is trying to maximize. What is at the top of the ladder? Is the organization in the business of maximizing short-term revenue or long-term

value? Do they want to maximize market share or to maximize profits?

(2) Decompose these metrics into smaller, manageable metrics that the organization could tackle independently. For instance, the revenue earned from a customer in a store could be decomposed into three distinct components, each of which can become activities that the organization should try to optimize. The first metric is traffic, the number of people who visit a store or its website. The second metric is conversion rate, the percent of those visiting who then buy something. And the third metric is an increase in basket size — the total number of dollars spent in a given occasion. The organization can now be very specific about marketing interventions — discounts, advertising, sampling, new products, absolutely anything from the panoply of the 4P arsenal — they use to manage each of these metrics separately.

(3) Construct the value ladder. Can the organization identify a number of discrete behavioral and attitudinal stages in the purchase decision — snapshots of customer behavior as they make decisions to visit a website, to purchase a product, or to make a repeat purchase? We suggest that organizations could, and should, document and formalize these steps in a value ladder.

(4) Model the value as a function of each stage. Once the ladder has been constructed, the organization could use various techniques discussed in this book to estimate the value of the customer at each stage. Note that we do not necessarily restrict ourselves to long-term lifetime value as the underlying metric of success; the organization could just as easily use revenue or profit depending on what its objective is. Attaching a value to each stage will allow the organization to estimate the benefit of moving each customer from his or her current stage to the next one. Once this is done, the organization can use the tools discussed in our framework to prioritize those customers on whom

to focus attention on and to determine how much to spend on each marketing intervention.

(5) Develop strategies, tactics, and execution plans. The organization is now in a position to develop strategies and tactics to manage customer value and to develop plans to execute these strategies by harnessing customer intelligence (insights gained about customers through data-driven marketing systems), pricing interventions, and loyalty programs.

This process is summarized in Figure 1.2.

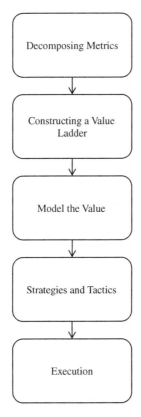

Figure 1.2 The Process of Managing Customer Value (MCV).

Why do we advocate yet another process framework when there is clearly no shortage of books in marketing? We believe that our approach is different in the following specific ways.

First, a lot of the work in marketing has talked about what organizations should do to add value for the customer. Recommendations include "satisfy and delight," "the customer is always right," and "live and die by the customer." We do not disagree. But we also posit that adding value to customers is worth it if and only if the customer will eventually add value to you, the organization. Managing this tension between creating value for the customer and growing value from the customer is central to our approach.

Second, because we propose an approach in which we decompose customer activity into discrete stages, we have the ability to direct marketing interventions that are very *specific* — that is, are designed to accomplish a very specific outcome, to move the customer to the next step of the ladder and do no more — and very *directed* — that is, they can be delivered only to those customers whose behaviors you would like to change and to no one else. The result is an efficiency in the use of marketing dollars!

Third, we develop a series of simple mathematical models to complement the framework. The models are intuitively very simple and we encourage the reader to develop a mastery of the intuition and not necessarily of the computational details. These models help the manager answer basic questions for which they have had little analytical support in the past: How much should I spend in trying to acquire a new customer of given characteristics? Which is more effective given my present objectives — a sales promotion or an in-store display? What is the value of increasing the life of a customer from three years to six years? What is the value of a 5% increase in repeat purchasing or loyalty rates?

Fourth, our view of the marketing function is integrative. In particular, we make a distinction between the marketing department (comprising people whose business cards feature the word "marketing") and the "customer value" function (comprising all individuals that directly or indirectly are responsible for value creation and value management, presumably a vast majority at most organizations). In the past, writers have looked at marketing as the customer-facing part of an organization. In that sense, the function has been trivialized, often unfairly so, as a mere conduit between the organization's strategic initiatives and its customers. Our integrative view suggests that it does not make sense to think about customers merely as an adjunct to strategy, finance, accounting, or human resource issues. So, while the focus of our book remains on customer activity, we work backwards to integrate the whole organization and to energize it toward actively managing and harnessing the value that arises from the customer.

While the MCV framework differs from existing process frameworks, the idea that people are different from each other, and that people in some groups might behave differently from people in other groups is common. An often-used concept in traditional marketing — segmentation — is central to our framework. In the language of our value ladder, segmentation shows up in three different ways:

Insight Box 1.2

MCV Insight

The MCV approach emphasizes both the value to the customer and the value of the customer. It is concerned not just with developing delighted customers, but also developing delightful (high-quality) customers.

---

(1) Segmentation by current status: At any given point in time, the aggregate customer base of a given organization will be dispersed across different steps of the ladder. Some customers will be *entry level* (say, at the lower levels of the ladder), others might be *loyal* (middle levels), yet others might be *extremely loyal with large spends* (high levels).

(2) Segmentation by opportunities for growth: Imagine a website or an app for whom revenue is a product of the number of unique visits and dollars spent per visit. Some customers might be visiting frequently but not spending much per visit, while others might be infrequent visitors yet spend a lot per visit. These represent two different segments because the *opportunity for growing* their revenues is different across the two. In the language of the ladder, this might mean that the *sequence of rungs* in the ladder might be different for the two groups. One group starts with increasing frequency and then increasing spends, while the other starts with increasing spends per visit and then increasing frequency.

(3) Segmentation by optimal location on ladder: The costs involved in moving customers from one step of the ladder to another might vary across customers. As a result, it might make sense (from a value perspective) to move some customers up and not others. More generally, the *optimal location* for different segments of customers on the ladder might be different.

In the past, segmentation was often done by using observable data (demographics or firmographics) that were expected to correlate with behaviors. Today, with greater access to data on actual behaviors and the speed with which these data can be analyzed, there is a greater reliance on real-time behavioral segmentation. In later chapters, we will highlight behavioral segmentation with examples.

One salient objective for many organizations is to maximize market share by increasing the number of customers who purchase the product. Our discussion on segmentation would suggest that a fixation on growing the total number of customers could be fraught with dangers, especially if there is insufficient attention paid to differences in customer quality. Admittedly, there is some value to be gained from increasing your customer base. It could signal quality and also take business away from competitors. However, it could come at a cost. For instance, imagine a simple world in which our analysis results in two segments — Segment H in which the optimal step is at the very top of the ladder (and hence each customer is worth a lot to the organization) and Segment L where the optimal step is at the bottom and each customer is not worth. In this world, Firm X that has 1,000 customers might prima facie appear to do better than Firm Y that only has 500 customers. Yet, if all of Firm X's customers were from Segment L and all of Y's from Segment H, then the organization with fewer customers might actually be more profitable.

1.3 Components of the MCV Framework

Any business can successfully model itself by using the metaphor of an online or physical retailer — where revenue is the product of traffic, conversion rates, basket size, and the number of occasions on which shopping is done (loyalty or repeat purchases). Figure 1.3 illustrates this decomposition and Table 1.1 applies the metaphor to a number of other industries.

Breaking down an aggregate metric like revenue into its constituent components has both a diagnostic as well as a management benefit. In one example, researchers found that the rank of products displayed in search advertising or in top 10 lists (e.g., by online retailers like amazon.com) influences revenues.[6] In particular, the higher a product is in the list, the greater is the revenue from that product. However, a more nuanced analysis showed that while rank influenced the likelihood that web visitors clicked on the relevant

---

[6] Ursu, R. (2018). The Power of Rankings: Quantifying the Effect of Rankings on Online Consumer Search and Purchase Decisions. *Marketing Science, 37*(4), 530–552.

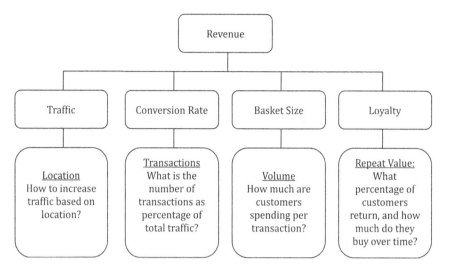

Figure 1.3 The decomposition of revenue.

link, it did not change the likelihood of purchase conditional on clicking. In other words, using the language of our retail metaphor, ranking of the product increased traffic via an increase in the number of clicks, but did not improve conversion rates. This decomposition allows a retailer to better understand why some design features of their website influence the aggregate revenue measure. It could furthermore also help the online retailer by identifying (and rectifying) deficiencies. In this case, the ranking had no effect on the conditional purchase of probability. This suggests that the retailer could think about additional interventions that might influence the likelihood that customers purchase after they have clicked through to a particular page.

More generally, decomposing an aggregate metric will allow a retailer to identify what components of their interventions are working and where there are deficiencies. This is helpful because prior research suggests that interventions that increase traffic are different from those that might influence conversion rates or basket size. It is also important to keep in mind that the specific interventions need to be customized to the target segment they have in

Table 1.1 Revenue models for different industries.

	Traffic	Conversion Rate	Basket Size	Loyalty
Rideshare services	Defined by: – Number of application installs – Acquisition of drivers	First trip booking rates	This is the total fare paid per trip, which is comprised of route-based pricing determined by a willingness-to-pay algorithm, gratuities, and ride upgrades. For example, the Uber premium lines (e.g., UberBLACK, UberSUV, and UberLUX) costs the rider more to ride in a luxury car	Achieved through providing convenience. For riders, this is gained through lower fares and wait times For drivers, this is gained through low barrier to entry. Additionally, loyalty is also promoted through points programs. For example, Uber promotes extensions to other product lines. Uber Eats users may use Uber Ride points
Customer packaged goods	Defined by selecting suppliers that can maximize customer visibility to the product – Large department stores versus convenience stores – Product positioning on shelves	Company's market share of a specific segment (e.g., shampoo)	Identified by the total number of products a given customer has purchased from the same company/brand. For example, shampoo, toothbrush, and deodorant from Proctor & Gamble	Achieved by providing incentives that minimize switching between brands

(Continued)

Table 1.1 (*Continued*)

	Traffic	Conversion Rate	Basket Size	Loyalty
Consulting	Defined by the total number **RFPs** (request for proposals) attempted by the firm	The ratio of total engagements and projects to the total number of **RFPs**	The ability for the firm to get involved in more than just one project pertaining to the same client	Achieved by providing quality consulting services and ensuring future business
Retail banking	Convenient branch locations and online presence to maximize visibility and traffic	The ratio of total number of clients (savings/ checking accounts, investments, etc.) to number of inquirers	Defined by added services such as credit cards, investments, and mortgages to the client's current account. The greater the basket size, the higher the switching costs	Achieved through providing superior services. As clients decide on other investment alternatives, they will remain loyal. Will also refer peers
Non-profit organization	Measured by overall rate of inquiry	The ratio of new members and contributors to the total number of inquiries	If a non-profit organization is promoting more than one cause, increasing basket size is the ability to commit members to all its causes (or more than just one)	Maintaining membership on a continuous basis. Achieving referral by encouraging current members to exert influence on their friends and families

mind. For example, the domain of physical retail, interventions used to build traffic might vary for a segment of customers without cars as compared to customers with cars. It is also worth noting that the decomposed metrics could (but do not always) represent sequential stages of value creation. For instance, traffic precedes conversion, which might in turn precede an increase in basket size and then repeat visits.

The second step in the MCV framework relates to the construction of a value ladder. Note that ladders could be constructed for different metrics and different units of analysis. For instance, if the organization is looking to convert a customer who is browsing on their website or in a store, the various stages of the ladder might include these stages — prospect (someone who is on your webpages), browser, somebody who has clicked through to a particular product, interested browser (somebody who has collected information about the product), add-on shopper (somebody who has considered additional products to add to their basket), a purchaser (someone who has completed a transaction), and a repeat purchaser (someone who has shopped on multiple distinct occasions). Alternately, a different business might construct a longer-term ladder for how to convert an entry-level customer into a high-value customer over time. For example, the ladder of a retail bank might start with a customer who has a basic bank account (checking and saving), then purchases additional loan products (credit cards or car loans), adds on larger lines of credit (mortgages), then opens investment accounts (retirement or personal investment), consolidates wealth into these accounts (withdrawing funds from other banks and depositing them here), and finally being an advocate for the bank and its services.

Ladders can be constructed through empirical observations, market research, or managerial judgment. Chapter 3 will provide a deeper dive into how ladders could be constructed. It is important that each step in the ladder should represent distinct observable stages that are different from the immediately preceding stage.

As long as each step is distinct, and as long as the organization has a clear understanding of what they could do to move the customer from one stage to the next, the value ladder will help the organization think about exactly how this can be done.

The next stage of the MCV sees the framework involves mathematical modeling to estimate the dollar value of each step on the value ladder. For the sake of exposition, imagine that the manager knew exactly what a customer that was on step one versus step two of the ladder in Figure 1.1 was worth in dollar terms. Imagine that they also know what the cost of the intervention to move the customer from step one to step two is. They can now make the assessment of whether it makes economic sense to move the customer in this direction. The heuristic is simple: if the marginal cost of moving the customer is lower than the marginal value of the customer, it makes sense to move the customer.

In Chapter 5, we will dive deep into the details of the mathematical formulation to compute the value of a customer. Here, we will start by outlining the basic building blocks of the framework that we will use in Chapter 5. The factors that determine the lifetime value of the customer (VOC) are displayed in Table 1.2.

The acquisition cost of obtaining a single customer is simply the cost of the marketing effort such as for direct in-store advertising, print and television media, direct mail, and sales staff commissions, spent to acquire a single customer. The *average contribution* of each customer is determined by the revenue-generating capabilities of that customer offset by the cost incurred in serving that customer. For a retailer, the contributed profits to its bottom line can be driven by the price per item sold adjusted for the various costs to serve that item (cost of purchase, labor, and other overhead costs). For a business to justify its existence, the average contribution of sales should generally be a positive figure. The *churn rate* is the rate at which a business loses an already acquired customer, and it varies across different businesses and industries. The churn rate is often higher for

Table 1.2 The building blocks of lifetime value.

Variables	Definition
1. Acquisition cost (AC)	The cost associated with initially acquiring the customer
2. Variable contribution (M)	(Revenue — Cost to serve)
3. Churn rate (g)	The rate at which the businesses lose customers
4. Expected return (i)	Will vary depending on the business

a retailer than for a financial institution. The rate at which customers leave a business will depend on factors such as the competitive environment, elasticity of demand for the product, and contract versus non-contract transactions. The *expected rate of return* is also unique to different companies and is based on the risk factors of that business.

Once the retailer has determined the above variables, it will then be able to estimate the value of its ideal customer by using discounted cash flow techniques to determine the present value of all future cash flows accruing from the customer. This approach allows the retailers to not only understand the components that determine the value of each customer but also appropriately make adjustments to the various factors as it sees fit. At Harrah's Entertainment, a casino that was struggling to compete in the intensely competitive Las Vegas market, executives began to make revisions to the different factors driving the value of the customer. Ultimately, by altering its offerings, introducing a loyalty program, and revising its pricing strategy, the company was able to maximize the value of its customers.[7] In later chapters, we investigate the implications of these four components on the predicted value of customers.

[7]Loveman, G. (2003). *Diamonds in the Data Mine.* Boston, MA: Harvard Business Review Press.

The fourth stage of the MCV framework relates to the organization's strategies and tactics to be aligned to deliver and manage value at various stages of the value chain. One example of a general strategy by an online retailer to maximize revenue might be captured by a statement such as, "We will revisit our customer service capabilities to ensure that we are offering the best possible service to our customers." Once the entire organization is aligned on the new strategy, management must identify specific tactics to achieve that strategy. These may include increasing investment in training sales associates, hiring more staff, or increasing sales incentives. The evaluation of the tactics will depend on the expected incremental value that can be achieved by implementing the tactic, as we determined in the previous step.

The final stage of the MCV framework is the execution of specific tactics. To set new customer service standards, the manager from our preceding paragraph will have to provide detailed guidelines to unit heads in achieving the new targets. Examples might include increasing staff by 5%, improving the app experience by adding two additional capabilities, signing new service-level agreements with vendors or shipping partners, or increasing incentives by 10%. Ultimately steps 5, 6, and 7 of the frameworks shown in Figure 1.2 must be aligned to help improve customer service, which will lead to an increase in customer experience, interest and trial, which will in turn lead to an increase in the conversion rate, finally achieving an increase in overall revenue.

It is important to note that both strategies and execution steps must be developed and carried out in conjunction with a broad array of departments within the organization. Just as launching a new product requires coordination across product, research, finance, operations, R&D, legal, design, sales, and marketing departments, so too does implementing the MCV framework. Imagine trying to convince the finance department to reallocate marketing budget from media to coupons without providing a context, or convincing the R&D department that a new product they have been working on will not serve a customer's needs without describing findings from customer observations. MCV should be the goal for the organization as a whole, not merely the marketing department.

1.4 What This All Means

The MCV framework provides the tools that are necessary for converting a potential customer into an ideal one. Through decomposition of the key success metric, decision-makers are able to diagnose the factors responsible for weighing down the overall metric. By linking the decomposed metrics to the steps in the ladder, organizations can isolate the customer behavior that is the direct cause of the revenue decline. Following the diagnosis, managers will know precisely how to advance a customer up the value chain through additional marketing efforts. By building the probability acquisition model, different marketing efforts can be easily quantified and therefore prioritized to maximize the expected value of each marketing effort. Ultimately, the MCV framework offers the most efficient use of scarce marketing resources in creating, acquiring, and retaining the ideal customer.

1.4.1 Guideline 1: What Does an Organization That Practices "MCV" Do? We Propose That it Does the Following

(1) The organization understands how to create value for its customers. It does so by identifying what behaviors are associated with their high-quality customers, and by building a ladder — a pathway — in which each step represents a distinct set of behaviors and outcomes.

(2) The organization understands how to create valuable customers — customers who add value to the organization. It does so with appropriate segmentation based on customer

quality, and by spending decisions that are guided by an analysis of marginal value and marginal cost. The organization wants to delight and surprise customers, but (a) only those that can be delighted profitably and (b) only by incurring an appropriate level of costs.

(3) The organization has the tools to measure and predict the dollar value of customers, or segments, and of marketing interventions. Advances in data science coupled with some of the value models we introduce in this book and the increasing instance of customer data make it increasingly likely that organizations can do this.

(4) The organization uses insights from the new disciplines of behavioral economics, machine learning, and data science in an ethical and respectful manner to better understand customer needs and behaviors, and hence to create value.

1.4.2 Guideline 2: This Framework is Applicable to All Kinds of Organizations, and Not Just to Firms That Are Looking to Maximize Profits!

At first blush, it might appear that the framework we propose applies only to for-profit businesses. Nothing is further from the truth! Even not-for-profits or governments need revenues to deliver on their mandates. The gain their revenues not from selling products, but through a wider range of sources such as grants and contributions, taxes, subsidies, or charitable donations. These organizations are not looking to make profits, but they are all in the business of behavioral change of various stakeholders, and as such they are definitely interested in achieving efficiencies in doing so. This allows them to expand the scope of their work with the limited resources they may have. As such, after accounting for the fact that different organizations will have different objectives and therefore a different definition of how to measure "value" of stakeholders, the concepts that we will cover in this book will apply to all organizations.

1.4.3 Guideline 3: Respect the Customer: Allowing Them to Make Choices and Ethics Are Central to MCV

As the world has changed over the past decade, it is now becoming easier to practice MCV. In particular, the quality and quantity of data continue to grow, competition is getting more intense, and the costs of

> **Insight Box 1.3**
>
> **MCV Insight**
> The MCV framework applies equally well to all kinds of organizations — businesses, not-for-profits, start-ups, and even government units.

collecting and analyzing additional data are rapidly declining. This creates the danger of organizations going too far! If the reader takes our framework merely as a mechanical list of things to be done, and forgets that customers are assets, we can foresee situations where overenthusiastic organizations create privacy concerns, ethical concerns, or feeling of being manipulated. Throughout the book, we will caution the reader at places where we feel that an imprudent and mechanical over-application of the tools and techniques can cause concerns.

1.4.4 Guideline 4: MCV ≠ Marketing

The "MCV" approach to marketing differs from the traditional approach in several important ways. First, the building blocks of MCV have to do with the behavior and activities of customers (the steps of the ladder) as opposed to activities of the organization (the 4 P's). Second, the unit of analysis in MCV is the customer — a true MCV-oriented organization might focus on customer managers or segment managers, while a marketing-oriented organization might

---
Insight Box 1.4

MCV Insight

With decreasing costs and increasing ease of using data and customer tracking comes the risk of overdoing it to gain short-term gains that can damage long-term value. We encourage managers to ensure that the foundations of their MCV efforts are built on the principles of customer choice and respect, ethics, and honesty.

---

focus on product managers. Third, a traditional adage in marketing is that the "customer is the king (sic)," a corresponding adage in MCV is that the customer is sometimes the king depending on their quality. Fourth, MCV is concerned to a greater degree than traditional marketing with both revenues and costs to serve customers.

More generally, an MCV-oriented organization sees customers as its assets, and thinks about portfolios of customers. Consequently, unlike traditional marketing which is often seen as a "going to market" facilitator, MCV is more deeply embedded in the operations of the organization.

A note on terminology: We recognize that many marketers have made distinctions between users (or consumers), customers (paying consumers), or funders (paying non-consumers). These distinctions have become even more nuanced in an era of digital- and platform-based markets. We will use the term "customer" throughout for simplicity of exposition, with the understanding that the term could refer to many different stakeholders. We also use the term "organization" rather than business or firm because the framework is applicable to all kinds and all sizes of organizations.

Looking ahead: This book is in three parts. The remaining three chapters in Part 1 explore each of the building blocks of this framework. In Chapter 2, we take a closer look at value — both the value (of the products and services) to the customer [VTC] and the value of the customer to the organization [VOC]. We will also start making distinctions between customers of varying quality. In Chapter 3, we will study the benefits and process of decomposing revenue, and learn the basics of constructing ladders. In Chapter 4, we will examine loyalty and repeat purchasing. The four chapters in Part 2 each tackle a specific tool or technique that organizations need to move people up a value ladder. In particular, Chapter 5 will present different ways of modeling and measuring value, Chapter 6 presents behavioral science as a vehicle for behavioral change, Chapter 7 speaks to the promise of data, Chapter 8 introduces Digital and Social Marketing, and Chapter 9 talks about Pricing. Finally, the two chapters in Part 3 provide prescriptive advice on "making MCV happen." Chapter 10 discusses ways in which the organization can be prepared, and Chapter 11 provides a practitioner's guide in the form of worksheets and frameworks.

Chapter 2

Value

Value: (1) A fair return or equivalent in goods, services, or money for something exchanged. (2) The monetary worth of something. (3) Relative worth, utility, or Importance.[1]

The word value has been one of the most used terms in both academic as well as managerial folklore. There are four common examples of the usage of the term value:

(1) "It has been argued that the primary goal of business is to create value for customers."
(2) "Retailers have claimed that they believe in the principles of value pricing."
(3) "A recent surge of academic work in the domain of customer value has put forth the notion of customer lifetime value."
(4) "A number of service providers have proposed that the most effective pricing structure is — what they call — value-based pricing."

Interestingly, while the general idea of value being something that gives utility or worth to an agent is common across the above-mentioned four examples, the more nuanced meaning of the term is different in each of the four examples. In general, there appears

---

[1]Value. (n.d.). *Merriam-Webster.* Retrieved January 1, 2020, from http://www.merriam-webster.com/dictionary/value

to be a lot of conceptual confusion about the definition of the term value.

Textbook definitions of the term "value" abound.

"Value is the ratio of perceived benefits to price."[2]

"Value can be defined as what the customer gets
in exchange for what the customer gives."[3]

Unfortunately, many of these descriptions share features common to the dictionary definition of the term. They are general and parsimonious (i.e., they capture a breadth of situations and are worded relatively simply); yet they are imprecise (i.e., they are not defined against the backdrop of a specific marketing task), ambiguous (i.e., they mean different things under different contexts), and immeasurable (i.e., they do not lend themselves to developing a model for quantifying the value).

While it may be argued that all of these problems are not unique to the term value, we believe that it is critically important to be nuanced in the definition of value, to understand different drivers of value, to develop a taxonomy for classifying value, and finally to develop a method for measuring value. Our approach to the management of customer value is based on the following principles:

(1) *What is value conceptually?*
    Managers need to know precisely what it is they are trying to maximize. Are they trying to maximize the value gained by customers, the value gained by the organization, or some other facet of value? Without a nuanced definition of value, there may be a "vocabulary gap" where multiple managers in a given organization do not complement each other's efforts because they are working with different objectives.

---

[2]Berkowitz, E. (2006). *Marketing* (8th edn.). New York: McGraw-Hill/Irwin.
[3]Donnelly, J. & Peter, J. (2002). *A Preface to Marketing Management*. New York: McGraw-Hill Professional.

(2) *How to create value?*

Managers need to understand what they can do to create value. Traditional approaches to marketing and strategy have talked about value creation through new products and services. We would like to go a step further and think about value creation as a function of what the product or service does for the customer. Does it help them save money? Does it make their processes more efficient? Does it make them happy? Does it allow them to do their business more effectively or efficiently? Understanding value at the level of the customer allows an organization to better think about other ways of value creation.

(3) *How much value to create?*

Managers need to be able to quantify value. Our emphasis will be on tools and models that will allow the manager to determine the dollar equivalent of the value they create. Without tools to quantify value, the manager is at a loss to determine whether their new products, services, or marketing efforts have truly been successful. However, we now have the tools to answer questions like these: What is the average customer worth to me? What is the difference in value between Segment A and Segment B? Therefore, how much should I spend to try and move a customer from one segment to the other? What is the effect of a particular product, service, or marketing program on the value of a customer and the value to a customer?

(4) *Which mechanisms should be used to increase value?*

Managers need to be able to influence value with the mechanism that gives the biggest bang for the buck. Chapter 1 introduced the idea of a value ladder. If the manager could quantify the value of at each step of the ladder, and also determine what it takes to move a customer from one step to the next one, they are now in a position to make several interesting analyses. Which movement on the value ladder yields the highest increase in value? Which ones are the cheapest to influence? What changes yield the highest bang for the buck? Which marketing intervention is the most cost effective in doing this?

In this chapter, we start addressing these building blocks of managing customer value. In particular, we distinguish between value to a customer and value from a customer. We think about different types and sources of value, and start identifying some simple principles that help quantify value. In Chapter 5, we will build on some of these principles and illustrate different approaches to the calculation of value, and what utility these value calculations have for the marketing manager.

2.1 When Is Value Created?

In order to develop a more nuanced definition of value, we return to the examples from the introduction. Recall that we gave four examples of the usage of the term value:

(1) *The primary goal of business is to create value for customers.*
    When used in this sense, the term "value" suggests that some form of utility is being added to the customer. As we will discuss later, this utility could be in different forms and could manifest itself in different ways.

(2) *Retailers have claimed that they believe in the principles of value pricing.*
    We interviewed several retailers to find out what exactly they meant when they spoke of "value pricing." Our investigations revealed that they used the term primarily to mean prices that were low given the cost structure of the retailer. One retailer said "Value pricing is all about giving the lowest possible price that is fair both to the customer and to the store." This retailer (and indeed many others) was using the term "value pricing" to mean low and fair prices — prices that were driven primarily by the costs of selling.

(3) *A surge of academic work in the domain of customer value has put forth the notion of customer lifetime value.*

In their seminar work on customer lifetime value, Gupta and Lehman write, "The lifetime value of a customer is the present value of all future profits generated from this customer.[4] Conceptually this is similar to the present value or discounted cash flow (DCF) approach used in finance to make appropriate investment decisions and to estimate the value of an organization.[5] A mathematical treatment of the customer lifetime value will be provided later on in this chapter, and in more detail in Chapter 5. However, for now we recognize the fact that this usage of the "value" term stands for the utility that a particular customer (or groups of customers) bring to the organization. It is the answer to the question — What is this customer (or segment) worth to me? Therefore, how much should I be spending in order to acquire and maintain the business of this customer? As we will see in Chapter 5, while the concept of customer lifetime value was created to understand individual customers, it can be used to determine a number of important customer-related indices, including the effectiveness of various marketing programs, the marketing return on investment, and marketing spending decisions.

(4) *A number of service providers have proposed that the most effective pricing structure is — what they call — value-based pricing.*

This usage of the term relates very closely to the first usage, and is distinctly different from the second usage. It says that the price that the organization charges a customer should depend on the dollar value that the organization creates for the customer. The greater the value an organization can create, the higher is the price it can charge for its product or service. This is dramatically different from the second usage — the concept

---

[4]Gupta, S. & Lehmann, D. R. (2003). Customers as Assets. *Journal of Interactive Marketing, 17*(1), 9–24. https://doi.org/10.1002/dir.10045
[5]Damodaran, A. (2011). *The Little Book of Valuation: How to Value a Company, Pick a Stock and Profit* (1st edn.). New Delhi, India: Wiley (India).

of "value pricing" which suggests that pricing is based primarily on costs. As we will see later in the book, the exact same service created with the same exact costs could create a different dollar value for different customers.

2.1.1 *The Value Grid*

Two big ideas emerge from this discussion. The first relates to the distinction between the value to the customer (VTC), and the value of the customer (VOC) to the organization. For simplicity, we will refer to the former as VTC and the latter as VOC. For now, let us assume that we can somehow quantify both these variables and plot organizations on a two-dimensional grid as in Figure 2.1.

The four quadrants in Figure 2.1 represent four stages in an organization's value evolution. Those organizations in quadrant 1 neither create VTC, nor gain value from the customer. These are either recent start-ups that are in their early days of operations and hence have no proven products and services, or organizations that have tried but failed to produce winning products.

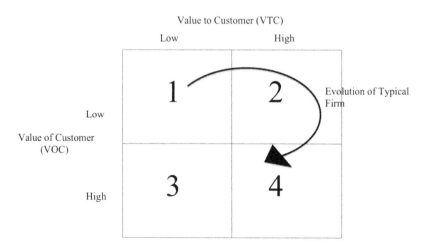

Figure 2.1 The value grid.

Most (eventually) successful organizations are born in this quadrant, but quickly move to quadrant 2. In this area, the organization can deliver value to customers through winning products and services. However, the organization hasn't yet been able to master the ropes of pricing and is therefore unable to extract value from their customers. This could either be the result of suboptimal pricing and selling policies, or the fact that the organization may not yet have a brand name and reputation that allows it to command a higher price. In either case, a start-up organization should not remain in this quadrant 2 for too long or else they may risk giving away value but not making any money for themselves in the long run. If the organization eventually gets its pricing model right, it should graduate to quadrant 4 — the bliss point in the matrix where the organization creates value for customers and also extracts value in exchange. In this book, we will use quadrant 4 as the goal of all the organization's efforts.

In our parlance, value creation occurs when both

(a) the organization has product and services that create utility for the customer, and
(b) that increased utility is reflected in valuable customers: customers that are valuable to the organization.

In order to understand whether value is created for the customer, we use a simple value heuristic which says:

You create value for the customer when you can do something for them that

(a) they — or anyone else — cannot do;
(b) you can do better than anyone else;
(c) you can do faster, cheaper, or more efficiently than anyone else; or
(d) somehow allows them to do their business better than they could otherwise do.

> **Insight Box 2.1**
>
> **MCV Insight**
> The VTC, the value of your product to the customer, captures the economic or emotional benefits that your customer gets from using your product rather than what they are currently doing.

Therefore, when you want to create value for your customers, one very simple approach is to understand how the customer does their own business and then ask the question: What is it they do that I can do more effectively for them? Are there activities that they would rather not do that would be relatively more efficient for me to offer as services? Or what can I do that makes their process and products better?

But creating value for the customer is only part of the overall value creation machinery. Put differently, overall value is created if and only if the creation of customer values has a direct and positive effect on cash flows accruing to the organization.

These increased cash flows could arise from the following:

(a) a greater willingness to pay for the product (e.g., moving from a freemium version of a digital product to a paid version),
(b) greater frequency of purchase,
(c) increased consumption per occasion,
(d) greater rates of usage over time and loyalty, and
(e) greater willingness to refer and recommend the product to others.

> **Insight Box 2.2**
>
> **MCV Insight**
> It is not enough to merely create value for the customer. Over time, the organization needs to ensure that customers are valuable to them.

In addition, traditional measures of success like market share and volume of sales also have the capacity to increase the cumulative VOC to the organization.

Occasionally, some organizations (or divisions of organizations) may find themselves in quadrant 3 of Figure 2.1. In this quadrant, the organization has a high potential VOC, but unfortunately the

VTC is low. Why does this happen? Sometimes the reputation of the organization or the hype created through advertising results in a large number of customers that are willing to try a new product or service. If the organizations were able to then follow up on its promise and deliver a truly value-add product to its customers, it could potentially land up very quickly in quadrant 4. Sometimes, though, organizations fail in this endeavor and find themselves in quadrant 3. In 1992, Crystal Pepsi was marketed as a caffeine-free "clear alternative" to colas, equating clearness with purity and health. Its marketing tagline was "You've never seen a taste like this." However, the taste was not significantly different from other colas; unlike other colorless soft drinks, which usually have a lemon-lime flavor, Crystal Pepsi tasted much like the original drink. Initial sales were good but quickly fell. Pepsi pulled the drink off the market, and pulled itself out of quadrant 3![6]

2.1.2 *Pricing*

The second major theme emerging from the discussion in this section is the importance of pricing in creating customer value. For the longest time, pricing has been treated as an ancillary function to the marketing function — a role conducted primarily by economists and the "numbers people." The centrality of pricing to value cannot be overemphasized. Effective pricing can acquire customers, it can grow value to customers, it can create the right incentives for customers, and eventually it can grow value to the organization. In addition to merely setting a price, the manner in which it is presented to the customer and the manner in which it evolves over time are critical to the organization's ability to manage value. We will discuss various aspects of the pricing decision in Chapter 9.

---

[6]Murguia, S. (2013). *Failure to Launch*. Westport, CT: Praeger Publishers.

2.2 Value to the Customer

In order to understand the drivers of customer value, we would like to present examples from a number of hypothetical organizations. In the examples that follow, we present a relatively impoverished description of these organizations, as well as their operations without any loss in generality. Put differently, while the descriptions are impoverished, they are sufficient to highlight the underlying principles.

2.2.1 *Coal Inc. Case*

The first example is of an organization called Coal Inc. This organization is in the coal distribution business — it transports coal from coal mines and sells it to manufacturers of iron ore. It uses primarily rail links to transport coal. On a fixed schedule (say once every week), a train laden with coal will make a journey from the closest coal mine to one of the customers, Iron Inc. and will deposit the coal on the customers' yard. The customer, in turn, manufactures iron by using a process called smelting in a tall structure called a blast furnace. When the furnace is run, coal and iron ore are fed continuously through the top of the furnace. Chemical reactions ensue, and after a period of time, the end products (the molten metal and waste) are taken off from the bottom of the furnace. Iron Inc. runs the blast furnace on a six-day schedule, and on every occasion that the blast furnace is run, it lays a series of conveyed belts from the yard onto which workers manually load the coal so that it could be fed into the top of the furnace. On an average, the coal sits on the yard for about eight days before it is used.

Note that it is highly improbable that one would find a freshly minted marketing MBA student working for Coal Inc. The MBA would find the product category relatively boring and their skills difficult to apply. However, suppose an ingenious student of "managing customer value" were to spend some time on the custom-ers site and to ask themselves, "now what could Coal Inc. do to add value to the customer?" This student could recall the value heuristic, map out Iron Inc.'s process and ask — which part of this process can I improve? One part of the process that should jump up at this stu-dent is the eight days of inventory carrying costs. If Coal Inc. could somehow manage to run a train twice a week and reduce the inven-tory to four days, which would represent a four-day inventory cost savings to Iron Inc. The student should be able to compute the financial impact of a lower inventory carrying cost, and therefore the dollar value of the benefit to Iron Inc.

That number, though, is not yet the value that has been created. In order to give this benefit to the customer, Coal Inc. themselves need to incur two additional costs. First, they now need to carry inventory for the four additional days. Second, there is the added expense of running trains on a more frequent schedule. If the total incremental costs are lower than the total incremental benefits, Coal Inc. will have created value. Figure 2.2 illustrates this idea schemati-cally on a value spectrum.

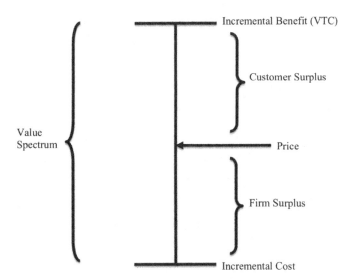

Figure 2.2 The value spectrum.

2.2.2 *The Value Spectrum*

Value spectrum = incremental benefit − incremental cost

In cases where either (or both) the benefits and cost extend over time, this relationship can be rewritten as:

$$\text{Value spectrum} = \text{NPV (incremental benefit)} - \text{NPV (incremental costs)}$$

where NPV stands for the net present value of all future and current cash flows.

Note that any price in the value spectrum results in a proverbial win-win situation for both the organization and the customer. The customer pays less than the benefits they get, and the organization earns more than their cost. Exactly where in the pricing spectrum should the price be set is a function of several factors, notable customer behavior, and the competitive landscape. However, it is clear that the wider the pricing spectrum, the greater is the organization's latitude in setting the price.

> **Insight Box 2.3**
>
> **MCV Insight**
> The Value Spectrum = The Incremental Benefit of the Product to the Customer − The Incremental Costs to the organization of delivering the product. Any price in the value spectrum creates value for both the selling organization and the customer.

Over time, organizations like Coal Inc. need to continually think of other ways of widening the value spectrum. One simple approach could focus on understanding their own processes and therefore cutting down on the cost of providing the service. A second approach could focus on the customer, and on identifying other value-creating opportunities. Our student might recommend further reduction in inventory carrying, just-in-time delivery (this would completely eliminate inventory carrying costs), direct deposit of the coal into the blast furnace (this would eliminate all coal handling costs for

Iron Inc.), and perhaps even consultancy services (aimed at helping Iron Inc. increase their productivity). By introducing innovations like these in successive time periods, Coal Inc. will give itself greater latitude and an ability to increase price — and therefore could increase the value of their customer — over time.

2.2.3 *TH Corporation*

Our second example comes from the market for construction equipment. TH Corporation is a manufacturer of excavators and other earth-moving machines, and its biggest competitor is XY Corporation. The blockbuster product for each form is a backhoe, a machine that scoops up earth at construction sites, lifts it in a bucket, rotates, and then deposits the earth on dumper trucks to be driven away to a different location. The primary specification in selecting a backhoe is the bucket capacity — the volume of earth that can be carried by the bucket of the excavator.

One of the biggest challenges facing TH Corporation is the fact that in addition to manufacturing earth-moving machines, XY also manufactures farm equipment as well as other industrial equipment. Given their larger scale and longer history of manufacturing, XY's cost to produce a unit of backhoe excavator are considerably smaller than TH's. In particular, a comparison of the 1 cubic meter capacity machine revealed that while the two products had the same digging power and capacity, TH's product cost 15% more than XY's. The sales force at TH constantly complained that they would never be able to compete with such a large cost differential.

In order to understand how the salespeople at TH could see the value-creating potential to their expensive-yet-superficially-identical product, we take recourse to Theodore Levitt's influential article on Marketing Myopia.[7] Levitt wrote about a number of different things

---

[7]Levitt, T. (1960). *Marketing Myopia*. Cambridge, MA: Harvard Business Review Press.

in the article, but his central premise can be loosely paraphrased as follows: Organizations need to broaden their view of the market. Rather than focus on the actual product they are selling, they need to focus on the underlying need of the customer.

At the risk of putting words in Levitt's mouth, he would probably argue that customers do not buy backhoe excavators; they buy the ability to dig and move earth expeditiously. So manufacturers of excavators can add value to their customers by increasing their ability to dig and move earth. Construction companies would love to increase the volume of earth moved in a given amount of time. The sooner they can do the job, the lower is the labor cost and other supporting costs, and the sooner they can actually start the construction.

The capacity to move earth depends not only on how much earth could be carried by the bucket, but also the speed with which the dig and scoop, rotate and deposit operations can be done. If the TH salespeople had studied the technical manuals carefully, they would have realized that the TH excavators come with a superior quality motor that completes one complete operation 25% quicker than the XY excavators. Over its lifetime, the TH machine can move 25% more earth than the XY machine. Using a relatively simple back-of-the-envelope calculation, they could now compute the NPV of incremental benefits and incremental costs (the greater purchase price, plus potentially greater maintenance costs) and calculate the VTC — the value to the customer of a TH excavator as compared to an XY excavator.

2.2.4 *Coal Inc. and TH Corporation: Economic Value Creation*

While the cases of Coal Inc. and TH are superficially different (i.e., Coal Inc. adds value by service enhancements, TH by a superior product), they share some common features. First, in both cases, they create value by helping the customer do their own business better.

Coal Inc. helps the iron production process by taking away the costs and hassles associated with handling coal, while TH uses the greater efficiency of its machines to help move more earth for the customer. Second, we keep in mind that while we discussed situations in which the organization successfully added value to their customer, the very same enhancements might not have added value for some customers. For instance, suppose Coal Inc. was dealing with a customer who was geographically so remote that adding more train services would be prohibitively expensive, then they might not be able to create this large value spectrum. Or if the volume of earth being moved by the construction company was small enough (or the cost of time was low) that XY's capacity would have sufficed, then TH would not have been able to add value with a superior product. More generally, the very same product, service, or innovation can add different levels of value to different customers.

But perhaps the greatest similarity between Coal Inc. and TH is this — the value they created for their customers is quantifiable, economic in nature, and can be predicted *a priori*. The product or service innovation can be translated into dollar terms (of course not accurately, but with a fair degree of precision) even before the sale is made. In our parlance, we will call this economic value creation.

2.2.5 *DS Airlines and RR Railways*

We now turn to two other hypothetical businesses: DS Airlines and the RR Railway network. Let us look specifically at a DS flight that operates overnight between, say, Mumbai and Shanghai: a flying time of approximately six hours. Likewise, an overnight nonstop train journey from Mumbai to Ahmadabad takes about six and a half hours. If both organizations know that the bulk of travelers on these routes are business travelers that are making a day trip to Shanghai and Ahmadabad respectively for work, what can they do to add value to these customers?

When posed with this challenge, the first set of responses from managers is unsurprising. They typically include (a) the provision of sleeper berths on the train and greater recline on plane seats, (b) the provision of sleeper suits and toiletries, (c) arrival lounges where passengers could shower and change before leaving for their meetings, (d) the provision of better meals on board, (e) airport transfers, and (f) the ability to check into their return flight or train at the time of departure from Mumbai. All of these actions are examples of what airlines and railroads often try to do for their business passengers. In general, given that passengers need to be well rested for their one day of work at their destination cities, the best way in which the transportation provider could help them is to ensure that they sleep well. However, note that while all of these activities are designed to improve the quality of sleep, they do nothing to help passengers get a greater quantity of sleep. In particular, a six-hour flight allows no more than four hours of sleep — seatbelt signs stay on for about a half hour, meals are served for the next 45 minutes, and then seatbelt signs are again switched on about 45 minutes from arrival. The lack of sleep is a particular problem for flights that cut across time zones and where jetlag is an added complication. That's why the commonly accepted term for overnight flights of this duration is a "red-eye" flight!

From the perspective of economic value, overnight flights are good because they eliminate the need for a hotel room (thus saving the passenger some money) and allow the customer to use their workdays more productively. The cost of this economic value is the red eye, and the benefit of saving hotel and meal expenses for the night.

The only real way of reducing or eliminating a red eye is to allow a greater span of time over which the passenger can sleep. This can be accomplished in two ways. First, keeping the flight (or train) arrival and departure times constant, as many nonsleep-related activities could be rescheduled to other parts of the entire experience. For instance, DS airlines could consider serving a meal in the arrival area, and hand out (and encourage the passenger to complete) all arrival documentation prior to boarding the flight, and as a more extreme measure, they could consider increasing the flight time; this simply entails flying the plane at a lower velocity so that the journey could now take, say, eight hours. In conjunction with the other measures, this could give the passenger up to seven hours of sleep on board. The practice of slowing down an overnight journey is not alien to the railroad industry.[8] In particular, railroads often have what is called a set-out sleeper train in which the train (or sleeper cars) are set aside into a railway siding at an intermediate station so that the full journey is extended in order to allow passengers a full night's rest.[9] Might an airline be able to use this strategy and extend its flying time? Would such an innovation make sense?

Three immediate thoughts come to mind. The first two thoughts relate to the concept of the value spectrum, which we defined as the difference between incremental benefits and incremental costs. It is apparent that the customer might not see the incremental benefit arising from this innovation *a priori*. Indeed, it is even possible that some novice (i.e., relatively inexperienced) customers might find the increase in flight length aversive and might decide to switch to other airlines. The more experienced customers, as well as those that are prone to inertia will stay on with the airline. After a couple of trips, though, these customers should get sensitized to the fact that they are indeed better rested for their workday, and hence end up having a more productive day. Put differently, customers may have to experience the innovation in order to fully appreciate the incremental benefit they are getting. Using our heuristic for overall value creation, though, we would argue that this improved experience should translate into a financial benefit — greater willingness

---

[8]Garratt, C. (2002). *The World Encyclopedia of Locomotives*. London, UK: Hermes House.
[9]*Ibid.*

to pay, improved frequency or loyalty, of greater rate of successful referrals — for value creation to have occurred.

The second thought relates to incremental costs — at first blush, it appears that a longer flight time would involve a greater expense on fuel. Surprisingly, we found out that the opposite was true; fuel efficiency actually increased if the flight operated at moderate speed.[10] The second family of costs has to do with opportunity costs. As the example of Southwest Airlines has shown us, capacity utilization results in greater profits.[11] Consequently, DS airlines would rather have their flight arrive early in Shanghai, turn it around with servicing, fuel, and a fresh load of passengers and get going onto its next revenue-earning flight. While this is a good general principle, its applicability in a given context might vary. For instance, if Shanghai is the hub for DS airlines, the opportunity cost of slowing down the flight is indeed high because there are other demands on the plane once it arrives from Mumbai. However, if Shanghai is only the terminal destination and the plane is going to idle at the airport before its return flight to Mumbai, then the opportunity cost of flying slowly is low, and extending the flight time might be a worthwhile strategy!

Our third thought is tangential at this stage, but refers to discussion that appears later in Chapter 3. It is difficult to imagine any traditional market research that would have prompted an airline to lengthen the duration of a flight. When asked what they would choose between an eight-hour flight and a six-hour flight, a customer is likely to emphatically say that they would rather take the shorter flight. In reality, the customer is better off with the eight-hour flight! As we will discuss later, survey research is often woefully

---

[10] Phillips, W. (2004). *Mechanics of Flight.* Hoboken, NJ: John Wiley & Sons; Durning, A. B. & Flavin, C. (1988). Don't Dim the Lights on the Energy Revolution. *Across the Board, 25*(5), 36–45.

[11] Henderson, D. K. (1991). Southwest Luvs Passengers, Employees, Profits. *Air Transport World, 28*(7), 32–41.

inadequate in helping organizations make decisions on how to add customer value.

In contrast to the economic value we wrote about earlier, we note that the value created in these examples was more experiential in nature. It did not directly improve cash flows of the customer, but indirectly helped them perform their activities better. *A priori*, it was not possible to predict the value that would accrue, and since the value was not measurable, it was not possible to create a value spectrum and use it to make pricing decisions. We also note that in our examples above, one could argue that the experiential value could possibly translate into an economic benefit through increased productivity. However, the causal linkage supporting this argument is tenuous and does not stand up to scientific scrutiny. The linkage is even more tenuous and likely nonexistent for other examples of experiential value; for instance, a relaxing massage treatment, a vacation, a dinner and movie out, and for our morning cup of expensive gourmet coffee. Often times, people are very willing to pay for experiences that do not have any obvious rational or economic benefits at all. Table 2.1 summarizes the differences between economic and experiential value.

2.2.6 *The Locus of Value*

In the previous section, we presented a few hypothetical examples to illustrate the concepts of economic versus experiential value. In this section, we turn to two the two biggest innovations in terms of how customers consume television entertainment from the turn of the past century — high-density television and digital video recorders (DVRs).

High-definition television (HDTV) is a digital broadcasting system with better resolution than traditional television systems. HDTV yields a better-quality image than standard television does, because it has a greater number of lines of resolution. The visual

Table 2.1 Economic and experiential value.

	Economic value	Experiential value
Value creation results in...	Overall dollar impact/ savings for the customer	A better quality of consumption experience that may or may not lead to productivity
Predictability	*A priori* prediction of value possible	*A priori* prediction of value not possible
Measurability	Easy to quantify	Difficult to quantify
Ease of selling	Relatively easy — the value model can be conceptually explained to customer	Difficult — customer often needs to experience the product or service to appreciate its value
Variability across customers	Possibly high, as a function of drivers of value	
End result	Ideally, greater VOC to the organization!	

information is some two to five times sharper because the gaps between the scan lines are narrower or invisible to the naked eye.[12]

DVRs are best exemplified by companies such as TiVo. These gadgets provide an electronic television programming schedule, and provide features such as predetermined recordings schedule (which ensure subscribers never miss an episode of their favorite shows) and Wish List searches (which allow the user to find and record shows that match their interests by title, actor, director, category, or keyword). Some systems like TiVo also provide a range of features when the TiVo DVR is connected to a home network. These features include movie and TV show downloads, advanced search, personal photo viewing, music offerings, and online scheduling.[13]

---

[12]Astra. (2009, January 11). *HDTV: Europe's Leading High-Definition TV Platform.* http://www.sesastra.com/business/en/solutions/media/hdtv/index.php
[13]Brochures and Graphics. (2009, January 11). *Tivo Gets It All!* http://www.tivo.com/assets/images/abouttivo/resources/downloads/brochures/TiVoSeries2_brochure.pdf

The primary value offered by HDTV is a better television viewing experience. The picture is of a higher resolution, transitions are not jerky, and the sound is better. The primary value offered by a DVR is one of convenience. The customer now does not need to be glued to the television set at, say 7:30 PM because that's when their favorite show airs. They can let the DVR record the show and can then watch it at their leisure. Basically, the DVR removes a set of constraints in the customer's schedule.

A closer inspection of these sources of value allows for a broader conceptualization of value to customer as a function of where the effect of the value creation resides. An innovation like HDTV improves the quality of the consumption experience itself; it improves the manner in which the target product is consumed. For example, HDTV gives a better viewing experience, fully reclining beds improve the level of comfort in a flight, and the latest cell phones give a better call quality. We refer to these as value with an internal locus. The term "internal" refers to the fact that value creation occurs through the consumption experience of the product.

In contrast, innovations with an external locus of value are those in which the customer gains utility not through the consumption experience itself, but through its implications for other activities they perform. DVRs do not provide better-quality television viewing on their own, but they do allow the customer greater flexibility in scheduling their time. A longer Mumbai–Shanghai flight does not necessarily improve the in-flight experience, but it does allow the customer to have a more productive day at work. And a handheld PDA device such as a Blackberry or iPhone does not necessarily improve call quality or make it easier to send email, but it does allow the customer to utilize their time more effectively. Table 2.2 provides other examples of value that is either internal locus or external locus.

Based on a survey with managers from 105 organizations, we concluded that a large proportion of all new products or

Table 2.2 Examples of internal and external locus of value.

Domain	Internal locus	External locus
Mattresses	Memory Foam mattress	**SleepTracker** SleepTracker is an alarm watch that wakes sleepers up only when they are in light sleep so that consumers will feel less groggy in the mornings. Research shows that people who wake up in the middle of deep sleep feel more tired during the day. SleepTracker adds value to the consumer (feeling more energetic) beyond its duty of waking up the consumer. Instead of improving the quality of a mattress or a bed, SleepTracker helps the consumer get more rest in a different way. http://www.time.com/time/business/article/0,8599,1129523-2,00.html;www.sleeptracker.com
Television	HDTV	**SlingBox** SlingBox is a DVR where it allows users to hook up their home set and can beam whatever is onscreen to any web-enabled device such as a laptop or a PDA. As such, if you were to be waiting for a plane in Paris, you can use your laptop and the airport's wireless network to watch the local news from back home, a DVD, or favorite TV show. http://www.time.com/time/business/article/0,8599,1129528-2,00.html; www.slingmedia.com
Car rental	Standard car rentals	**ZipCar** ZipCar is a model for automobile transportation where cars are parked around a city for members to drive by the hour instead of owning their own vehicles. Compared to the rental services that typical car rentals offer, ZipCar adds value to drivers because it saves them to convenience of having to go through tedious registration procedures of renting a car while getting the same driving experience that they would from a rental. www.zipcar.com
Retail mirrors	Regular fitting room mirrors	**IconNicholson's Magic Mirror** The Magic Mirror is a new dressing-room technology designed for retailers. It is a high-tech, three-paneled interactive mirror that has two cameras located on either side. Clothes shoppers can transmit an image of themselves wearing a new outfit to friends and family to get feedback. The mirror also displays recommendations of other styles and accessories that shoppers can try on. Retailers who purchase the Magic Mirror for their dressing rooms can experience additional sales growth that would exceed the growth that they would experience from investing in renovations to the dressing room. http://money.cnn.com/2007/01/22/news/companies/retail_innovation/index.htm; http://www. iconnicholson.com/nrf07/

innovations were of the internal locus variety (approximately 70%). We also concluded the following:

(1) It was relatively easy to do a concept test for an innovation that was internal locus than one that was external locus. Customers were able to comprehend better what an enhancement to an existing product meant, but were not as quick at grasping how the product might change their other (nonproduct) activities.

(2) Managers reported that external locus innovations were much more sustainable in the long run. These innovations lasted longer, and rates of customer acceptability increased with time.

Insight Box 2.4

MCV Insight

An internal locus of value creation occurs when the innovation enhances the consumption experience of the product or service. An external locus occurs when the innovation creates a benefit outside of the consumption experience. While internal locus innovations are more easily understood and adopted by customers, the external locus innovations are more sustainable in the long run.

2.3 Value of a Customer

Authors in marketing and strategy have for long believed in the idea that a stable and loyal customer base is like any asset that an organization possesses. However, the practice of treating customers as assets, and using the principles of finance to make decisions like how much to invest in a customer, or how much to spend upgrading a customer, is relatively new. In fact, it is only in the last few years that we have seen a surge of interest in the application of finance to marketing decisions.[14] The building block of this approach is the

---

[14]Doyle, P. (2000). *Value-Based Marketing: Marketing Strategies for Corporate Growth and Shareholder Value*. Chichester, England: John Wiley & Sons; Gupta, S. &

Insight Box 2.5

MCV Insight

The Value of the Customer is the answer to the question: What is this customer worth to me in dollar terms? What is the net present value of all cash flows that can be attributed to this customer?

---

calculation of the value of a customer to the organization. The VOC (also called customer lifetime value, CLV by some authors) is the answer to the question: What is the NPV of all cash flows that can be attributed to that particular customer? It is also the answer to other related questions: (a) if I were to acquire the business of this customer today, how much should I spend on doing so? and (b) if I "sold" my customer to another service provider how much should I charge for the customer? (silly as this idea may sound; this is pretty much what happens when one organization gets acquired by another).

Why is it important to calculate the VOC? This calculation allows the manager to make a number of important sets of decisions with the help of rigorous analysis, which would not have been possible without estimating the VOC. In particular, it could help answer the following questions.

2.3.1 *VOC Analysis and Decision-Making*

(1) How much should I spend on acquiring a customer? If the manager has a profit margin or a return on investment in mind, knowing the customers' VOC allows them to decide how much to spend on acquisition. At the extreme, the manager should spend no more than the VOC on acquiring the customer; spending anything more results in unprofitable customers.

(2) Should I launch a new marketing program? Should I launch a new product? Is it cost effective? In order to assess the cost

---

Lehmann, D. R. (2003). Customers as Assets. *Journal of Interactive Marketing, 17*(1), 9–24. https://doi.org/10.1002/dir.10045.

effectiveness of a program, the manager needs to estimate the effect of the program on drivers of value, and therefore on the VOC. The program is cost effective to the tune of the gap between incremental VOC and the cost of the program. If C represents the cost of the program, then the return on investment can be expressed as $ROI = \Delta VOC/C$.

(3) Which of many marketing programs should I introduce? Which of many products or services could I introduce? The approach to these decisions is similar to the approach above. The manager needs to estimate ΔVOC arising from each program and — depending on the specific goals of the program — choose the one with greatest ΔVOC or the greatest ROI.

(4) I have some extra money in my marketing budget: to which customers should I allocate it to? Traditionally, marketers have segmented customers as a function of demographics, psychographics, or behavioral variables where the unit of analysis is a customer; the entity is a human being. We propose that marketers think about customers as a collection of multiple stages. Suppose the steps on a bank customer's value ladder look as follows:

Entry level (checking account only) → Credit user (checking + credit card) → High-value credit customer (checking + credit card + mortgage).

We can now segment customers as a function of which stage they belong to. In this highly simplified example, the manager can either invest the marketing dollars in moving customers from entry level to credit users, or from credit users to high-value customers. For each transition, the manager should be able to estimate ΔVOC. Further, knowing the cost of the marketing efforts needed and the success rates of these interventions, they should be able to compute the effective cost of each transition. Like before, the manager could then choose to spend the extra marketing dollars on the transition that provides the highest incremental value, or the highest ROI.

(5) How can I prioritize my customers on a "quality scale"? If the goal of the organization is to maximize long-term value, the manager simply needs to estimate the VOC of each customer (or segment). The most valuable customer is the one with the greatest VOC.

2.3.2 *How to Calculate VOC*

Financial analysts often use the principle of DCFs to value projects, with a view to answering similar questions.[15] A customer is like any other project that an organization may engage in — the organization needs to spend money to acquire them; they earn revenues from them on each sale over a period of time; they need to spend money on the customer over time in order to maintain, grow, and strengthen the relationship; and the customer typically has a finite length of relationship (lifetime) with the organization. Given that organizations would rather prefer a dollar in the present to a dollar in the future and hence all future cash flows need to be discounted, the lifetime value of any customer can be simply expressed using standard NPV equations.

As the simplest illustration of how to calculate VOC, let us consider a customer in Hong Kong who buys a bottle of shampoo every six months. Let us assume that the contribution (Contribution = Price – all variable costs, the free cash flow that arises out of the sale of each unit) from each bottle is HK$50, and the relevant discount rate is 10%. Let us also assume that the customer life is infinity and

---

[15]International Federation of Accountants. (2009, January 11). *International Good Practice: Guidance on Project Appraisal Using Discount Cash Flow.* http://www.ifac.org/Members/DownLoads/Project_Appraisal_Using_DCF_formatted.pdf; Pratt, S. P., Reilly, R. F., & Schwihs, R. P. (2000). *Valuing a Business: The Analysis and Appraisal of Closely Held Companies.* New York: McGraw-Hill Professional; Damodaran, A. (1996). *Investment Valuation: Tools and Techniques for Determining the Value of Any Asset.* New York: John Wiley & Sons.

that all cash flows accrue at the end of the year, so the VOC can be modeled as a perpetuity. Given that the annual contribution is $100, a simple formula from finance tells us that[16]:

$$VOC = A/r = 100/0.10 = \$1000$$

Whenever this example is presented in an MBA class, however, a number of hands shoot up immediately challenging the concept of VOC. "This is absurd, no customer can live forever," is the most common complaint. Others are equally vociferous. "People's consumption rates might change," one student argued. "Some of us tend to lose hair," one of the older men in class remarks. Or, "people switch brands all the time."

While each of these criticisms is valid, they are easily handled with suitable mathematics. The following equations can be drawn from any standard finance textbook of finance that discusses DCF analysis.[17]

(1) No customer can live forever: This issue can be easily handled by using a formula for an annuity instead of a perpetuity. In particular, when the lifetime of the customer extends over *t* years:

$$VOC = \Sigma t \, (A_t)/(1 + r)^t$$

(2) People's consumption rates may change: Again, finance theory offers us formulas on how to calculate the NPV. If *r* is the discount rate and *g* is the growth rate:

$$VOC = A/(r - g) \text{ for a perpetuity}$$
$$VOC = [A/(r - g)] \, [\, 1 - \{(1 + g)/(1 + r)\}^t \,] \text{ for an annuity}$$

---

[16]Damodaran, A. (2011). *The Little Book of Valuation: How to Value a Company, Pick a Stock and Profit* (1st edn.). New Delhi, India: Wiley (India).
[17]*Ibid.*

(3) People switch brands all the time: This is indeed a problem with the VOC equations as they have been discussed above. However, we can use probability theory and the tools of decision analysis to derive a suitable approach on how to tackle VOC calculations for situations in which brand switching could occur. We will revisit this issue further in Chapter 5 where we discuss the mathematical modeling of customer behavior in a greater level of detail.

Given that we are now in the realm of a discussion on customer as assets, an important question that needs to be asked is this: What is the appropriate discount rate that should be used in valuing customers? Several options come up for contention: the weighted average cost of capital, the market interest rate, and the internal rate of return. As with most questions in the field of business strategy, the answer to the question of which is the best discount rate to use is — It depends! The key question is this: What does it depend on?

The appropriate discount rate depends on what it is that the manager wants to do with the VOC calculation. If VOC is being calculated to determine whether the organization should launch a new product and this launch would require the establishment of a new manufacturing facility (i.e., new capital investment), then the cost of capital seems to be the most appropriate discount rate. If the VOC calculation is generated to guide the manager on whether to launch a new marketing campaign for which the organization may need to borrow from the market, then the interest rate is the appropriate discount rate. Finally, if the goal of the VOC analysis is merely to prioritize customers on a quality scale, then any reasonable discount rate should work (unless, of course the cash flows from the customers are so skewed that some customers return revenues very early in the lifetime and others do so only very late in their lifetime). Irrespective of which discount rate is actually used, we strongly encourage the manager to run sensitivity analysis to ensure that the conclusions are robust to small changes in the discount rate.

2.3.3 *The Criterion for Success in VOC Analysis*

Thus far, we have presented a relatively simple, conceptual model for how to think about the VOC. In Chapter 5, we will take this building block and present several illustrations of how this simple tool can be used to make relatively important customer-related decisions. We will also discuss several approaches (including sensitivity analyses and what-if analyses) for making the VOC formulation more pragmatic, more usable, and more consistent with the way in which managers traditionally think about the customer.

For now, however, we could like to take a moment to put the VOC variable in the broader context of our framework. We proposed that a retailer's business model serves as a useful metaphor for thinking about any type of business. We extend this idea further by modeling the business along the following principles. See Figure 2.3 for a schematic illustration of this framework.

(1) *Principle 1*: All customer-related activity can be decomposed into two distinct phases. The first set of activities, acquisition, refers to everything that the organization does in order to attract the business of the customer. In the case of a retailer, all traffic-building activity that gets the customer to visit the store for the first time can be grouped under the acquisition umbrella.

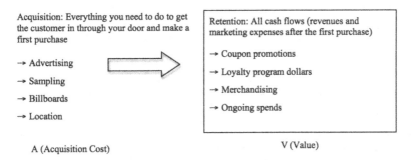

Figure 2.3 The retailer metaphor.

Everything that happens after the customer is in the store falls into the value of customer umbrella.

(2) *Principle 2:* If the cost of acquiring a customer is $A, and the value of the customer is denoted by $VOC, the net value of the customer is [VOC − A]. Acquisition cost, A, is a function of the cost of activities like sampling, direct sales, sales force, advertising, couponing, and traffic-building incentives; as well as the success rate of these vehicles (the probability with which a prospective customer exposed to these vehicles actually ends up being a customer). It is the average cost that is spend per customer who arrives at the door of the store. And as discussed earlier, VOC is a function of all positive cash flows (contribution revenues) as well as all expense flows (marketing expenses, loyalty programs, cost to serve the customer, etc.).

We have talked about three metrics thus far: A, VOC, and VOC − A. The reader may ask this: Which of these metrics is the real criterion of success? As the reader probably knows by now, the answer to that question is, again, that it depends! In the context of the value ladder, the manager might need to make decisions at two points in time. The first is pre-acquisition. Suppose the manager needs to decide between two groups of customers, and she has data on the predicted acquisition cost and VOC for each group. In this case, VOC − A is the net value of each customer for a forward-looking manager, and hence this net value should be the appropriate metric for deciding which customer group to choose. Now suppose the manager has already acquired a large pool of customers, and must decide which subset of this acquisition pool she should further invest in. Since these customers have already been acquired, A is a sunk cost and hence the forward-looking manager should now only target customers with high predicted VOC. Finally, if we are looking at a business in which the variance in VOC is expected to be low, then acquisition cost is the only relevant metric and the manager should select groups of customers that have the lowest A.

2.3.4 *The Customer Portfolio Matrix*

In this chapter, we have argued that with the right data, it is possible not only to estimate the VTC, but also the VOC to the organization. In some cases, especially those in which the direct costs of producing, selling, and servicing the customer are highly variable, it is relatively easy to get all the data to come up with appropriate estimates of VOC. In other cases, however, it is not as easy to compute the cost of serving a customer.[18] Consider an organization in which a large proportion of the total costs are S, G, & A (selling, general, and administrative) costs. If this organization is engaged in the business of distributing, say office supplies to various customers, all of their fixed distribution and customer-servicing costs get lumped into the "S, G, & A" bin. In trying to estimate the cost associated with each customer, this organization may simply divide the total cost by the number of customers to yield an average per customer cost.

This approach will result in all customers being treated equally on the cost dimension. However, any manager will be quick to point out that this is misleading; some customers are more demanding than others, and the manager intuitively knows that the former group costs more to service than the latter. We surveyed two groups of managers, one in the financial services industry and the other in the business-to-business distribution industry and asked them to list the features that distinguished their good customers from their bad customers. A summary of their responses is shown in Table 2.3.

A good system of measuring customer value will incorporate differences in customer behavior and the associated costs into the VOC computation. Unfortunately, the traditional accounting systems used by many organizations do not allow the organization to

---

[18]Johnson, H. T. & Kaplan, R. S. (1987). *Relevance Lost: The Rise and Fall of Management Accounting*. Cambridge, MA: Harvard Business School Press; Cooper, R. & Kaplan, R. (1988). Measure Costs Right: Make the Right Decision. *Harvard Business Review, 66,* 96–103.

Table 2.3 Behaviors of "Good" and "Bad" customers.

Good customers	Bad customers
High order quantities	Low order quantities
Order standard products	Order customized products
Predictable orders	Unpredictable orders
Order high-margin products	Order low-margin products
Standard requirements over time	Changing requirements over time
Low level of sales support needed	High level of sales support needed
No dedicated inventory needed	Dedicated inventory needed
Electronic processing of order	Manual processing of order
Infrequent bank transactions	Frequent bank transactions
Use cheaper channels (ATM and online)	Use expensive channels (tellers and advisors)

answer questions like "what is the cost of making a just-in-time delivery?" or "what is the cost of clearing one cheque?"

These questions can be answered by adopting an activity-based costing (ABC) system.[19] The philosophy of traditional costing is that objects consume costs. Therefore it costs money to make a unit of product, say a pencil or this book. Costs that can be directly attributed to each unit of the product are assigned to it, those that cannot be directly attributed are lumped together into S, G, & A, which is a period cost. ABC has a different philosophy. It believes that activities consume costs, and that activities are needed to produce output.[20] Figure 2.4 shows a schematic representation of the philosophy behind ABC and more traditional costing methods.

That said, ABC is a long and expensive exercise, and while organizations are now increasingly adopting ABC, it is still relatively rare. In the absence of good cost data (which impairs the ability

---

[19]Cooper, R. & Kaplan, R. (1988). Measure Costs Right: Make the Right Decision. *Harvard Business Review, 66,* 96–103.
[20]Johnson, H. T. & Kaplan, R. S. (1987). *Relevance Lost: The Rise and Fall of Management Accounting.* Cambridge, MA: Harvard Business School Press.

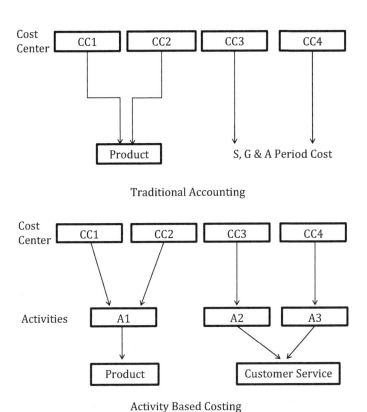

Figure 2.4 Traditional Accounting and ABC.

to conduct diagnostic VOC calculations), what tools can an organization use to manage customer value?

We note that the two key drivers of value are the revenue potential of the customer and their cost potential. Assuming that the organization has the ability to place their customers relative to each other on both of these dimensions, they could produce a grid like Figure 2.5, which we refer to as the customer portfolio matrix. The customer portfolio matrix is an interesting encapsulation of some of the ideas that we have presented thus far, and a good taste of what is to come later in this book.

The four quadrants in this matrix represent four different groups of customers. Customers in the bottom right corner are

	Low Cost	High Cost
High Revenue/ Benefits	STARS	Pursue cost-reducing strategies
Low Revenue/Benefits	Pursue revenue-increasing strategies	DOGS

Figure 2.5 Customer portfolio matrix.

customers who are the lowest in the pecking order; they have low profit potential and they are also "high maintenance" customers. If the organization had cost data, they would discover that these customers probably create negative value for the organization. Purely from a mathematical perspective, the organization can actually increase value by dropping these customers. We borrow a term from the original product portfolio matrix designed by the Boston Consulting Group and label these customers as "dogs."[21] On the contrary, customers in the top-left corner are the star customers. They yield high revenues and are easy and inexpensive to serve. The organization is best advised to continue engaging with these

---

Insight Box 2.6

MCV Insight

Create a customer portfolio matrix by placing each customer on the "revenue potential" and "cost to serve" scales. The matrix gives a clear visual understanding of what the manager needs to do with different sets of customers, as well as a glance at what the composition of the customer portfolio looks like.

---

[21] Hedley, B. (1977). Strategy and the Business Portfolio. *Long Range Planning*, *10*(1), 9–15.

customers, and to continue adding value through the delivery of innovative value-adding products and services.

The two off diagonal quadrants are more interesting. Those in the top-right corner yield high revenues, but are also costly to serve. They are probably neither very profitable nor highly unprofitable. The organization could try and create incentives for these organizations to shift to cheaper channels of communications (e.g., banks that give incentives to customers that bank online or using ATM's instead of teller services) or put pricing structures in place that influence customer behavior (e.g., a distributor is extremely willing to offer services like just-in-time delivery, but will charge for it; forcing the customer to think about whether they really need the extra service).

Customers in the bottom-left corner have low revenues, but are also inexpensive to serve. Again, they are probably neither profitable nor unprofitable. The organization should aim to keep these customers on their books, and over time try and increase the revenue potential of these customers by trying to upsell (i.e., attempt to sell a high-margin product when the customer has decided to purchase a low-margin product), cross-sell (i.e., attempt to sell a second product when the customer has purchased the first), or to increase usage rates or purchasing frequency.

What should the organization do with the dogs? Clearly they consume service but do not pay for it. For instance, consider a bank customer who has very low balances but makes a large number of teller transactions. One specific strategy is to set up a pricing structure that forces the customer to pay for every unit of service consumed. For instance, in the recent past many banks have announced that customers who have less than a certain amount of cumulative balances would need to pay, say $5 for every teller transaction they make.[22] A large number of customers would probably never

----

[22]Holton, L. (1995, April 26). Visit a Bank Teller, Pay a Fee // First Chicago to Impose $3 Charge. *Chicago Sun-Times*; Gibson, R. (1995, April 27). Some Think the Bank Robbers Are on Wrong Side of the Window. *Wall Street Journal*, B1.

experience this teller fee. For the rest, the dogs, this could have one of three effects. First, they might pay the fee and hence cover the costs. Second, they might have the incentive to consolidate balances from other banks, hence increasing the revenue to the organization. Third, they might be unhappy with the fee structure and might defect to another bank. This too is not an undesirable option. The dog metaphor is not accidental; we note that dogs are extremely loyal creatures and the same principle works in business. Unprofitable customers do not easily leave the organization, and one of the biggest challenges facing organizations today is to determine how to get rid of their dog customers.

Before we conclude, we would like to make three observations about the customer portfolio matrix:

(1) We made the point that the matrix could be used in situations in which the organization does not have the cost data to make VOC calculations. However, we would like to clarify that even when the organization can make VOC estimates, the matrix provides additional insights that can help manage customer value. Why? While the VOC presents one number that serves an index of customer quality, the matrix allows the manager to decompose it and visually analyze customer quality along two separate (revenue and cost) dimensions. This gives the manager a better idea of what specific marketing activities to target to what groups of customers.

(2) We presented the customer portfolio matrix as a 2×2 matrix for the ease of exposition. However, if the manager wants to get a more fine-grained analysis, she could decompose organization rankings into quartiles or deciles and work with, say a 10×10 matrix. In this approach, the goal of each marketing activity can be defined as the transition of a customer from one particular cell of a matrix to another cell of the matrix. While a detailed description of this approach is beyond the scope of this book, we have used this approach successfully in research and consulting projects.

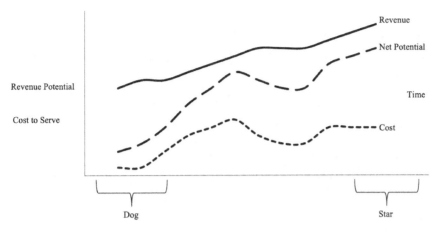

Figure 2.6 A representation of a customer's quality over time.

(3) The third driver of VOC, the time course of costs and revenues is not captured in this matrix. While it is relatively easy to capture the time course in a matrix format (see Figure 2.6 for an example), a full treatment is not easy to illustrate on paper.

2.4 What This All Means

Our goal in this chapter was simple. We wanted to articulate what "value" truly means, and outline a framework that managers could use to understand the tension and interplay between VTC and VOC to the organization. But what does this all mean for the manager? We offer a few prescriptive guidelines for managers.

2.4.1 Guideline 1: Understand How You Can Create Value

Recall that earlier in the chapter, we formulated a simple heuristic for when value is created:

You create value for the customer when you can do something for them that

(a) they — or anyone else — cannot do
(b) you can do better than anyone else
(c) you can do faster, cheaper, or more efficiently than anyone else, or
(d) somehow allows them to do their business better than they could otherwise do.

Given this simple heuristic, we suggest that managers proactively look for ways in which they could add value to their customers by deeply understanding how customers go about consuming their products and services. In work we have done with our clients, we have often used a simple diagram that describes what happens to our products after they are delivered to customers. For instance, in the example of the Coal Inc. discussed earlier, the diagram might look like Figure 2.7, and we call it the "consumption flow-chart." Note that Figure 2.7 is an extremely simplified version of a flowchart — simplified only for expositional purposes. Note also that this flowchart might look different for different customers.

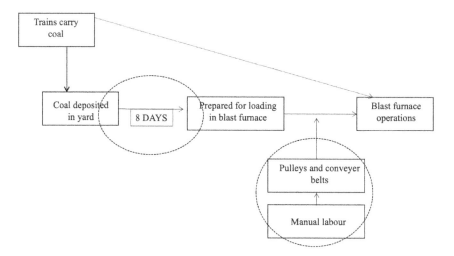

Figure 2.7 Coal Inc.: Consumption flowchart.

Armed with a flowchart like this, the manager could now scrutinize every step in the chart and ask themselves — "is this something I could do for my customer, and if so would I be creating value?" In Figure 2.7, the manager might find three opportunities for value creation as indicated by dotted lines.

2.4.2 Guideline 2: Create Value to the Customer First; Value to the Organization Will Follow

As Figure 2.1 suggested, organizations can only develop a portfolio of high-value customers if they can create VTCs. In later chapters, we will develop a family of examples and frameworks to show that the best results are often achieved when the organization tirelessly strives to create value for its customers without being too concerned for profits in the short run. In our view, too many organizations lose the plot because they are impatient in earning money from customers. We look at customers as assets — they need to be invested in for a period of time before they start yielding returns.

That said, we also encourage the reader to eventually go beyond creating VTC and think about converting that value — the goodwill that they have been created — into value for the organization. One of the biggest tools to do this is through effective pricing strategies. In Chapters 3 and 4, we will discuss specific ways in which the organization can develop customers over time, and in Chapter 9, we will discuss some of the pricing strategies that can be used to better create and grow organization value.

2.4.3 Guideline 3: Create Models of Value of Customer

After getting a good understanding of what value your products and services add to customers, we would strongly recommend that the manager create a conceptual model of the VOC to the organization.

A number of tools presented in this chapter are useful here: (a) using the retailer as a metaphor for identifying acquisition costs and value of customer, (b) the idea that customers can be modeled as gambles, and (c) the DCF approach to computing the VOC. We note that in using these tools as an aid into decision-making the manager should use a forward-looking approach — sunk costs should be ignored and only incremental costs and benefits should be used in making the relevant analyses.

Why is it important to create these conceptual models of value? They allow the manager to understand the underlying drivers of value which in turn will allow them to determine how exactly to manage the process of adding value to their customer segments.

2.4.4 Guideline 4: Treat Different Customers Differently

We presented a customer portfolio matrix — a method of visually locating all the customers of an organization on a two-dimensional grid as a function of their revenue potential and their cost to serve. The practical value of this grid is immense — it allows the manager to view their current portfolio of customer assets as a snapshot, and to then think about how to treat each of those customer groups differently in order to achieve the same underlying goal — the creation of value to the organization. This notion of treating different customers differently will be one of the central features of the discussion later in this book.

Thus far in this book we have outlined our one-stage-at-a-time view of the world, and have articulated what we mean by value. How does the reader go about identifying stages? What metrics do they use to quantify success? How can the reader change their mental models of customer management from one in which they are thinking about aggregate outcomes (e.g., revenues or profits) to one in which they think about smaller stages at a time? We start addressing these questions in Chapter 3.

The Value Ladder

Ladder: (1) A structure for climbing up or down. (2) A series of usually ascending steps or steps.[1]

In Chapter 2, we discussed the notion of value to customer (VTC), the value of customer (VOC), and the need to maintain a balance between the two. VTC should translate to an overall increase in value to the organization in the form of revenues and profits through an increase in customer loyalty, increase in the rate of referrals, lower churn rate, and decrease in marketing costs and costs to serve customers. In this chapter, we focus on the organization's potential for revenue growth, and growth in VOC. In particular, we will illustrate two sets of ideas:

(1) An analysis of the revenue model: we will illustrate how the organization can decompose its key performance index (KPI) and use the decomposition to better focus its efforts on improving the KPI efficiently.

(2) Constructing value ladders: we will discuss how marketing research can be used to construct a value ladder that can then be the basis of improving the value of the customer over time.

---

[1]Ladder. (n.d.). *Merriam-Webster.* Retrieved January 1, 2020, from http://www.merriam-webster.com/dictionary/ladder

3.1 The Revenue Model

In simplest terms, a revenue model can be defined as a mathematical representation of the organization's answer to the question of how they will make money. Businesses often have more than just a single revenue stream — different means of generating and collecting revenue. The business should have revenue models that describe each revenue stream and the way the business expects to generate income from each of them. It is important to note that a single revenue model cannot be applied to different lines of businesses. Every business has its own unique revenue streams.

While the term "revenue model" is often used in the context of for-profit businesses, the general principle of identifying a "top line" inflow of funds is common to all organizations. For instance, a charity might be interested in maximizing the total donation dollars collected; a government might be interested in maximizing tax revenues; a not-for-profit might be interested in increasing grants and contributions; and a publicly funded university might seek to maximize its inflows from government support, tuition fees, endowments, and grants. While these not-for-profit entities might not explicitly go out of the way to increase revenue, they still need a revenue model to help them manage their inflows so they can operate at their desired levels.

Table 3.1 provides examples of revenue models for various types of organizations, while Figure 3.1 provides a visual breakdown of the revenue model for a retailer. Revenue is a function of the sum of price (see Chapter 9) multiplied by units sold across all its products. In turn, units sold is a function of market share and category growth. Furthermore, market share is a function of not just the organization's marketing efforts but also the efforts of its competitors. Category growth is a function of changes in customer taste and in population growth rate and demographics.

Table 3.1. Revenue model for different businesses.

Business	Revenue Model
Retailer	Average price per unit × total units sold
Credit card firm	(Annual fee × Members) + (Average credit balance × Interest rate) + (Average credit purchases × Retailer fee)
Not-for-profit	Total public donations + Total government donations
Consultants	Average rate per hour × Total hours billed
Grocery delivery service	Percentage of sales revenue × Total grocery partner order volume + Delivery fees

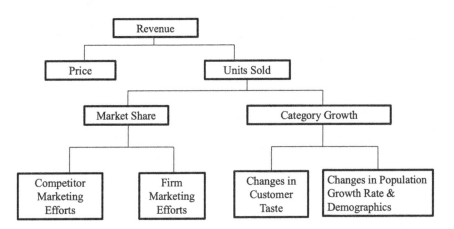

Figure 3.1. A decomposition of the revenue for a retailer.

Suppose that in the month of April, a global clothing retailer saw a 12% decline in its denim revenue. Since the price of its denim had been constant during that period, the decline is due to fewer units being sold. Further analysis revealed that there were no changes in category growth but there was a decline in market share. An analysis of the competitive environment revealed no new marketing activity by a major competitor, leaving management to conclude that the decline in units sold had to do with a decline in its own marketing efforts. It is now looking to arrest and reverse the decline in denim revenue. What are the next steps? Where and how does management deploy the marketing efforts to increase the sales? Should they offer a special denim promotion? Should it increase the style variety of its denim brand? Or should it offer discounts on other merchandise in the hope of attracting more people into its stores?

3.2 Decomposing Revenue

To address these questions, management will need deeper insight into the revenue model that will serve the following two purposes:

(1) Ability to diagnose specifically which piece of the revenue function requires adjustments, resulting in direct and efficient use of marketing efforts.
(2) Ability to define revenue strategies which are aligned with the nature of the business.

A traditional revenue analysis approach has led management to link the decline in revenues to their marketing efforts. But this initial diagnosis is potentially inadequate. If this store was not blessed with an overabundance of marketing dollars (which is the case for most businesses), the organization would benefit more from a precise knowledge of the area in which to direct its efforts in order to achieve specificity, targetedness, efficiency, quantification, and prioritization of marketing efforts. In other words, the retailer needs to target efforts toward specific elements of the revenue model which will yield the highest value for the manufacturer. As illustrated earlier in Chapter 1 (and summarized in Table 3.2), this can be accomplished by decomposing the metric of success — in this case, the revenue.

Table 3.2. The drivers of long-term revenue.

Function	Definition
Traffic	Total average number of customers visiting a business at a given time.
Conversion rate	Number of transactions as a percent of total traffic.
Basket size	Total dollar value of each customer.
Customer repeat/loyalty	Frequency of a single customer's repeated visits and transactions, and the basket sizes purchased in those repeat visits.

Note: Short term revenue = Traffic × Conversion rate × Basket size.

3.2.1 *Why Decomposition Helps*

An organization has developed a new type of widget for which the marketing manager must select the most effective marketing strategy. They dither between two bundles of marketing interventions that each involves some elements of sampling, couponing, advertising, and after-sales support. However, the first bundle has an innovative sampling and couponing element, while the second one has an innovative advertising and after-sales support element. In order to determine the better bundle of marketing, the manager tests each one in a different city — matched on all dimensions other than the marketing bundles — for four consecutive months. The two selected cities, C1 and C2, display similar characteristics, such as population size, demographics, average income, and population density. Note that in our stylized example, (i) the manager has selected C1 for the sampling-and-coupon intensive bundle and C2 for the advertising-and-support heavy strategy; (ii) market share is the metric used in evaluating the success of each marketing effort; and (iii) during the study, transactional data is collected on each customer interaction.

At the end of the four months, the market share for the new product in both cities amounts to exactly 20% for each. This result creates a dilemma for the manager who has spent four months of organization resources to run the study and is still uncertain about which strategy to use. It is evident that market share information alone is insufficient in

Insight Box 3.1
MCV Insight
Simple market share percentages fail to extract the revenue components which drive the overall market share. In ignoring revenue decomposition, opportunities to apply best practices for revenue generation across the organization can be easily missed.

determining the more effective strategy. However, if market share is broken further into two components — trial rate (defined as the percent of the market that makes one purchase) and stable repeat purchase rate (the percent of triers that continue to purchase the product after three months) — there may be hope in providing more detail for the analysis. In particular, we note that the market share is the product of the trial rate and the repeat purchase rate.

The sampling program in C1 resulted in a strong trial rate and the advertising and support campaign in C2 produced a desirable repeat purchase rate. With this information the manager can combine the elements that work for a high trial rate and the elements that work for a high conversion rate and apply them to the launch. Through decomposition of market share, the manager can hone in on the key elements driving the success of each measure and provide a compelling story for the importance of applying both marketing strategies across different launch regions (Table 3.3).

Our retailer can benefit from a similar approach. Given that revenue is the product of traffic, conversion rates, basket size, and number of repeat visits (loyalty) in a given period, the store will need to track each of these elements separately over time to determine which of these is responsible for the decline. Table 3.4 provides the definition of traffic, conversion rate, basket size, and loyalty for different businesses; and Table 3.5 gives a non-exhaustive list of approaches to influence the first three of these elements.

Table 3.3. Decomposition of market share.

	Trial Rate	Conversation Rate	Total Market Share
C1	**70%**	20%	15%
C2	30%	**70%**	15%

3.2.2 *Traffic*

Consider two types of retailers that are looking to increase traffic: one a bookstore and the other a department store. The bookstore changes its window display merchandise depending on the time of day. In the mornings when most shoppers are stay-at-home parents, the store displays children's books. In the afternoons — around the time students are out of school — the store displays books on sports, pop music, and culture.

In comparing two department stores, Walmart and Macy's, the differences in their traffic strategies are evident. Walmart builds its stores in suburbs and customers are forced to drive long distances to reach

> **Insight Box 3.2**
>
> **MCV Insight**
> Traffic is not merely a matter of location. Given location, traffic can be influenced through directed marketing strategies aimed at increasing traffic for the business.

them. However, Walmart continues to attract traffic into its stores by offering rock-bottom prices and convincing its customers of its everyday low price strategy. Macy's, on the other hand, is known to locate its stores in prime locations. For example, Macy's in Manhattan is located at one of New York's busiest shopping areas and Macy's in San Francisco is located at the heart of downtown in Union Square. Unlike Walmart, customers do not associate Macy's with rock-bottom prices and many probably are not willing to travel far distances to shop at a Macy's. The store's strategy is to locate itself in the prime location of any major metropolitan and ensure traffic via browsers who might wander into the store to kill time between other activities.

3.2.3 *Conversion Rate*

Home Depot — an American retailer of home improvement and construction products — came up with a creative strategy to include women in the shopping experience. In order to convert the women

Table 3.4 Defining the elements of decomposed revenue.

Business	Traffic	Conversion Rate Determinant	Basket Size Determinant	The Definition of Loyalty to Different Businesses
Consumer packaged goods	Defined by suppliers that agree to carry your products. Driven by the size and location of the suppliers and product placement on shelves. Determined by obtaining records on sales of a certain good segment (e.g., Shampoo) at the various distribution locations.	Firm's market share of a specific segment (e.g., Shampoo): The ratio of firm sales to total segment sales.	Total number of the same branded products (from different categories of goods) in a single customer transaction.	Achieved by providing incentives that minimize switching between brands.
Consulting	Determined by the total number of client opportunities for potential firm pitches.	The ratio of total engagements and projects won to the total number of pitches.	Total value of a client comprised of more than one case.	Defined by superior services that meet and exceed client expectations. Achieved through repeat business where the firm does not have to prepare an RFP (request for proposal) in selling its next case.

(Continued)

Retail banking	Defined by branch locations and online presence. Determined by the total number of clients who seek banking services at a given time.	The ratio of total number of clients (savings/ checking accounts, investments, etc.) to number of inquirers.	Customer's purchase of different services offered by the same bank (credit cards, investments, mortgages, etc.).	Defined by superior service and incentives. Achieved through client repeat business and portfolio enhancement.
Non-profit organization	Defined by effective use of sponsorships, partnerships and advertisements, which create visibility. Determined by total inquiries.	The ratio of new members and/ donators to the total number of inquiries.	If the not-for-profit is involved in promoting more than one cause: gaining member commitment to the different causes.	Defined by continuous membership and an increase in friends and families' referrals.
Retailer	Determined by total number of customers who visit the retailer's location at a given time.	The ratio of total number of transactions to the total number of retailer visits.	Number of units of different goods sold in a single transaction.	Achieved through incentives. Defined by increase in returning customers.

Table 3.5 How to influence traffic, conversion rate, and basket size.

	How to Impact Traffic
Cause	Action
Competitor traffic	Observe and track traffic for major competitors.
In-store displays	Observe customer attention and reaction to in-store displays.
Awareness	Track media advertising aimed at creating brand awareness.
Promotion	Design promotions that drive customer visits to a store to (a) buy deeply discounted products, (b) redeem gifts, or (c) sample products or lifestyle awards.
Customer service	Observe customer reaction to staff.
	How to Impact Conversion Rate
Cause	Action
Competitor conversion rate	Compare conversion rate to that of the competitor's.
Customer service	Observe customer interaction with staff and service provided in completing transactions.
Product/service positioning	Observe customer attention and reaction to product/service positioning within the store.
Customer incentives	Offer incentives for customers to complete their transaction. Track the impact of the incentives.

(Continued)

Strategies to Increase Basket Size

Strategy	Definition	Example
Up-selling	To promote or sell to customers a higher-priced version of the product/service they intend to purchase (or have purchased in the past)	Vintage wine stores employees are incentivized to suggest more expensive wine recommendations to the consumers.
Cross-selling	To promote or sell to customers who are considering a purchase decision related to a (complementary) product/services	Online music and bookstores (e.g., iTunes and Amazon) do an excellent job at cross-selling. They are able to suggest to consumers similar songs or books based on their previous purchases.
Penetration-selling	To promote or sell more of the same product/service to a customer making a purchase decision	Mobile service providers often offer family mobile packages to head of households where for a lower price, each person in the family can own a cell phone.

Insight Box 3.3
MCV Insight
Naturally, the more time customers spend shopping or contemplating purchase decisions, the greater the likelihood of them making a purchase.

into actual shoppers, Home Depot introduced "Do-It-Herself" workshops for women only. This strategy not only increased the number of shoppers to include women but also prolonged the time an average shopper spent in a Home Depot.[2] As the above example illustrates, management can influence the rate at which customers purchase their products by modifying customer service, positioning, and incentives. In fact, often simply getting customers to spend more time in a store can increase sales.

3.2.4 *Basket Size*

The value of the basket of goods/services can be structured in numerous ways. For instance, customers often purchase more units of lower ticket items and fewer units of higher ticket items. Hence, different strategies to increase basket size will be needed, depending on the type of product/service being offered. Figure 3.2 provides a numerical example of two baskets with different product compositions. The first is a "high value basket" since the price/unit is $100 and the second basket, a "low value basket," has a price/unit value of $27, despite there being more units.

Insight Box 3.4
MCV Insight
Product relevancy and customer path predication can influence basket size.

Typically, there are three strategies to increase basket size: up-selling, cross-selling, and penetration-selling. We start off by noting that the idea

---

[2]Waters, J. (2007, October 10). Home Depot Sets to Test Stores Geared to Women. *Wall Street Journal* (Eastern edition), B.11B; Williams, N. (2006, April). Women: Initiative: Home Depot/Chatelaine. *Strategy* (Toronto, Canada), 52.

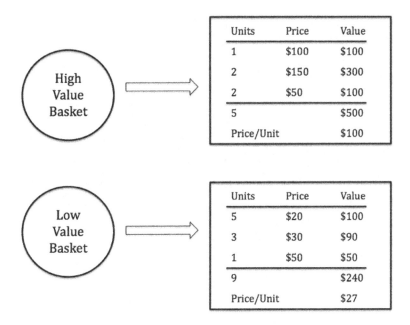

Figure 3.2 Calculating basket size.

of increasing basket size should not be misinterpreted as the skill associated with selling customers products that they will not need. While this might increase immediate revenue, it also comes with the risk of the customer not returning to the store! We encourage organizations to ensure that their basket-growing approaches are ethical and respectful to the customer, and are based on an understanding of their needs.

The Swedish retailer IKEA provides an excellent example for how design features of a store — in this case, store layouts — can be used to increase basket size. A marked path for customers takes them first past necessities — items that they typically came to the store to purchase (e.g., a living room furniture set). Next, the path takes them past aisles laden with high-margin impulse items that complement the items already purchased, increasing the likelihood that the customer may be tempted into purchasing — or recall the need to purchase — these items, resulting in a larger basket size. Other design features may include merchandising (displaying complementary products in physical proximity) or in-store signage.

3.2.5 *Loyalty/Repeat Purchase*

Customers' repeat purchase and loyalty rates are a function of consistently meeting customers' needs and expectations and surpassing the efforts of competitors. As mentioned earlier, the cost of serving a loyal customer is much lower than acquiring a new customer. Once a business has acquired a customer, it becomes ever more critical for it to maintain that customer through continued service and relevant (customized) incentives that encourage repeat visits.

Our discussion of loyalty is brief here as Chapter 4 offers a more comprehensive analysis on the management of loyalty for value creation using data-driven systems to generate loyalty programs. For most competitive businesses, loyalty programs are critical for not only attracting new customers but also retaining current ones. The travel and tourism industry has benefited greatly from loyalty programs. Most major airlines provide their customers with frequent-flyer programs where customers can collect points based on the total number of miles traveled per trip. The points in aggregate can be redeemed for merchandise, money, or even free air trips. Hotels are another industry which use loyalty programs to increase repeat business. It is not uncommon for airlines to partner with hotel ladders wherein customers can accumulate points for both businesses under one program. What is important to note here is that each business needs a program unique to the needs of its customers. An airline program cannot simply be transferred to a retailer or a fast food chain. It is important for managers to understand the precise needs of their customers and offer programs that are relevant and valuable to them.

3.3 Market Research for Building Ladders

Now that the retailer has a clear understanding of which specific element of their revenue model they need to work on, it will need to build a ladder to guide their efforts. Recall that a value ladder provides a one-step-at-a-time pathway between a prospect (or a new customer) to the best customer. A ladder provides a pathway that the organization can guide the customer along; and therefore, a guiding path for its customer value function.

We first note that ladders could be built more generally for the whole business, or for a specific element of the revenue model. Depending on what the goal of building the ladder is, the start and end points will be different. Consider two examples:

(1) A store manager is looking to increase conversion rates. In particular, they are focused on trying to get people who walk into their store (or arrive on their website) to make a purchase. In this case, the bottom of the ladder represents a prospect that has just walked into a store, the top represents a customer that has just made a purchase, and each step in the ladder is a specific behavior that successively leads toward a purchase.

(2) A chief marketing officer is looking to develop profitable customers. In particular, they are looking to attract new customers that will eventually resemble their current "stars customers." In this case, the bottom of the ladder represents a prospect that the business development manager is considering, the top represents a customer that behaves like their current stars, and each step in the ladder is a specific set of behaviors (e.g., types of products purchased, frequency of purchase, or volumes purchased), with each step resulting in a customer that is more valuable than the previous step.

Ladders are best constructed using appropriate research methods. In the next section, we overview key market research methods and illustrate how they could be used to generate ladders.

3.3.1 *Traditional Market Research*

The primary purpose of market research is to identify, gather, and analyze information related to customer preferences, behavior, and consumption. In inferring customer behavior, traditional market research uses transactional and market research data. However, as we discuss in the following, these techniques may not have the ability to allow an organization to map out a representative ladder of its customers.

(1) *Transactional data*: As its name implies, transactional data refers to information gathered based on actual transactions between the company and its customers (or between a company's competitors and its potential customers). These data include details of the actual transaction (e.g., units purchased, price paid, time and date of purchase, and how the payment was made) as well as other demographic information that may be routinely collected as part of the sales process (addresses, phone numbers, etc.). These data can be particularly handy in allowing us to determine revenues (and value) associated with a given customer at different steps of a ladder. However, transactional data do not reveal any insight into underlying behaviors that result in a purchase. For example, it is very difficult to infer the conversion rate of the business from transactional data, or to identify what factors trigger a purchase, a click on a website, or a donation to a charity. Therefore, these data along might not be helpful in *constructing* ladders.

(2) *Survey-based market research:*
Traditional marketing also
uses market research to
test new products for innovation, to modify existing
products, or to understand
the size and structure of
new potential markets.

> **Insight Box 3.5**
>
> **MCV Insight**
> The insight from transactional data is limited to quantitative analysis. To stretch the application of such data into customer purchase behavior will increase the result of inaccurate and vague conclusions.

There are two types of research that most companies employ in understanding new markets — product-focused research and culture-focused research.[3] Product-focused research uses surveys, focus groups, interviews, and home visits to ask customers about existing or prototypical products or services. Culture-focused research uses measures like census data and demographics in evaluating the general aspects of a culture. According to recent estimates, the bulk of research activity across a wide range of industries is focused on collecting and analyzing survey-based data. Statistical considerations like the ability to obtain large sample sizes as well as managerial preferences for numerical estimates drive this predominance of survey activities. However, recent research in behavioral science raises questions about the validity of survey-based research. It suggests that survey data is adequate for collecting factual information. However, to (a) identify steps in a purchasing process (steps in a ladder) and (b) to offer an enhanced approach to the process of product innovation, survey data will be insufficient. In particular, we discuss six axioms (assumptions that are usually taken for granted) underlying market research and discuss the reality.

---

[3]Kumar, V. & Whitney, P. (2010). Faster, Cheaper, Deeper User Research. *Design Management Journal (Former Series)*, *14*(2), 50–57. https://doi.org/10.1111/j.1948-7169.2003.tb00041.x

Axiom 1: Customer preferences are deeply ingrained and customers are able to articulate these preferences reasonably well.

Reality 1: Research shows us that in many cases customers do not have good insights into why they made purchases or displayed certain behaviors. When asked questions, they create stories to appear consistent and logical — they construct responses to questions rather than retrieve them from their memory. This occurs simply because it is very difficult for customers to know what they want when they have not yet experienced it. As customers, even if we don't like certain things about a product, we tend to make compromises without putting much thought into it. We become habituated with current conditions and learn to accept them as they are so that we fail to ask for a new solution. Market research is useful when testing customer preference in selecting one product over another. The technique becomes impractical though when the company is in search of developing a new product (or technology) not yet familiar to customers. Hence, research could suggest a decision-making process which doesn't actually exist in the real world and is merely an artifact of the method used to collect the data. Table 3.6 looks at Research in Motion's Blackberry as an example of a product that customers were never explicitly able to identify as a need but which has evolved to become a necessity for many.

Axiom 2: Customer responses are invariant to the type of questions asked and the specific frame used.

Reality 2: In line with the argument that respondents construct responses, a stream of research suggests that the exact question serves as a crutch for respondents' construction efforts, influencing their response. There is a need to balance different ways of framing

Table 3.6 Can customers predict the value of an innovation?[4]

Blackberry is an innovative wireless handheld device introduced by Research In Motion (RIM) in 1999. Since its initial launch the product has grown from a simple two-way push e-mail and messaging device to a complex gadget with mobile telephone, push e-mail, text messaging, Internet faxing, web browsing, instant messaging, and many other capabilities. At the time of its launch — still during an era when mobile cell phones where still an anomaly, most customers did not have a need for a mobile e-mail device; hence RIM targeted the Blackberry at C-Level executives and government officials. It took five years from the time of its launch for RIM to reach 1 million subscribers, another year to reach 2 million, and by mid-2008, Blackberry's total subscribers amounted to over 14 million. How was RIM able to foresee a customer need that at the time of its launch, customers didn't recognize themselves? Today, it's not just the C-Level executives of top firms and government officials that carry Blackberries; it's the undergrad analyst, the MBA associate, the keen marketer, the busy construction worker, and the diligent parent.

The reality is that RIM was able to create a market that everyone else is now chasing. The executives at RIM recognized an opportunity to increase corporate efficiency by offering a product that mobilized e-mail sending and receiving — a task that was achievable only by remaining fixated at a personal computer. Keeping in mind that this is a product that customers did not recognize as a need, RIM did not waste marketing efforts on advertising and promotion. Instead, it invested in product samples allowing potential customers to experience the benefits of Blackberry prior to making a purchase. It didn't take long for executives to realize the converted downtown (e.g., traveling to meetings, waiting at airports) into productive time as well as the immediacy in responding to urgent matters. Today, the Blackberry is a "must-have" for all employees in a large organization. A device that just a decade ago wasn't even considered a need by customers is now nicknamed "Crackberry."

a question to gain quantitative answers with open-ended questions effective for qualitative analysis. Researchers are also known to develop questionnaires that direct respondents to a predefined path in order to prove their own hypothesis. For example, asking

[4]Based on the following references: CBC. (2008, February 21). *RIM Sees Strong Gain in BlackBerry Subscribers.* http://www.cbc.ca/consumer/story/2008/02/21/rimoutlook. html; Massachusetts Institute of Technology (2007, April 1). Finding the Right Job for Your Product. *MIT Sloan Management Review.* https://sloanreview.mit.edu/article/ finding-the-right-job-for-your-product/; EWEEK. (2004, November 22). RIM, Seven Gain Support. https://www.eweek.com/mobile/rim-seven-gain-support/

customers whether they were "satisfied with an experience" causes them to seek reasons for being satisfied, while asking them if they "found any reason to be dissatisfied" causes them to seek different evidence. In a recent study, we were asked by a large multinational bank to examine their customer satisfaction scores. This bank had intercepted customers leaving several branches and asked them "Were you satisfied with the service you received today?" Ninety-one percent said yes. The study was repeated shortly thereafter, with the following, slightly modified question. "In your opinion, could the bank have done anything differently to provide you with excellent service? Were you dissatisfied with the level of service today?" Seventy-seven percent said yes. Thus the bank found 91% satisfaction and 77% dissatisfaction — both in the same time period — the difference was generated only because of the different framing of the question.

Axiom 3: Market research that strips the context away from the customer decision-making process makes it more generalizable. They are presented with only a simple choice/task between products.

Reality 3: Research shows that customer choice is meaningless in the absence of context, and choice between products swings dramatically as a function of (a) what else is available; (b) what the consumption occasion is; (c) what social and emotional factors surround the purchase occasion; and (d) other visceral factors like need states and arousal and background factors like mood, ambience, etc. While traditional economic theory (which was the basis of survey approaches to study customer choice) treats context as an unnecessary nuisance and attaches all the value of the product to the product itself, new research in behavioral decision-making suggests otherwise. In fact, as we will discuss in Chapter 6, context is the soil in which customers sink the roots of their utility/value functions, and ignoring its relevance is one of the biggest problems in marketing research.

Axiom 4: Simple questions (multiple choice or scales) and simple responses are preferred to open-ended questions.

Reality 4: The only reason for preferring simple responses is that they are convenient to code and analyze for the researcher. Arguably, forcing respondents to pigeonhole responses into categories that do not represent how they think results in responses that are an artifact of the manner in which responses were coded.

Axiom 5: Customers are able to recall and share their insights about their post-product experiences.

Reality 5: Research shows that insights on how to improve a product or service often strike customers as they use a product or service but these are lost in retrospective surveys. Certain valuable customer insights and opinions can only be captured at the time of the experience as it becomes more difficult for customers to recall what they might consider to be insignificant thoughts.

Axiom 6: Customers' experiences can be captured in numeric and text format.

Reality 6: The richness in data can be enhanced by capturing customer experience through visual and auditory means. Visual and auditory data can provide cues to customer behavior that cannot be captured from numeric and textual data. These cues may include triggers of product use, frustrations, and other intangible product-related attributes. In an experiment to understand customer frustration with public transportation, we equipped several commuters with audio recorders and asked them to record their daily experiences with public transportation. This exercise enabled us to capture the feelings associated with various day-to-day commuter frustrations that would have otherwise gone unobserved with the use of a post-experience survey.

Biases in customer responses to survey questions can be minimized through multiple question framing. In large surveys, the researcher is encouraged to frame questions in multiple ways and then randomly set up different versions of the questionnaire so that different respondents see different frames. In cases where responses are invariant to the manner of asking questions, the data is valid. Table 3.7 offers a table summarizing the myths of traditional marketing, the realities, and ways of fixing the problems inherent in the method.

(3) *Observation Research:* The observation of behavior is an alternative approach to transactional data and market research used to uncover customers' preferences and gain an insight into their decision-making process while making a purchase. Unlike surveys, interviews, and focus groups, where customers are placed in artificial settings that differ from their day-to-day routine and activities, customer behavior observation takes place in the customer's own environment. This approach to market research will yield five types of information, which would otherwise not be possible to gather through traditional market research — triggers of use, interaction with the user's environment, user's customization, intangible attributes of the product, and unarticulated user needs.[5]

We note that while observation research can often be a fairly involved and effortful process in the brick-and-mortar world, it is relatively trivial in an online digital world. An online retailer might have the potential to observe previously difficult-to-assess data like what sequence a customer searches in, how she sorts her search result, how long she tends to view each item, or whether she leaves items in her cart for a period of time before making a final purchase

---

[5]Leonard, D. & Rayport, J. F. (1997). Spark Innovation Through Empathic. *Harvard Business Review, 75*(6), 105–108.

Table 3.7. The myths, realities, and fixes for survey-based approach to market research.

Myth	Reality	Fix
Customer preferences are deeply engrained	Customers do not have a good insight into why they make purchases	Multiple question framing
Customer responses are invariant to the type of questions asked	An exact question serves as a crutch for customer's construction efforts, and hence could change the response	Greater reliance on context-rich environments through observation
Good market research strips the context away from the customer decision-making process	Choice is meaningless in the absence of context	Create experiments where researcher can "manipulate" a number of factors and see which of these actually cause customers to change behavior
Simple questions and simple responses are preferred than open-ended questions	Only reason for preferring simple response is that they are convenient to code and analyze for the researcher	Use of technology to listen to customer
Customers are able to express insights into product preferences and modifications	Insights often strike customers as they use a product or service, but these are lost in retrospective surveys	Capture data by asking customers to carry an audio recording device during shopping and purchase decision experiences
Customers' experiences can be captured in numeric and text format	The richness in data can be enhanced by capturing customer experience through visual and auditory means	Create experiments involving customers using cameras and videos to capture experiences

decision. Unfortunately, this ease of gathering data has meant that sometimes organizations have gone too far in tracking online behaviors, thereby creating concerns about loss of privacy.

Metaphorically speaking, a walk on a beach will leave behind a set of footprints that others who walk can see and track. However, these footprints are temporary because tides will usually wash them out. The online marketplace can be metaphorically modeled as a scenario in which the footprints are indelible and can never be removed. These footprints can be shared by anyone anywhere in the world.[6] Online behaviors can, in theory, never be a personal experience. In Chapter 7, we provide further details on different approaches to privacy. For now, we simply urge managers to make sure that the low costs of online observation do not result in a violation of customer privacy, and that the principles of choice, respect, and the right to not be identified are maintained in online data collection.

These traditional approaches to research can be complemented with alternative approaches.

3.3.2 *Alternate Approaches: Using Non-Text Media*

Data on customer behavior can also be gathered from visual, auditory, and sensory cues. Technology can and should be used to institutionalize the kinds of information and customer insights that were previously available only through personal interactions. For example, a hotel can monitor guest preferences about things like what kind of pillows they request or what time of day they typically check in by using simple listening devices (of course, with consent). Use of photography and videography can provide cues to subtle behaviors that may go unnoticed to a casual observer.

The use of photography can be helpful in involving customers in the research process as well. Recently, a customer behavior data

---

[6]Kim, M., Ly, K., & Soman, D. (2015). *A Behavioural Lens on Consumer Privacy*. Toronto, Canada: Behavioural Economics in Action at Rotman (BEAR) Report Series, available at http://www.rotman.utoronto.ca/bear.

study was conducted in an attempt to assist the provincial government of a major city to increase usage of its public transport system. In this study, a sample of daily transit commuters and daily car drivers was selected and divided into two groups, "transit users" and "drivers." Each group was given the responsibility of putting together data that best represented their commuting experience. The researchers provided the transit users with a disposable camera for one week and directed them to take pictures of *all things* that created an emotional reaction during their public transit commute. The drivers were asked to write a diary of their daily commute experience for one week. They were asked to provide details of their thoughts, emotions, and emotional reactions to events, objects, and other drivers on the road. At the end of the study, members of the research team sat with both groups to conduct one-on-one interviews.

The transit users were asked to (a) place the pictures in an order that conveyed a story, (b) describe each picture in detail, and (c) provide reasons for taking the picture. Following this assessment, research team members categorized each picture as people, objects, environment, messages, and services (POEMS). This framework helps researchers tag observations by categorizing them under one or more of the five listings.[7] If the purpose of the picture was to display frustration with overcapacity in transit vehicles, then the picture was tagged with a "P" for people. At the end of each interview, we were able to compare POEMS that made public transportation enjoyable versus ones that made it unpleasant. Similarly, team members met with the drivers to discuss each diary and their emotional and behavioral experiences. As the subjects reflected on each diary, team members categorized their experiences into POEMS. We were then able to establish common causes for different types of emotions between the two study groups.

---

[7]Kumar, V. & Whitney, P. (2003). Faster, Cheaper, Deeper User Research. *Design Management Journal, 53*, 50–57.

Insight Box 3.6
MCV Insight
To hand over the task of data gathering to users or customers themselves improves the validity of data and provides a more accurate insight into the customer's intention and behaviors.

As another example of using photographs in market research, we were approached (in 2003) by a property development firm in an Asian city that wanted to develop a radically new format for a shopping center — one that was better aligned with what customers truly believed was a good shopping experience. The developer wanted us to help them understand the elements of the shopping experience for different groups of customers. Before approaching us, they had commissioned a market research agency that had decomposed the shopping experience into a series of attributes (these included location, ambience, parking, variety in store types — unfortunately, all very vague and not actionable) and administered a lengthy survey to a large group of respondents. Many weeks and dollars later, the agency had come back with a fancy report showing that most customers reported that most of the attributes were important in deciding where to shop.

We adopted a different approach. We recruited a number of customers — sampled to include a sample representative of the target population and gave them 24-exposure disposable cameras. Our instructions were simple: "take up to 24 pictures that best represent what a complete shopping center visit means to you." As in the earlier example, participants then debriefed us on their photographs and used them to tell stories. Some of the most interesting insights we got were by comparing the photographs taken by different subgroups. For instance, when comparing men and women, we found that most men took their first picture in the parking lot or while entering the shopping center whereas many women took a picture at home getting organized to go shopping. Men took pictures of store signs, products, and price tags. Women took pictures of the coffee shop, the concierge service, the lounge areas, and of other groups of people who were enjoying themselves in the shopping center. Distinct behavioral patterns emerged when we compared the young with the old and smaller families with larger ones.

Another use of innovative media in market research comes from yet another example for mass transport, this time in Hong Kong. The goal of a market research project was to compare the effectiveness of survey-based research that asked users of the mass transport system for their suggestions on improvement with that of a "real time" survey methodology.[8] In conducting the survey that asked respondents to recall and report recent consumption experiences, the students targeted a group of commuters exiting Hong Kong subway stations and asked them for suggestions on how the mass transport company could improve their service. To conduct the real-time survey, a group of respondents were each given a handheld audio recorder and asked to carry it around for a period of a week. They were given the following instructions:

Often when we ride the MTR (subway), we have complaints or suggestions that pop up during the experience; we wish that the MTR did things differently. Every time you have such an "I wish" moment, please speak into the [audio recorder].

At the end of the week, the audio recorders were collected and the suggestions transcribed. Comparing the two methods showed that the real-time methodology resulted in approximately 12 times as many suggestions per capita as the traditional survey, and — based on the evaluation of an expert panel — a significantly higher quality of creative and innovative ideas. The real-time survey method is especially useful in situations where experiences extend over time, and in which each small suggestion might be small enough not to be remembered — or be considered too trivial to report — but a collection of such small suggestions might result in significant improvements.

[8]Soman, D. (2004). *The Pitfalls of Market Research*. Teaching note, Hong Kong University of Science and Technology.

The underlying idea of gathering real-time data on customer behavior is to capture customers in their normal settings as they carry out routine activities. Now although the use of technological devices certainly simplifies the investigative process, simple observation of customers can also lead to ample discoveries of the subconscious behavior of customers. Store managers can discreetly follow and observe the actions of their customers without videotapes and photos. A great deal of skill is required in order to detect subtle behaviors; with practice, though, managers will be able to sharpen those skills.

3.3.3 *Alternate Approaches: Using Technology*

Continuous advances in the field of technology provide us with ample tools, techniques, and options to methodically observe and gather customer behavior. Instead of asking customers about hypothetical choices, researchers can observe real choices in their contexts of situational, social, psychological, and emotional factors. A recent publication recognizes several unconventional approaches for data collection and active market research in gathering information on a customer's path data; the article defines path data as a record of a person's movement in a spatial configuration, or, how a person interacts with his or her environment. For example, tracking customers' paths during grocery shopping can easily be achieved by installing Radio-Frequency Identification Tags (RFID) beneath shopping carts.[9] The RFID tag emits a uniquely coded signal every five seconds indicating the location of the cart. Purchase records can be obtained from scanner data and matched to the path of the cart, providing a complete record of the shopping trip. This gadget can provide store managers with various kinds of information such

---

[9]Hui, S., Fader, P., & Bradlow, E. (2009). Path Data in Marketing: An Integrative Framework and Prospectus for Model Building. *Marketing Science, 28*(2), 320–335. Retrieved May 2, 2021, from http://www.jstor.org/stable/23884266

as the most visited zones or the most utilized grocery paths. Managers can employ the data to determine the optimal layout of the store to increase shopping efficiency or to increase customer shopping time. Another noteworthy method of data collection includes eye tracking — the subject's eye movement is captured while viewing an advertisement using infrared corneal reflection technology. This device gives advertisement developers valuable data into customers' behavioral reactions to different ads. One more commonly used tool is web browsing — an internet website that tracks the movement of shoppers and browsers to predict online shopping behavior. It goes without saying that it is important that in the age of privacy and customer protection, that marketers are being transparent about the data they are collecting, how they're collecting it, and what they intend to use it for. Customers should have control over their data and the tracking mechanism.

3.4 Building Value Ladders

How can research inform the construction of a value ladder? To best understand the process, we would like to look at a project in which researchers were asked to (a) visit an apparel store, (b) select a target segment, (c) make observations about the shopping behavior of the target, and (d) develop a preliminary ladder map for the apparel store. In selecting an apparel store, students were advised to pick a convenient store to visit where shopping activity is frequent yet allows adequate time and space for observations. Note the parallels between a physical store and an online business; and that in the online world, the data collection efforts described here are significantly easier.

Prior to making in-store observations, researchers are directed to observe the level of traffic outside the store entrance — activities such as shoppers' interaction with the store's window display — and to ask themselves the following questions: Does the display attract the shopper's attention? Does it invite them to visit the store? How do shoppers interact with neighboring window displays? Similar observations can be made outside a competitor's store to help students understand the impact of displays on shopper traffic.

Once inside the store, the focus of the study is to observe the patterns of activity between people and objects in the store. Researchers think about how people arrive at a place, how people and goods flow, and what the natural stopping points, thinking points, and talking points are for the customers. Ultimately, they have to look for the non-obvious ways customers make decisions and the subtle cues or interactions that impact their behavior. Table 3.8 provides a list of behaviors that observers should consider and document.

The third step is an analysis of the notes taken during the observation period. Researchers are asked to think about what they wrote and to ask themselves why they attended to those specific items and

Table 3.8 Checklist of actions and behaviors for observers.

Actions and Behaviors
Upon entering the store, at which points of the store path does the customer pause to think, observe, and evaluate?
What are the natural transition points (e.g., mirrors, mannequins, walks, display tables, etc.) in the store?
What catches their attention, what doesn't?
What do they touch or not touch?
What do they pick up or shake?
Does the customer check the price tag immediately upon coming in contact with merchandise?
What path does the customer follow throughout the store? Is it seamless?
Does the customer immediately walk to a specific section or follow a predefined path?
Is the customer attracted by the "sale" section?
How much time does the customer spend in each section of the store? How much time do they spend in aggregate?
How many items does the customer take into the fitting room?
How does the customer react to sales people?
Does the customer take note of the mannequins in the store?

Prospect → Browse → Interest → Try → Add-On → Purchase → Repeat

Figure 3.3 Steps on the value ladder.

not to others. How do their assumptions influence their observed data? What are some of the trends and commonalities in actions and behaviors of shoppers? The analysis assists them in structuring their observations into concepts and categories and in looking for relationships between the categories. This structure will help the researcher clarify the persuasive influences created by the environment and the people in it.

The final step of the project is the development of a preliminary ladder. If, for example, the data suggests that in most situations customers browse through the shelves and racks prior to displaying an interest in any particular item, then one can assume that "browse" and "interest" are two separate stages. To increase value for the store and to move the customer up the ladder will require behaviors to be categorized into additional stages. The outcome of this exercise might be a ladder that looks like the one in Figure 3.3.

3.4.1 *Evaluation of the Ladder*

The key to validating a ladder is to look at each step and determine whether or not that particular step changes the probability of the occurrence of the final outcome (say, purchase) or of other subsequent observable steps. For example, we can test the "browse" step by documenting the total number of customers who *browsed* through merchandise and ended up *trying* it, or the total number of customers who *browsed* and eventually made a *purchase*. We can then compare the percentages of total *browsers* that led to *try* or *purchase* and can conclude that *browse* either results in a *purchase* or it does not. If *browse* does lead to *purchase*, the manager will know that by getting more people to browse through the store's merchandise will increase the probability of purchases.

It is important to realize that (a) not every retailer will have the same set of ladders and (b) ladders evolve over time and therefore need to be revised. Hence, managers should conduct customer observations on an ongoing basis.

3.4.2 *A Manager-Determined Ladder*

In all the discussions and examples thus far, we have implicitly suggested that the act of identifying a ladder is essentially the act of imposing a structure on extant customer behavior. This imposition of a structure would allow us to observe actual customer behavior, propose a ladder, and then validate it by additional data collection from observations and/or transactional databases.

In some situations, however, an organization may actually want to create a desired ladder and encourage customers to behave according to that desired path. We illustrate this point with an example. Consider an organization that offers a premium product that only a very small proportion of the population has any degree of expertise and interest in. Examples abound, and include fashion brands such as Coach and Prada, luxury cruise vacations, first-class airline travel, and spa and golf club memberships. The potential clientele of, say, a luxury cruise line is small and the organization could be relatively efficient in marketing its product to a small group of high-income households. The organization could also introduce a loyalty program for its patrons. That said, the cruise product category is such that it is difficult to get people to consume much more beyond a certain limit. At some point, the organization will need to think about marketing its products to people outside its initial target segment.

How would a luxury cruise liner appeal to someone who has never experienced the concept, especially given that fares on cruise ships are high? For instance, cruises in the Mediterranean from Southern European ports on the Queen Elizabeth 2 cost upwards of $2,000.[10] While a lot of people who could afford the occasional cruise would be intrigued by the possibility, it is highly unlikely that they would put down $2,000 for something they have no experience of. In response, the manager could put together a ladder whose steps look like as follows:

Prospect → Sampling Ambience → Entry Level Customer → Long Cruise Customer

The goal of the marketing efforts would now be to create products and services that allow a prospect to move up the ladder, one step at a time. This is important because people need to gradually learn the value of the $2,000 cruise vacation, because the likelihood that they would contemplate an expensive product having never purchased it in the past is very low. In particular, the organization could allow prospects to sample the ambience of the cruise ship by organizing events onboard when the ship is docked in major cities. Perhaps the cruise line could allow corporations and others to organize private events — retreats, weddings, or parties — on the ship. This would give guests the opportunity to learn about the ship and the facilities aboard. The organization could also introduce a short cruise with a low price — one that allows interested and intrigued guests to sample what a full cruise might look like. Star Cruises, a cruise line operating out of Hong Kong (and several other cities), offers a one-night cruise departing from Hong Kong in the late

---

[10]Cunard. (2009, February 4). *On Diverse Voyages in 2008, Queen Mary 2 and Queen Elizabeth 2 Continue to Offer Cunard's Unique Brand of Elegance and Refinement.* http://www.cunard.com/uploads/2008QM2QE2Programme.pdf

> **Insight Box 3.7**
>
> **MCV Insight**
> Think of the value ladder as the guiding steps along which you want to move customers. Each successive stage in the value ladder results in a greater value to the customer, as well as greater value of your customer bases.

evening and returning to shore the next morning.[11] Finally, the organization could target these customers with marketing that encourages them to graduate to full-length cruises. Note that at each level of this ladder, there are additional intermediate steps that the cruise line could think of — cross-selling offshore excursions, food and beverage packages, and flight and hotel packages. By mapping out a desired ladder, an organization can think about any desired end state (here, purchasing a high-ticket cruise) and create a pathway for customers to follow to learn about, and eventually reach that outcome (here, purchase the product).

3.5 What This All Means

In this chapter, we had two goals of (a) articulating the benefits of decomposing revenue into components, and (b) outlining ways in which research could be used to construct ladders. We offer a few prescriptive guidelines for managers.

3.5.1 Guideline 1: Understand and Decompose the Revenue Model

Early in this chapter, we claimed that every business possesses a unique revenue-generating model. That revenue model should next be decomposed into its constituent elements, such as traffic,

---

[11]Star Cruises. (2009, January 27). *Star Cruises Superstar Aquarius.* http://www.starcruises.com/newweb/ebrochures/PDF/SSQ/ssq_itin_oct08-apr09_en.pdf

conversion rate, basket size, and loyalty. Each element of the revenue model could be linked to a specific set of customer behaviors, and allow the manager to answer questions such as "what behaviors would I like my customers to display more of in order to increase value?" Revenue decomposition will allow for focused and targeted marketing efforts.

3.5.2 Guideline 2: In Developing Value Ladders, Both Research and Managerial Intuition and Experience Can Play a Role

Managers are often the best equipped in an organization to make inferences on customers' actions. This capability is perhaps driven by the nature of their role, which demands frequent interactions with customers. Customer-facing managers should be encouraged to interpret data from research, and to contribute actively to ladder-building activities. Likewise, encouraging customer-facing staff to maintain notes on their observations about customer behaviors will also help greatly in refining and updating value ladders over time.

> **Insight Box 3.8**
>
> **MCV Insight**
>
> Not all customers will climb the entire value ladder. Some will stop at intermediate locations, and others will drop out completely. Identify customers who show the greatest propensity to move up, and target marketing interventions to those customers.

3.5.3 Guideline 3: To Ensure Accuracy, Validate the Ladder

Perhaps one of the most critical steps in developing ladders is to test for their validity. The key question to be answered using data is

"Does each step in my proposed ladder influence the final outcome, or any of the subsequent steps?" If the answer is no, then that step is irrelevant and will needlessly lengthen the ladder, resulting in efforts. For example, let's take a manager of a retail bank who has identified "in-store price comparison" as a step on their ladder. In an effort to move customers past the "price comparison" step to the subsequent step, the manager decides to directly publish ads and promotional material which speaks of the bank's pricing advantage versus that of its competitors. If, in fact most customers conduct price comparison research at home via the internet, the manager would have wasted efforts in getting people to move to a step that will likely not change the final outcome.

3.5.4 Guideline 4: In Addition to Current Approaches to Segmentation, Managers Need to Think About Grouping Customers as a Function of Where They Are on a Value Ladder

In addition to traditional methods of segmentation, we call on managers to think about their customers as being grouped by which step on the ladder they are at. We recommend that managers ask themselves the following questions:

(1) What has triggered a customer to visit my business?
(2) How engaged is the customer with the products or services they encounter?
(3) How is the customer making decisions — seeking employee assistance, using brochures and promotional material, or taking advantage of trial opportunities?
(4) How intricate is their purchase decision process?

3.5.5 Guideline 5: Not All Customers Should Climb the Ladder Completely

We underscore the idea that while a ladder might represent the guiding rail that connects an entry level customer — or even a prospect — to the best possible customer, not all entry level customers should climb to the very top. Given their diversity in needs, some may not go beyond the first few steps in the ladder. And given the diversity in the firm's cost to serve them, the optimal step for each customer might be different. Deciding which customers to focus on and which ones to allow to stabilize at interim points is done by estimating the value of the customer at various steps, and by using the customer as a gamble metaphor to model the incremental value of a given transition.

Chapter 4

Loyalty

Loyal: (1) Unswerving in allegiance: as (a) faithful in allegiance to one's lawful sovereign or government, (b) faithful to a private person to whom fidelity is due, and (c) faithful to a cause, ideal, custom, institution, or product.[1]

Retention programs, often called loyalty programs, are all around us. Consider the following commonplace examples:

- A mobile-app-based meal delivery service offers points for each purchase. The number of points earned depend on the number of orders, as well as the dollar spent on each order. Collecting points allow customers to unlock different levels of rewards and discounts as they surpass preset milestones of cumulative points earned.
- An apparel retailer has a "Preferred Customer" card program. Customers can apply for the card by filling out a simple application form, and this entitles them to discounts in the store as well as other service benefits. Likewise, petrol pumps, fast food outlets, department stores, and even coffee shops use card-based programs.
- Most airlines offer frequent flyer programs. Travelers accumulate miles by taking flights and can then "spend" the miles in

---

[1]Loyal. (n.d.). *Merriam-Webster.* Retrieved January 1, 2020, from http://www.merriam-webster.com/dictionary/loyal

exchange for free flights, upgrades to higher classes of service, or access to airport lounges. Travelers who have accumulated a certain number of miles are accorded additional privileges like priority boarding, dedicated seating, and separate lounge areas.

- Many of the airline programs have evolved away from being pure "airline" programs and have now grown to include other products and services. For instance, Cathay Pacific's Asia Miles program allows a member to earn miles at hotels, car rental firms, and other retailers, and to similarly redeem these miles at various member locations.[2]

- In the past, a sandwich shop offered patrons a stamp card. Every sandwich purchased on the card earns a stamp, and a card with 10 stamps on it can be exchanged for a free sandwich. Similarly, a music retailer in India offered stickers for each purchase that can be exchanged for free merchandise.

- Third-party loyalty programs like Air Miles and credit card-based points programs allow the cardholder to collect points at a number of different locations, and to redeem them at either the same — or any other participating location.[3]

- Membership-based retailers like Costco and Sam's Club require customers to pay an annual membership fee in exchange for the privilege of shopping at their locations at low prices.[4] These memberships are annual. In a slightly different example, an Asian grocery supermarket rewards customers with free gifts and special promotions as a function of their cumulative spending over the calendar year.

---

[2]Asia Miles. (2009, January 17). *About Asia Miles.* http://www.asiamiles.com/am/en/about
[3]Air Miles. (2009, January 17). *About Us.* Airmiles.ca. https://www.airmiles.ca/arrow/AboutUsAmrp?referrerUrl=AboutUsHome
[4]Costco. (2009, January 17). *Costco.* http://www.canadaloyalty.com/Programs/costco.html; Sam's Club. (2009, January 17). *Sam's Club.* http://www.canadaloyalty.com/Programs/sams_club.html

- A department store in Canada — Canadian Tire — used to issue points in the form of "Canadian Tire money" which is designed to look like dollar bills as a reward for making purchases in the store.[5] Over the past few years, this program is now digital — though the points are still called Canadian Tire money, they take the form of electronic records on reward cards. The Canadian Tire money can be used as cash for making purchases at a later date.

The fundamental goal in each of these examples is the same — to get a customer who is presently a purchaser of the organization to make yet another purchase with the organization. At the barest bones, that is what a loyalty program is all about.

We can divide all marketing interventions into two different groups. Interventions that get a customer to land on a website or visit a physical store are acquisition activities, and those that occur after the first time that the customer is first in the store onwards can be called retention or loyalty activities. Therefore, loyalty activities can be decomposed into a large number of specific behaviors. These may include:

- A repeat visit to the store
- Increasing the basket size of purchases, through cross-selling and up-selling
- Increasing the frequency of store visits and therefore purchases
- Movement to higher margin products and services
- Referring the store to friends and family members

We will refer to the collection of activities that allow a manager to encourage these behaviors as a loyalty program. In this chapter, we address the following issues:

---

[5] Canadian Tire. (2009, January 17). *Canadian Tire Money.* http://www.canadaloyalty.com/Programs/canadian_tire_money.html

(1) What are the different types of loyalty programs and when should they be used?
(2) What are the underlying goals of a loyalty program?
(3) How can I design a loyalty program to explicitly reward the desired behaviors?
(4) How should I go about setting up a loyalty program?

4.1 The Different Flavors of Loyalty Programs

In each of the above-given examples, the organization is targeting a current purchaser of the product by using some form of a mechanism designed to incentivize that customer to purchase the same product — or all other products from the same organization — again. That said, there are a number of specific differences across the loyalty programs. In some, customers earn the incentive at the end of a single purchase while in others, they have to wait for a number of purchases. In some programs, the benefit is in the form of lower prices; in others it is in the form of gifts and other forms of recognition. Some programs buy loyalty (i.e., they require the customer to commit upfront to purchase, say a membership or apply for a card before they can start earning rewards) while others reward loyalty (i.e., they offer the customer a reward contingent on the number of purchases). And these programs differ in terms of the time horizon over which loyalty is rewarded. The sandwich card offers a reward at the end of every 10 purchases; the Asian supermarket offers a reward for purchases made over a calendar year.

But perhaps the two biggest variables that differentiate loyalty programs are whether (a) they use historical data in triggering promotions and (b) whether the program is operated by the selling organization and transactions to the program are only between the customer and the organization (an "in-house" loyalty program); or is operated by a third-party organization that operates the programs, but signs on a number of different vendors who transact with the

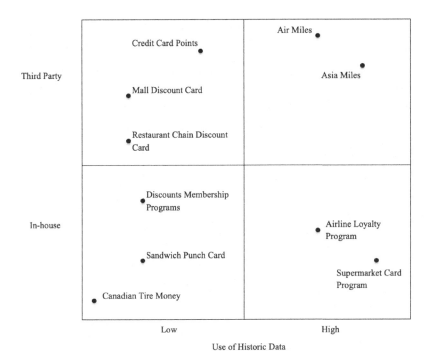

Figure 4.1 A typology of loyalty programs.

customer through the program (a "third-party" or "consortium" program). Figure 4.1 shows a few examples of loyalty programs as a function of these two dimensions.

Let us first focus on the ability of the program to track and leverage historic transactions data. As we will discuss later in the chapter, the ability of a program to build a good database of customer intelligence is perhaps one of the biggest values of a loyalty program. Therefore, we believe that any program that does not have the ability to harness historic data is incomplete at best. In essence, many of the programs that have no memory are structurally similar to price discounts applied over a number of purchases. That said, we can certainly identify with the point that such programs do have a role to play in some conditions, especially to generate relatively quick repeat purchase rates, or perhaps even to accelerate the consumption of the product by impatient customers who are eager to get their free unit, or other gift.[6] Also, such memory-less programs could be used as part of a larger basket of loyalty offerings.

Perhaps the one question that has received the least amount of research effort by both academics and practitioners relates to the relative benefits for an organization of having their own, in-house loyalty program, or to be a member in what are often called third-party (or, sometimes, consortium) loyalty programs.

Insight Box 4.1

MCV Insight

Third-party loyalty programs are offered by external providers. Vendors subscribe to the program, and customers can earn and redeem points across all participating vendors. They are cheaper than in-house loyalty programs, and particularly beneficial to small and growing organizations seeking to establish a reputation.

We conducted a series of interviews with a number of managers in customer facing roles in four different verticals: restaurants, retail, leisure and transportation, and entertainment and asked them for the relative pros and cons of in-house versus third-party programs. The following emerged as key issues:

(1) *The Richness of Data*: This point raises an interesting paradox. Given that a third-party program allows customers to collect and redeem points at an assortment of vendors, it has the capacity to generate a rich dataset that can be used to paint comprehensive behavioral profiles of customers. For example, the American Express or Airmiles database might be able to generate a richer set of customer insights and segments based on travel patterns, hotel preferences, spending levels at restaurants and wine bars, and even patterns of retail shopping. Conversely on the other hand, a bookstore loyalty card can only inform the organization about book-buying behavior. Herein

---

[6]Li, X., Shi, M., & Soman, D. (2007). *Multi Media Rewards Programs*. Rotman School of Management Working Paper, Toronto, Canada: University of Toronto.

lies the paradox. While an in-store program gives more impoverished data, the organization has more control on the data, and indeed the data sits on their computers. In the case of a third-party program, the data is owned by the organization running the program. In some legal frameworks, it might be illegal for this organization to sell the comprehensive dataset to its vendors, although it might be possible for them to provide customer intelligence consulting services.

(2) *The Brand*: Small and relatively new brands can benefit from the established network of a third-party program to drive traffic to their stores. Large established brands get no such benefits.

(3) *The Size of the Establishment*: Smaller establishments like coffee shops and neighborhood stores have neither the volume nor the financial wherewithal to support a loyalty program of their own. The larger the establishment, the more likely is it to be able to support its own loyalty program.

(4) *The Goal of the Program*: For small- to medium-sized establishments, most of our respondents felt that third-party programs were favored if the primary goal of the organization is acquisition and early stages of growth. However, as the relationships of customers with the organizations lengthened, and the goal moved toward retention and value creation at the higher levels of the value ladder, in-house programs are seen as being more valuable. This conclusion makes perfect sense — at the early steps of the value ladder, an organization will indeed benefit by creating incentives for customers of other organizations. And as the length of relationship increases, the focus should shift away from what the customer buys elsewhere to how value can be added once the customer is "in house."

(5) *The Nature of the Product*: There are some products that customers buy infrequently; there are others that are consumed more frequently. Third-party programs make more sense for the former as in-house programs are more valuable for frequently consumed items or frequently visited establishments.

From these responses, we conclude that as a new and small organization enters the marketplace in a quest for customers, it might want to consider enrolling itself in a third-party program. However, as it evolves and starts building a reliable core of customers, it could consider starting an in-house program of its own. An alternate approach is to be involved in both a third-party program as well as an in-house program simultaneously.

4.2 The Motivation for Loyalty Programs

In our framework, a loyalty program refers to any collection of marketing activities that allows an organization to build value from existing customers. When defined in this manner, the question of why a loyalty program is needed is rather tautological.

That said, the concept of a good loyalty program fits perfectly with our "one-step-at-a-time" approach to managing customer value. Keeping in mind the principle that different customers are at different steps of the value ladder, and that the activities and behavioral outcomes that the organization needs to achieve in order to grow their value is therefore different, we claim that good loyalty programs should do the following:

(1) *Create differentiation*: Specifically, they should allow the organization to treat different customers differently.

(2) *Enable marketing interventions to be targeted*: In particular, the program should identify which customers would grow in value as a result of a given intervention, and target that intervention only to those customers.

(3) *Deliver marketing interventions that elicit specific behavior*: Rather than the vague goal of increasing sales or profits, interventions should be designed to elicit specific behaviors like increasing basket size, increasing frequency of store visitations, etc.

Why is it important for the organization to be able to differentiate, and to be able to be targeted and specific? Think about a simple
business model, say an ice cream parlor that sells flavors of ice cream
that vary on margin. Any customer consumes just once a day, but
could choose a small (one scoop), medium (two scoops), or large
size (three scoops). The more frequently they make a purchase,
the more they will consume in a given interval of time. In this
simple, stylized world, there are three drivers of the value of the
customer — the specific flavor they purchase, the frequency of
visitation, and the size of purchase.

First, let us assume that the parlor does not have a loyalty program. The vendor sells ice cream as the demand arises, but does not
have the ability to identify specific customers and to pull out their
purchasing histories. The owner, though, is savvy and recognizes
that he can increase value by encouraging people to buy high-
margin flavors, by increasing the frequency of visitation and by
encouraging referrals. He might influence these behaviors by
spending money on (a) redesigning the displays and offering a
coupon for a high-margin ice cream sample, (b) offering a frequent
buyers discount through — say, a stamp card which is punched for
every visit, and (c) offering an explicit incentive like a volume
discount for increasing consumption per occasion. After pushing
the numbers on costs and increases in value (using analyses like the
ones shown in Chapter 5), the owner decides that the activity with
the highest yield is the one that increases margin through flavor
choice, followed by the one that increases frequency, and finally the
one that increases volume.

Suppose he decides on a coupon-based sampling program to
influence flavor choice and a stamp card to increase frequency. These
interventions might work well; but there is one big downside — there
may already be a number of customers who purchase high-margin
flavors and/or who purchase very frequently, and who don't need to
be incentivized to do so. The owner should not have to spend on

these customers because he would get no additional benefit. So while the goal of the marketing intervention is specific, the owner may end up spending money on behavior that already happens. This is a common problem with many types of businesses, say retailers or business-to-business services. No matter what marketing intervention is used, there will already be a number of customers already displaying the desired behavior, and hence a portion of the marketing spend will be wasted.

Assume for a moment that the ice cream parlor had the ability to track and identify all of their customers through a loyalty program. Customers get a card that can be swiped at the cash register, so that all of their purchases (flavors and quantity) and the date and time of purchases could be recorded. In order to get the card, the customer needs to fill a short form asking for their name, and basic contact information. The customer could also choose whether or not they would like to receive any marketing offers in the mail or electronically. At any point in time, the owner has the ability to generate a framework like the one shown in Figure 4.2.

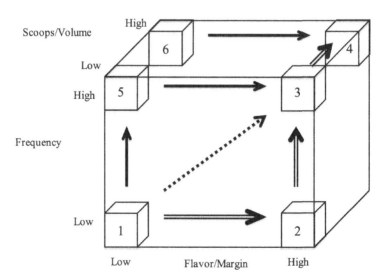

Figure 4.2 The customer value model for an ice cream parlor.

This framework will allow the owner to segment the customer base as a function of behavior. For instance, we have identified three groups of customers on the figure, the Entry-Level Group (Group 1), the Frequency-Opportunity Group (Group 2), and the Volume-Opportunity Group (Group 3). The first group (Group 1) represents customers who are new and have just signed up for the loyalty card. The owner could increase value from them by encouraging any of the three behaviors, but given that flavor choice gives the highest yield, he could send these customers a coupon for a high-margin flavor sample. If the intervention succeeds, they would now look like customers in Group 2.

We refer to this second group as the Frequency-Opportunity group. The reason is simple; now that they purchase the highest margin product, the next opportunity to increase their value comes from trying to get them to consume more frequently. Thus,

> **Insight Box 4.2**
>
> **MCV Insight**
>
> Identify the drivers of customer value (VOC), and then identify the appropriate value ladder that you would like your customers to traverse. This value ladder provides the guiding rails for your loyalty program.

the owner could now give customers in Group 2 — and only those in Group 2 — an offer that gives them an incentive contingent on a specific frequency of purchasing. Likewise, customers in Group 3 are volume-opportunity customers, and they could be given a volume discount offer. We note that the path from Group 1 to Group 2 to Group 3 to Group 4 marked with a solid arrow represents a value ladder, and the owner now has the ability to calculate the value of the average customer in each of these four groups and to model transitions from any one step to any other using the gamble framework that will be introduced in Chapter 5.

More generally, we refer to the ability to create segments based on differences in opportunities to grow the customer as opportunity segmentation. This is a specific form of segmentation by where customers are on a value ladder.

> **Insight Box 4.3**
>
> **MCV Insight**
>
> If a customer group does well on one driver of value (say, frequency of purchase) but poorly on another (say, spending per occasion), they could be considered an opportunity segment. In particular, the group of customers represents an opportunity to add value to the organization if they can be incentivized to improve along one value driver.

By identifying specific behavioral segments and differentiating the marketing offers that are given to them, the owner can ensure that

- Only those customers that need an incentive to display a given behavior receive that incentive.
- Customers that already display a behavior do not receive any incentives.
- The incentive rewards a very specific behavior (i.e., flavor choice, frequency, or volume).

The obvious benefit of such a loyalty program is that it reduces wastage and stretches the marketing dollars. Additionally, it allows for more precise segmentation and creative marketing interventions because of its ability to retain customer-level data. A number of recent articles have been written about the ability of the organization to slice and dice the data and therefore to harness the customer intelligence generated by the loyalty program.[7] Therefore, in addition to being effective (i.e., producing the desired behavioral changes), this program is also efficient (i.e., it does so without wasting marketing dollars).

This system of delivering differentiated offers to different groups of customers is contingent on the ability of the organization to deliver these offers in a targeted manner. The ice cream parlor may be able to distribute offers through the mail, or electronically if the customer gives them the permission to send out such offers. What

---

[7]Loveman, G. (2003). *Diamonds in the Data Mine.* Cambridge, MA: Harvard Business Review, 4–5.

could they do if they do not have permission? Thankfully, technology provides a solution in the form of point-of-sale coupon dispensers.[8] These handy gadgets are connected to the point-of-sale terminal, and can quickly print out an offer — perhaps on the back of the receipt — after being triggered by the loyalty card swiped at checkout. Since the database can easily link a particular card to a customer group, it is easy to print out customized offers at the point of sale. The terminal could also print out customized advertising along with the coupons.

Loyalty programs therefore have the potential to create two sets of benefits for the organization — first, it allows the organization to differentiate between different groups of customers; and second, it allows the organization to build and harness customer intelligence. While the two are not perfectly exclusive, we will focus on the differentiation aspects of loyalty programs in this chapter and present a framework for how to harness customer intelligence in Chapter 7.

> **Insight Box 4.4**
>
> **MCV Insight**
>
> Good loyalty programs are specific and targeted. A specific program gives the customer an incentive contingent on them displaying a very specific behavior. A targeted program allows the organization to deliver the incentive only to those customers who currently do not display the desired behavior. Targeted and specific programs are important to increasing the efficiency of your marketing dollars!

4.3 Differentiating Customers

On what basis could an organization differentiate between customers? There are three approaches to determining the basis to be used for differentiating customers.

---

[8]Pancras J. & Sudhir K. (2007). Optimal Marketing Strategies for a Customer Data Intermediary. *Journal of Marketing Research, 44*(4), 560–578.

4.3.1 *Differentiation on the Basis of History*

In the example of the ice cream parlor, we illustrated the use of current and historic data to make decisions about how to serve customers differently. Organizations have long differentiated between customers as a function of historic purchasing. In the domain of business-to-business marketing, the earliest approaches to Key Account management were based on segmenting customers as a function of cumulative dollar volume of business (either to date, or over the past year) and then giving preferred treatment to the best customers on that metric.[9]

Airline loyalty programs have traditionally followed the same approach. Passengers earn points (that are called miles) as a function of the length of flights taken. Miles earned in a given calendar year are tallied up and passengers are then sorted on the cumulative miles flows. Those at the very top of the chart are typically called the best customers (e.g., Platinum members), followed by the Gold, Silver, and then the regular members. The benefits and rewards that passengers earn vary as a function of their membership.

The philosophy behind historic programs is simple — the organization essentially tells the customer, "You prove your loyalty first, I will then reward you." It is a simple give and then take relationship. It has been shown to work well when customers are deeply entrenched in the loyalty program, but it is not that clear that this approach does a very good job of drawing new customers into the loyalty fold, and even less clear that it is able to influence behavior in a systematic and targeted manner.

There is another problem. Suppose that Bhanu travels a lot on business, but because he lives in Hong Kong, he always flies Cathay Pacific Airlines. He is a platinum member of their program: at the

---

[9]Capon, N., Potte, D., & Schindler, F. (2006). *Managing Global Accounts: Nine Critical Factors for a World-Class Program.* New York: Wessex Press; Capon, N. (2001). *Key Account Management and Planning.* New York: The Free Press.

very top of the loyalty pyramid. He accesses their premiere lounge, always gets upgraded to first class, enjoys priority boarding, and is allowed to check in close to the flight departure time. One particular week, he happens to be in Toronto and the only flight that meets his travel needs is an Air Canada flight. Unfortunately, he has no history with Air Canada, so for the very first time in many years, Bhanu is forced to check in early, wait in the crowded seating areas, and has to jostle with others to board the flight and get to his middle seat at the rear of the plane. Air Canada has squandered a wonderful opportunity to try and woo a potentially valuable customer. They could have remedied the problem by using a system of differentiation based on predicted value.

4.3.2 *Differentiation on the Basis of Predictions*

How can an airline or, for that matter, any other organization make predictions about the value of the customer? To illustrate, let us consider a hypothetical online retailer of music and movies, Ganga Inc. Like many online retailers, Ganga encourages users to create a profile in order to facilitate easy ordering. For example, when a customer Anu signs on at the website, she enters her identifying information, as well as responses to several other questions:

- Her gender
- Her age range
- Her music genre preference (rank ordered)
- Her movie genre preference (rank ordered)
- Her occupation

Ganga Inc. now has six pieces of information about Anu. However, the reader may argue that these data hardly seem sufficient — and perhaps not even relevant — to make predictions about Anu's future value.

If these data were truly the only assets that Ganga had, the reader would be absolutely spot on. However, Ganga also has data on several thousand of their existing customers for the past three years. Ganga can now rely on a family of techniques called collaborative filtering (CF). CF refers to the process of filtering for information or patterns using techniques involving collaboration among multiple agents, viewpoints, data sources, etc. In the discussion that follows, our goal is simply to present the reader with an intuition about the logic structures that approaches like these would use. The actual mathematics and computational details are beyond the scope of the present book — but as we will reiterate in Chapter 5, we reiterate that it is crucial for the manager to understand and develop the intuition, and outsource the actual model building efforts to people with the relevant expertise.

In this particular case, a customer analyst at Ganga could say, "We now have data on customers who have shopped with us for the past three years. We can calculate the VOC for them. We know who are our high value customers and our low value customers. As the first step, we can identify what differentiates our best customers from our worst customers." Suppose that three things matter — music genre preferences, film genre preferences, and age range. The best customers in their database prefer action films, then comedies and finally regional films; prefer Indian classical music, then rock and finally pop; and were in the 30–36-year-old age range when they first signed up. If Anu responded in the same manner, Ganga would predict that Anu has the potential to be one of the best customers. More generally, Ganga could use its database of current customers to generate a regression type model of the effect of various factors on customer value and then use the model to make predictions about new customers.

Alternatively, Ganga could use another logical model for making predictions, not just about the value of Anu but also about specific behaviors. When Anu first provides the six pieces of information about herself, Ganga's computer algorithm can search its database to find the answer to the following question: "Can I identify (say) one thousand customers who are closest in profile to Anu?" Without much computational complexity, Ganga's database should be able to do this by using the Euclidean distance as a measure of similarity.

The algorithm could now make the following claim: Given that I know nothing else about Anu, I believe that the average behavior of the 1,000 similar people best represents Anu's predicted behavior. Note that this is nothing different from what traditional segmentation tells us. For instance, if these 1,000 customers on an average make movie purchases once a month, we would predict that Anu would purchase once a month. If the average spends $50 on each purchase occasion, we would predict that Anu spends $50 on each occasion.

Is this prediction — or the prediction of Anu's value — accurate? No. That said, it is definitely better than having no prediction at all. However, if we can design a system where the accuracy of the prediction improves over time, then the organization can better manage the process of differentiating offers.

As Anu continues to patronize Ganga, the website continues to track Anu's behavior as time passes by. After a month or two, it might monitor Anu's behavior in order to determine whether its predictions were accurate. If Anu bought only once in two months, and spent $100 on each occasion, the algorithm learns that it needs to update itself. As an illustration, it might keep track of how often she logs on, what genres she browses and in what sequence, which songs or movies she samples, and how long she browses before making a purchase decision. Instead of the 6 pieces of information it had about Anu, Ganga Inc. now has 11 pieces of information. It repeats the process of sampling based on Euclidean distance, and using the sample characteristics to revise predictions. In essence, Ganga Inc. has a model of the customer's behavior, which is (a) based on collaborative principles — that is, uses the individual data but also draws from other existing customers, (b) dynamic — that is, which updates itself over time and, therefore, (c) a model, which learns and improves over time via an active feedback loop.

Note that the model might predict that Anu's value is high in the future; while it is presently low (she might just be an entry-level customer). How does this help the organization? First, it allows the organization to prioritize their marketing dollars for new customers — the organization should spend first on those with higher predicted value. Second, it gives the organization some guidelines in terms of what to do in order to move the customer up the value ladder. It could simply look at the time-varying purchase patterns of customers similar to Anu and then try to get her to follow the same course. Finally, as discussed in the next section, the organization could start engaging in marketing interventions that are specific and targeted.

Insight Box 4.5

MCV Insight
Marketing programs that differentiate across customers on the basis of their predicted value are more valuable than those that use historic purchases only. In particular, prediction models that learn and improve over time are especially useful.

Insight Box 4.6

MCV Insight
How can you make predictions about customers that you have no history about? Use collaborative models — models that allow you to rely on similar other customers to make predictions.

As we will discuss in Chapter 5, the utility of customer value models depends entirely on how much data is fed to them. CF models are very similar — the larger the existing database, the richer the insights that can be drawn and the more accurate the predictions that can be made about new customers. However, this level of accuracy can never be reached unless the organization starts with a database! Even with a new database, however, we believe that the value of a simple prediction-based approach is tremendous. Without any such system, the organization will possibly lose all customers like Bhanu from our earlier example — customers who are potentially very valuable, but on whom the organization has no historical data.

4.3.3 *Differentiation on the Basis of Desired Outcomes: Behavioral Shaping*

After a number of iterations to its predictive model, Ganga Inc. now has a model of Anu's music and movie buying behavior that meets their statistical criteria for validity and reliability. In essence, they now have a mathematical model of Anu that can faithfully replicate her behavior over time. From here on, Ganga's philosophy toward Anu is this: if Anu's consumption falls below what the model predicts, the model is not to be questioned — it is Anu who is probably too busy with work! For instance, suppose the model predicts that Anu purchases every three weeks, and it is now over four weeks. The discrepancy between predicted and actual interval could trigger an email message to Anu offering a reminder, and then — if the discrepancy grows by an additional week — an attractive price offer on music that the website knows Anu will like. In fact, if Anu is in the highest-value bracket of customers, she might receive increasing levels of offers with the goal of getting her to return to the store at the earliest. However, if Anu is not deemed to be a valuable customer, there may probably be only one reminder email. Figure 4.3 shows the logic structure of algorithms like the ones we described here.

The underlying goal of such interventions is to reduce the predicted versus actual gap. Using the language of psychology, we refer to these interventions as behavioral shaping interventions.

Discrepancies between actual and predicted behavior are only one kind of gap that shaping interventions can aim to eliminate. In a business service setting, for example, we could use shaping to reduce the gap between one customer, and the best customer in that particular industry vertical. Alternately, as discussed in the ice cream parlour example, shaping could be used to add value to a group of customers by identifying an opportunity to increase consumption.

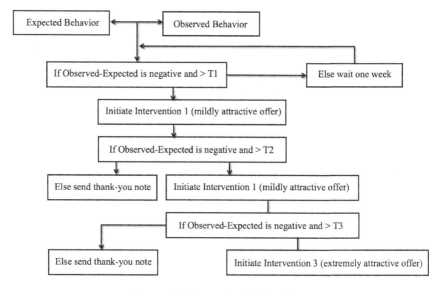

Figure 4.3 Ganga Inc.'s algorithm.

4.4 Creative Implementations of Loyalty Programs

Imagine that a grocery supermarket has implemented a card-based loyalty program, and they now have several years' worth of data on every single customer. What sorts of analyses could they do with these data and what could they use these analyses to do? We will present a few stylized examples, but will again emphasize that the use of data needs to adhere to principles of customer consent and respect for their privacy.

4.4.1 *An Analysis of Shopping History*

At the very minimum, the first thing that the grocery supermarket could do is a historic analysis of their databases. Recall that we decomposed customer value into four broad components — traffic, transaction rate, basket size, and repeat purchasing. At the first cut, the analyst could look at, say a window of the one year immediately preceding the analysis and compute the total number of dollars spent by customers. This would allow them to rank order all of their customers by total spends, perhaps into ten deciles from the highest spends (platinum customers) to the lowest. The store could also do what we call a stability analysis. Rather than doing the analysis on an annual window, they could do a similar analysis on a monthly basis. The question that they should seek to answer is this: Does the same group of customers remain platinum every month, or does membership change from month to month? If the membership is not very stable, then these people might not be very loyal despite being called Platinum customers. Those customers who are stable platinum customers might then be given rewards in the form of gifts, discounts, dedicated checkout lines, and other service benefits.

The analyst could also do a similar analysis on frequency of shopping, spends per trip, and number of categories shopped in. Cross-tabulating these data will allow the analyst to construct frameworks similar to the one in Figure 4.2, and therefore to identify opportunities for adding incremental value.

4.4.2 *Specific and Targeted Promotions*

The supermarket could identify specific behaviors that it wants to encourage in specific customers, and deliver incentives to do so. For instance, the analysis may reveal that while the Sengupta household is a frequent and regular shopper in the meat and produce categories, they never shop in the snacks or soft drink aisles. The store could then simply run an algorithm in which the Senguptas are offered an attractive reward — an offer delivered either via mail or via a point-of-purchase printer — if they shopped in the currently under-shopped categories. Alternatively, analysis might show that the Mitra household consistently purchased bread from the branded bakery section, but not from the in-store bakery (which yields higher margins). The store could use what we call a track-and-trigger algorithm — specific actions are tracked, and their occurrence triggers off a marketing intervention. In this case, on every occasion that the checkout scanner sees the Mitra card and the UPC for a branded loaf bread together, it could print out a coupon that encourages them to purchase from the in-store bakery on the next occasion.

Perhaps the most interesting idea example for a track-and-trigger promotion is a hypothetical one, born out of a creative brainstorming session with a group of students.[10] It involves the merchandising of dog food. The traditional manner of promoting dog food is to drop coupons using store flyers or via direct mail. However, given that only 37% of households in the United States at that time had a dog as a pet, much of this effort is wasted.[11] In addition, research suggested that for many species of dogs, it is difficult to change their preferences for dog food once they are used to a particular type of dog food. Therefore, for a supermarket selling dog food, the best use of their acquisition dollars is toward households that have recently acquired a new pet dog.

Insight Box 4.7

MCV Insight

Technology makes it easy to implement track-and-trigger promotions — when a customer displays a certain behavior, they can be given an incentive or a marketing intervention to try and change or build upon that behavior.

The Jones family shops at a supermarket using a loyalty card program. A look at their history of purchasing reveals no sign of dog food purchasing. However, for the first time in three years, their data file records a purchase in the dog category. After waiting for a second purchase to increase the likelihood that the Jones family has

---

[10]This series of brainstorming sessions was done for a consulting project on customer relationship management for a client.
[11]The Humane Society of the United States. (2007, March 18). *U.S. Pet Ownership Statistics.* Retrieved January 26, 2008, from http://www.hsus.org/pets/issues_affecting_our_pets/pet_overpopulation_and_ownership_statistics/us_pet_ownership_statistics.html

recently acquired a pet dog (rather than merely sitting a neighbor's dog), the store could act on this trigger and send the Jones family a package that might contain samples as well as a small gift for a dog. In doing so, the store would have eliminated wastage, and in the language of the customer as a gamble — focused the acquisition dollars on a small number of targets to increase the probability of converting them into potentially high lifetime value customers.

4.5 Building a Loyalty Program

Much has been written about the mechanics of establishing a loyalty program. In particular, Berman provides an excellent guide on how to go about developing a loyalty program.[12] According to his framework, there are 10 steps in the process (see page 132 of the original article):

(1) Outlining the objectives
(2) Developing a budget
(3) Determining program eligibility
(4) Selecting program rewards
(5) Considering partnerships with others
(6) Building an appropriate organization
(7) Developing and maintaining a database
(8) Managing an internal data warehouse and data mining capability
(9) Evaluating the success and failure of the program
(10) Taking corrective action

We would like to highlight one specific step in the process of building a loyalty program, a step that Berman and others have not

---

[12]Berman, B. (2006). Developing an Effective Customer Loyalty Program. *California Management Review, 49*(1), 132.

discussed in depth. Recall that the core value of a loyalty program is linked to its ability to generate a time series stream of customer-specific data. In some industries, it is relatively easy — and sometimes even part of the routine process — to link every transaction with the identity of the customer. For instance, every bank transaction is recorded against an account number, and the bank can easily link different account numbers (e.g., savings, checking, credit cards, mortgage, loans, and investment) to a specific customer. Likewise, airlines, hotels, online businesses, and business-to-business sellers have the ability — at least theoretically — to be able to pull a customer file and see all of their transactions and other recorded behaviors.

However, most forms of retailers do not enjoy this luxury. With the advent of scanner technologies, retailers are able to analyze the contents of shopping baskets in great levels of detail. However, retailers cannot associate those baskets with individuals, unless they have the ability to digitize the identity of the customer. Likewise, third-party programs need to create their own identity for members. The most popular and reliable way of digitizing the identity is by using a vehicle (a card, or perhaps even a chip embedded into a key ring) that can be read electronically. In essence, the critical factor that will determine the success or failure of the program is the retailer's ability to ensure that as many of their customers carry and use the card. This is not a trivial task. Most people today already carry a very large number of pieces of plastic in their wallets that they will want to know, "what is it about this new piece of plastic that is so valuable that I should replace one of my other pieces of plastic with this one?" Unfortunately, many loyalty programs do not pay enough attention to what we call "loyalty card marketing" — making the card so valuable for customers that they have the incentive to carry and use it every time they shop.

What can one do to maximize loyalty card penetration? Here are some specific examples of best practices:

(1) Identify a common activity that a large percent of the target market engages in, and link the card to that activity: Octopus, a Hong Kong-based program (which is not a true loyalty program but a micro-payment mechanism) and GetSmart, a Shanghai based third-party program, were based off cards that can be used to pay discounted fares for mass transit. In Hong Kong, most residents use public transit and hence the Octopus card reached unprecedented levels of penetration. Other examples of common activities might include payment of highway tolls, parking payments, going to the movies, or even eating at popular fast food chain restaurants!

(2) Use the card as an electronic coupon: many retailers worldwide use in-store promotions like coupons or bonus buys, or out-of-store promotions like coupons and rebates to create short-term incentives for customers to buy particular products. An in-store coupon is typically available from a display right next to the product display, and can be redeemed at the checkout counter for savings. While this might appear to be a relatively trivial task, research shows that the redemption rates of in-store coupons are nowhere close to a 100% (and in fact in some cases was lower than 50%).[13] People who really valued the savings made the effort of saving and using the coupon (Segment A), while those that didn't really value the promotion forgot about it, or otherwise failed to redeem at the time of checkout (Segment B). If the retailer now used the card as an electronic coupon (i.e., the discount was given as long as the card was used), it would cost them a lot more because now, they would need to give the reduced price to both Segments A and B. Yet, both segments will appreciate the added convenience of the card, and Segment B would be especially grateful that they are now able to avail of lower prices.

---

[13]Dhar, S. K. & Hoch S. J. (1996). Effective Price Discrimination Using In Store Coupons. *Journal of Marketing, 60*(1), 17–30.

(3) Use co-op and affiliate partnerships: A retailer might consider entering into a partnership with other organizations that their target customer might enjoy benefiting from. Under these partnerships, a member of the program might be able to use the card for free parking, discounted admission to the movies, or a free meal at a popular restaurant. While these promotions will cost the retailer, they will help in adding value to the card.

> **Insight Box 4.8**
>
> **MCV Insight**
> When building a loyalty program, invest heavily in increasing the penetration of the loyalty card. One of the greatest benefits of a card-based program is the data.

(4) Add other forms of utility to the card: the retailer might consider partnering with a bank to issue a credit card that could carry the loyalty program number, or perhaps partner with a local library and have the loyalty card double up as a library membership card. The opportunities to partner and add value are many and limited only by the imagination and initiative shown by the organization.

4.6 What This All Means

In this chapter, we discussed different forms of loyalty programs and their ability to manage customer value. In the following paragraphs, we offer prescriptive advice to the manager in the form of six guidelines.

4.6.1 Guideline 1: The True Value of a Loyalty Program is in the Quality of the Data

We reiterate our position that loyalty programs that only deliver rewards and incentives rather than using customer touchpoints as opportunities to gather data and learn about the customer do not deliver on the full promise that they are capable of. As the manager makes decisions about the kind of program they would like to use and its specific design features, we encourage them to keep this first guideline at the back of their minds. During the design process, we encourage the manager to be on the lookout for data collection techniques and to explicitly build these opportunities into the architecture of the loyalty program.

4.6.2 Guideline 2: In-House Loyalty Program or a Third-Party Consortium Program?

Our research suggests that a third-party program could be valuable in driving traffic and increasing transactions at a fledgling business, or one whose brand awareness is not very high. For more established brands with large volumes of extant customers, it is likely that the focus is more on loyalty and the "upstream" portions of the value ladder for which an in-house program might be more appropriate.

4.6.3 Guideline 3: Articulate Your Value Ladder Before Designing Your Loyalty Program, Not After

We view a loyalty program as an instrument to try and move customers along a value ladder. Therefore, it is perhaps almost tautological to argue that the manager must articulate the value ladder before designing their loyalty program. Without the guiding rails of the value ladder, it is not clear what the loyalty program is designed to do!

4.6.4 Guideline 4: Identify the Best Approach to Differentiating Across Customers

In this chapter, we made a distinction between three approaches that could be used to differentiate across customers: their history, predictions of future behavior, and the gap between desired and actual behavior. Obviously, the specific means that the manager chooses as the appropriate basis depends on the kinds of data available to the organization, and the ability of the models to convert the insights into appropriate marketing interventions.

In previous chapters, we had identified a couple of different frameworks to manage customer value — in particular, the customer portfolio matrix and a simple prioritization of the value of the customer (VOC). Note that each of these frameworks could be based on historic or predicted data. As a longer data stream becomes available to the organization over time, it will develop the ability to feed the data back to its models and allow them to become more accurate and diagnostic with time.

4.6.5 Guideline 5: Always Be on the Lookout for Opportunity Segments and Then Deliver Specific and Targeted Offers!

Imagine that in a given situation, there are three drivers of value: the specific product purchased (its margin), the frequency of purchase, and the volume of purchase per occasion. An opportunity segment is one in which customers already demonstrate some of the value-creating behaviors but where you could add value by changing another specific value. For example, the opportunity for a customer who already buys a high-margin product is to increase their frequency of consumption, and then their volume of consumption. Identifying these opportunity segments allows the organization to deliver marketing interventions that are specific and targeted, thereby stretching the marketing dollars available to it.

4.6.6 Guideline 6: Don't Skimp on Loyalty Card Marketing!

The core value of a loyalty program is linked to its ability to generate a time series stream of customer-specific data. In essence, the critical factor that will determine the success or failure of the program is the organization's ability to ensure that as many of their customers carry and use the instrument used to capture identity — in most cases, a loyalty card. Unfortunately, many loyalty programs do not pay enough attention to what we call "loyalty card marketing" — making the card so valuable for customers that they have the incentive to carry and use it every time they shop.

In the first four chapters comprising Part 1 of the book, we have introduced our basic framework and the value ladder as a metaphor, described what we mean by value, distinguished between value to the customer (VTC) and the VOC, and developed an understanding of the four components of the decomposed revenue metrics. We also suggested that the keys to moving customers up the value ladder included analysis that would inform the manager about the marginal benefits versus marginal costs of the move, an understanding of behavior change techniques, data that could support the analysis, and a nuanced knowledge of communication and pricing techniques. Five chapters in Part 2 of the book will provide the tools to be able to do this.

PART 2

Chapter 5

Customers as Gambles

Gamble: (1) To play a game for money or property. (2) To bet on an uncertain outcome. (3) To stake something on a contingency: take a chance.[1]

The goal of this chapter is to provide a mathematical approach for conceptualizing, measuring, and influencing value to the customer (VTC), as well as the value of the customer (VOC). We will build on concepts of VTC and VOC, develop them in mathematical detail, and then apply them to some of the key ideas generated in Chapters 3 and 4 to demonstrate how the analysis could be used to help a manager in making meaningful marketing decisions.

While the central idea of this chapter is mathematical modeling, we would like to emphasize that our objective is not to drown the reader in a swamp of unintelligible mathematical mumbo-jumbo. Instead, what we would like to achieve is to be able to give the reader some very clear intuition behind the mathematics. In particular, we could like the reader to be able to

(1) Understand the parameters of the customer management problem they are facing
(2) Structure the problem using very simple mathematical tools
(3) Work out the logic by which the problem could be solved

---

[1] Gamble. (n.d.). *Merriam-Webster*. Retrieved January 1, 2020, from http://www.merriam-webster.com/dictionary/gamble

Once the manager is able to achieve these three, they could simply outsource the actual mathematics/analytics to any of the large number of bright undergraduate students of science or mathematics. The trick in making any customer analytics work well for the manager is not in the spreadsheets or the actual mathematics (which can be conveniently outsourced to Mike the Mathematician), it is in the manager's ability to structure the problem effectively and to supply the analyst with the logic and intuition needed to analyze the problem. This chapter does precisely that, and so while the material appears superficially dense and complicated to read, we encourage the reader to stay with us through these pages and guarantee that you will have a very different way of thinking about marketing analytics.

5.1 Modeling Customer Value: The Building Blocks of Gamble Analysis

We start our discussion on the modeling of customer value (both VTC and VOC) by offering two building blocks for our analytical treatment.

5.1.1 *The Retailer Metaphor*

The first building block was introduced in Chapter 1 and illustrated in Figure 1.3. All customer-related activity can be decomposed into two distinct phases. The first set of activities, acquisition, refers to everything that the organization does in order to attract the business of the customer. In the case of a retailer, all traffic-building activity that gets the customer to visit the store for the first time can be grouped under the acquisition umbrella. Everything that happens after the customer is in the store falls into the value of customer umbrella. In ongoing discussion, we will refer to this building block as the "retailer metaphor."

5.1.2 *The Stochastic Model*

The second building block is a seemingly unusual, yet a very intuitive metaphor. Any visitor to the casinos of Macau and Las Vegas will know what gambling is all about. It is about inserting a token worth, say $1, into a slot machine, pulling a handle, and hoping that the player hits jackpot and wins, say, a thousand dollars. Likewise, any reader of quantum physics will know that when a thin sheet of metal is bombarded with energetic photons, the photon is absorbed with some probability and the atom transitions from a lower energy level to a higher energy level. Indeed, a simple stochastic model in which a given action results in a particular outcome with a probability p that is less than one is a very simple model to represent a very large number of real-world phenomena both in the natural sciences as well as in business administration. Quantum transition probabilities, the likelihood of finding oil on drilling in a field, many aspects of financial markets, and all forms of gambles have been successfully modeled using standard and simple stochastic models.

We model customers as gambles. Much like an individual inserting a $1 token into a slot machine and hoping for some reward in exchange, or a scientist firing a photon into an atom hoping to move it to a higher energy level, we think about organizations as initiating a marketing intervention targeted at a particular individual with the hope of moving that individual from one step in their value ladder to the next step. Moving people from any one step to the next step is like playing a gamble; the organization decides to introduce a particular intervention that, with a certain probability, moves the customer up the value ladder to the next step. The game

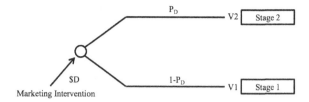

Figure 5.1 Customers as gambles.

can then be played again until the customer goes up the value ladder successively over time.

Insight Box 5.1

MCV Insight

Think about every marketing intervention as playing a gamble. With some probability of success p, the customer moves from one step of the value ladder to another step. The expected value of the gamble represents the net value of the marketing intervention. Your goals are to (a) identify interventions that maximize the probability of success, yet (b) result in high net value!

Figure 5.1 shows the simplest possible stochastic representation of the gamble metaphor. Consider a manager trying to move a customer from one step to another, where the value in the first step is V_1 and the value in the second step is V_2. Let us assume that the manager spends $\$D$ to try and engineer this upgrade and at that level of spending, the probability of success is p_D. Using the basic principles from probability and decision trees, the net expected value of this gamble can be written as:

$$EV \text{ (customer gamble)} = p_D * (V_2 - V_1) - D$$

5.2 Customer Gambles

5.2.1 *The Gamble Is Merely a Mathematical Metaphor*

A few discussion points are in order here. First, the term gamble as it is used colloquially in the English language has two connotations;

it is often used in the context of either fun or danger, and it suggests that the probability of the desired outcome happening is beyond the control of the gambler (that said, a number of successful gamblers at casinos and the race tracks would argue otherwise). When used in the context of customers, though, we abstract ourselves from any emotional content of gambling and focus purely on the ability of the gamble to give us a mathematical crutch for modeling value. Moreover, we do not believe that the act of playing a gamble for a customer is a passive one in which the manager simply sends out a marketing intervention and sits back and "hopes" for a customer to move up a value ladder. In fact, nothing could be further from the truth. When seen in the gamble analogy, however, marketing interventions take on a different conceptual definition. We can now define the goal of any marketing intervention as optimizing the value of each gamble. One manner of achieving this is to improve the probability of success, the probability with which the customer moves up along the value ladder. As we will see later, however, optimizing the value of a customer gamble does not necessarily mean that p should be extremely high. That said, if the manager has access to data on what the probabilities of success of various marketing interventions are as a function of how much is spent on that interventions, s/he will be able to develop a decision support tool to help determine which intervention to select.

5.2.2 *Customer Gamble and Relevant Costs*

Second, what is a marketing intervention and what costs should be modeled when trying to study customers as gambles? In our conceptualization, an intervention refers to a single or multiple activities that are designed to stimulate a move along the value ladder. These could include, but are not restricted to advertising, direct mail, sampling, couponing, mail-in rebates, catalogue promotions, phone sales, financing plans — absolutely anything designed to elicit a specific action. Note that an intervention could comprise of a combination of two or more individual actions as well. For instance, a retailing organization might choose to convert prospects to customers via a combination of sampling and low introductory prices. In real practice, however, there is never crisp and clear demarcation between different marketing activities and their consequences. If a potential customer responded to a direct mail solicitation, one might conclude that it was the direct mail that moved the customer from being a prospect to making their first purchase. However, other marketing actions might have also played a part. It could have been possible that, undetected to the organization, the customer also saw some advertisement and heard some good word of mouth about the organization. Therefore, the advertising and word of mouth would have also contributed to moving the customer up the value ladder. Similarly, the direct mailing might have effects beyond simply triggering the first purchase. If the mailing was attractive, or had some utility (e.g., included a wall calendar), it might also serve as a reminder and trigger repeat purchasing. Figure 5.2 shows a

	Traffic	Purchase	Multiple Purchase	Repeat Purchase	Loyalty to Brand	Create Referrals	Increase Frequency of Shopping
Samples		X	X			X	
Guerilla Marketing	X	X				X	
Word-of-Mouth Advertising	X	X				X	
Loss Leader							
Point-of-Sale Display	X	X					
Phone Sales	X	X			X		
Direct Mail		X					
Company website	X					X	
Mail-in rebates		X	X				X
Premium Promotion		X	X				
Personal Sales		X		X	X	X	
Financing Plans		X					
Buy-one-get-one-free promotion			X				
Price Promotion based on Volume			X				
Price Promotions (Discounts)		X	X	X			
Catalogue Promotions Coupons		X	X				
Reward Programs					X	X	X
Customer Relationship Management Systems					X	X	X
Loyalty Programs					X	X	X
Refer-a-Friend Promotion						X	

Figure 5.2 Marketing activities and behavioral outcomes.

number of different marketing activities as well as possible behavioral outcomes arising from them.

Our approach addresses this imperfect association between action and outcome in a number of specific ways.

(a) *Apply the models in controlled environments*: There are a large number of situations in which an organization decides to introduce only one marketing activity at a time, especially at the level of a geographic or demographic segment, and for different products. In such instances, the likelihood of contamination is low especially if the activities are done in a manner in which each segment is not exposed to interventions meant for other segments. For instance, a conversation with the operating officer of a large retail bank suggested that this bank sent electronic messages to the younger segment, phone calls to the older segment, and direct mail that differed in geographic reach for different product lines. When they analyzed the effectiveness of their marketing vehicles, they would treat each vehicle independently after verifying through some simple market research that the customers had not received any other communication and their decision to act was based on the specific marketing activity that had been targeted to them. In such instances, the schematic in Figure 5.1 does a fine job of modeling the effectiveness of the marketing activity.

(b) *Apply the models at the margin*: A second approach to applying the approach is to use it "at the margin." We illustrate what we mean with a specific example. Suppose a manager at a spa salon has decided on a two-pronged strategy to acquire new customers — initially a long running advertising campaign to increase awareness and liking, followed by a series of more specific programs (e.g., couponing to one group of prospects, sampling to another, a buy-one-get-second-free offer to a third group). It is obvious that the advertising will influence a prospect's decision to try the new service for all these groups of customers. Hence, each customer could be influenced by two different marketing activities, and a clean application of the gamble framework would not be possible. However, the manager could choose to analyze this by considering the entire campaign (advertising, couponing, sampling, and the offer) as the universe. In this universe, advertising could be considered as a fixed cost — and indeed a sunk cost when it comes time to spend money on the more specific programs. In this case, the manager could treat each of the three specific programs as a gamble at the margin, and noting that now — at the margin — the three programs are independent, use the framework from Figure 5.1 to analyze their effectiveness and value.

(c) *Apply the models at a broader level of analysis:* Sometimes the manager might choose to use marketing activities in conjunction with each other, and the assumption of independence between different marketing actions might not hold true. For instance, an organization might choose to use a direct mail program in conjunction with a sampling program for the very same target segment, and with the very same value ladder objective (e.g., converting a prospect into an entry-level customer). In this case, our approach would be to broaden the level of analysis and treat the combined marketing activities as the unit of analysis. The manager then might not be able to reach a nuance conclusion on the effectiveness of direct mail vis-à-vis sampling, but would be able to analyze what happens when both are used in conjunction with each other.

(d) *Allocate costs:* In some cases where the manager expects contamination across two marketing activities, it might be able to estimate (either using syndicated data or custom market research) the degree of contamination. For instance, suppose it is known that 10% of all customers received both direct mail and sampling, while 45% received only one of the two. In this case, the manager will be able to treat this program as comprising three different marketing activities: (a) sampling, (b) direct mail, and (c) direct mail and sampling. The manager can allocate costs appropriately across these three, and apply the gamble model suitably.

5.2.3 *Using Portfolio Approaches to Manage Customers*

The third discussion point is metaphorical yet very meaningful. Now that we have conceptualized customers as gambles, we can think about the organization as an entity that manages a portfolio of gambles. Any student of finance knows that this is exactly what a portfolio manager in a financial institution — or a wealth manager looking after your assets — does. The portfolio manager wants the portfolio to be diversified and balanced in a manner that is consistent with the client's goals. Likewise, the organization should seek to maintain a balanced portfolio of customers. This activity requires an ongoing audit, acquisition, investing in, and letting go of customers. The customer portfolio matrix presented in Figure 2.5 is one way to think about how to manage customers. However, there are other ways, notably a risk versus reward approach to categorizing customers and segments. We will discuss some of the tools needed to approach these decisions later in this chapter.

5.2.4 *Customer Gambles and Accuracy*

Fourth, we could like to comment on the accuracy of the analysis that will emerge from our framework. We will be the first ones to admit that the numbers that arise from the Customer Gambles will not be accurate. It is easy to question the assumption of independence in many cases, and in the event that the manager decides that independence is not valid and that costs need to be allocated suitably across different activities, the manner in which allocation is done could be questioned. Whenever analytics like the customer gamble model, or VOC and VTC calculations are presented in class, the first set of responses always tends to focus on challenging the underlying assumptions and hence the accuracy of the calculations.

We reiterate that the models presented here might not necessarily yield accurate answers. However, we also make the counterclaim that accuracy is NOT the goal of any of our models. In many cases, we estimate customer gamble models and VTC/VOC models in order to forecast the worth of a customer, or to decide on which

---

Insight Box 5.2

MCV Insight

The goal of using customer gamble analysis is not accuracy. It is to help the manager make choices between marketing interventions, different levels of spending, and different steps in the value ladder to target. Don't be too hung up about accuracy, but do ensure that the analysis is forward looking and diagnostic!

---

marketing activity to choose. By definition, forecasts cannot be accurate. While we don't necessarily aim to be inaccurate, our goals in conducting the analytics are twofold: first, we would like to give the manager some direction in terms of how to make decisions like which marketing action to employ, which part of the value ladder to focus on, how much to spend on trying to upgrade a customer, and so on. Note that traditional approaches to marketing do not give managers any quantitative guidelines. In fact, when we surveyed managers and asked how they made such decisions, the overwhelming majority responded with "intuition," "seeing what the competition does," or "continuing what seems to work in the past." Therefore, while we acknowledge that the answers from our models might not be perfectly accurate, however, we posit that they are very valuable when benchmarked against having no model at all.[2] The second goal

---

[2]See Dawes, R. M. (1979). The Robust Beauty of Improper Linear Models in Decision Making. *American Psychologist*, 34(1979), 571–582; Hoch, S. J. & Schkade, D. A. (1996). A Psychological Approach to Decision Support Systems. *Management Science*, 42(1), 51–64.

of analytics is to give the manager discriminability — the ability to discriminate between
groups of customers, marketing
actions, or steps in the value
ladder.

Insight Box 5.3

MCV Insight
In choosing the level of complexity
for analyses, do not use a cannonball
to kill a mosquito!

Oftentimes, these calcu-
lations are done only to prioritize actions or customers; and hence it
is not that important to be accurate as it is to give the manager the
ability to discriminate. Finally, we follow the principle often attributed
to Confucius when he said, "Do not use a cannonball to kill a
mosquito." In the context of our framework, the implication of this
principle is that managers should not be too hung up on accuracy,
because they may not actually need the levels of accuracy to make
effective decisions. We encourage the reader to keep this philosophy
at the back of their minds in order to be able to better appreciate the
utility of the modeling approach presented in this chapter.

5.3 Customer Gambles: Numerical Illustrations

In this section, we start with a very simple, stylized situation and analyze it to illustrate the basic method of the "customers as gambles"
approach. We then add increasing levels of complexity to the situation in order to illustrate how real-world situations could be
modeled.

5.3.1 *Scenario 1*

As our first illustration, consider a simplistic scenario in which a
manager is faced with the choice between two methods of acquiring
a customer, direct mail or telemarketing. For simplicity, let us
assume that the manager has historic data on the costs of each activity and the success rate. In particular, suppose that in the recent

past, each piece of direct mail costs $6 and it is sent to 5,000 prospects, 5% of which made a purchase and became an entry-level customer. Likewise, each phone call costs $10 and 10,000 prospects were called, 15% of which made a purchase and became an entry-level customer. Note that the costs above include all of the direct costs needed to implement the marketing activity — these might include direct labor, postage, calling charges, computer support, materials, and supplies. Finally, note that the goal of this marketing intervention is to move customers from one step to the next of a very simple value ladder:

> Prospect (P, someone touched by the organization's communication) → Entry-level customer (E, someone who has made their first purchase)

In our language, we are comparing two gambles, each of which converts the target from state P to state E with a probability p. Historic data tell us that the value of p is 5% and 15%, respectively for direct mail and telemarketing.

As our first analysis, we employ the retailer metaphor, which says that everything that happens up to the time that the customer "enters the store" is treated as a cost. So, assuming that any customer is as valuable as any other customer should they buy at the store, what is the acquisition cost of a customer using each of the two methods? Figure 5.3 shows the steps of the value ladder, the associated data as well as the process of calculating the average acquisition cost. In essence, we need to calculate the total cost of acquisition, and allocate it equally across all those individuals who eventually make it to state E for each of the two methods separately. Using this procedure, we find that if there is complete independence between the two methods, the acquisition cost for a customer using direct mail is $120; and using telemarketing it is $66.67.

Note that the resulting number is not indicative of the degree of difficulty of getting a particular customer; rather it is the function of

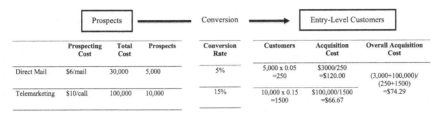

Figure 5.3 Acquiring a new customer.

both the cost per prospect as well as the success rate. Each customer costs the organization a lower amount for direct mail ($6 versus $10), but because direct mail is not as effective as telemarketing, it ends up being more expensive.

What is the utility of this analysis? For one, it tells the manager that if there is complete independence between the two methods of acquisition, and if the resulting customers are the same in terms of their value to the organization, it would make sense to spend more of the acquisition budget on telemarketing because it costs less. If, however, the manager does not believe that there is independence but rather that there is synergy between direct mail and telemarketing, the acquisition cost can be calculated at the level of the overall campaign. As Figure 5.3 shows, the total cost of the campaign is $130,000 [$100,000 + $30,000] while the total number of acquired customers is 1750 [1500 + 250]. Hence the average acquisition cost is $130,000/1750 = $74.29. The manager now also has an additional piece of insight — to the extent that the $74.29 cost is accurate, they know that they should ensure that the VOCs they acquire using this campaign should exceed this amount for the exercise to be a valuable one! This gives them a numerical goal for managing the VOC.

5.3.2 *Scenario 2*

Let us now think about acquisition processes that are a bit more complex. Consider a bank that is trying to acquire credit card customers through one of three means: direct (targeted solicitations by mail), take-ones (a highly technical term for leaflets left at various locations with a sign asking people to "Take One"), and through an affiliate partner (e.g., a co-branded card where the solicitations are mailed out by the branding partner). Selling a credit card, though, is different from selling a carton of milk or a vacation package. For the milk and vacation packages, revenue accrues at the time of the transaction while for the credit card, revenues typically occur — if at all — with a significant time delay through interest charges, defaults fees, and other charges. Therefore, the bank will not grant a credit card to anyone who asks for it, but only to applicants that qualify. Likewise, the credit card choice process is not an easy one for customers. Some customers, especially first-time credit card applicants, likely apply to a number of different issuers and, if successful with more than one issuer, might end up turning down a credit card offer. Consequently, the acquisition process could be further decomposed into the following steps:

Prospect → Respondent (a prospect who responds to the solicitation) → Qualified respondent (those respondents that meet the criteria) → Customers (those that eventually accept).

Suppose that a bank knows the following, simply by keeping track of historic acquisition attempts. The per-unit cost of a direct solicitation is $12.50, a take-one is $1.00, and an affiliate solicitation is $3.50. Response rates are highest for direct solicitations (20%), followed by affiliate solicitations (10%), and lowest for take-ones (3%). Since the direct solicitations are better targeted, about 70% of the applicants qualify for the card, while this number is significantly lower for other methods (40%). Finally, the bank estimates that 75% of all qualified respondents eventually become customers. Using these data and starting with 1,000 prospects for each method, Figure 5.4 shows the steps of the value ladder, the number of people at each step, and hence the acquisition cost of each method, assuming independence.

	Prospects	Conversion Rate	Respondents	Conversion Rate	Qualified Respondents	Conversion Rate	Customers	Total Cost	Acquisition Cost
Direct Mail	1,000	20%	200	40%	140	75%	105	12,500	119.05
Take-One	1,000	3%	30	70%	12	75%	9	1,000	111.11
Affiliate Partner	1,000	10%	100	40%	40	75%	30	3,500	116.67

Figure 5.4 Multiple steps of acquisition.

The cheapest method of acquisition using these data is take-ones, closely followed by affiliate solicitation, and then by direct solicitation. Suppose there is complete independence between the three activities. A novice bank manager might be tempted into thinking that take-ones is probably the cheapest method, and hence may allocate a large share of the acquisition budget to take-ones. However, two caveats are in order.

The first caveat is that this analysis captures dollar costs, not hassle costs or strategic costs. For instance, if the organization has trouble recruiting sales staff, or has strategically decided to adopt a lean strategy and to outsource all non-core activity, then the hassle costs or the strategic costs of direct sales will be higher than the dollar costs. Of course, over time the cost estimates made by the manager would reflect these strategic costs. The second caveat goes back to the point we made in Figure 2.6 — the decision to go with the cheapest acquisition method only makes sense if the manager expects all customers to have the same value potential. However, this assumption seems intuitively incorrect in this particular instance. Customers who are directly targeted by the bank are probably more valuable than those acquired by take-ones because one would assume that the targeting mechanism explicitly focuses on high-quality customers. Hence, even if there is complete independence between the three activities, the manager might want to track customers who were previously acquired via each of these methods, estimate their value (VOC) to the organization, and then use [VOC — A] as the relevant metric to base their decision on.

5.3.3 *Scenario 3*

Thus far, we have worked with historical data in which the organization had already decided to spend a certain amount on a marketing intervention with the hope of moving the customer along a value ladder. However, the decision of how much to spend rests with the organization. How could we model the decision to decide how much to spend on a marketing intervention?

In structuring this decision problem, we use the approach first proposed by Blattberg and Deighton in their 1996 *Harvard Business Review* article.[3] These authors propose that the relationship between how much an organization spends on acquisition (more generally, on a given marketing intervention) and the probability of success can be modeled as a variant of the so-called exponential curve (see Figure 5.5 for examples of the relationship). In particular, if we denote $X as the money spent per prospect on, say direct mail; and p_x as the probability of converting the prospect into a customer, Figure 5.5 suggests that

(a) The relationship between X and p_x is monotonically increasing; the more one spends, the greater is the probability of conversion.

(b) There are diminishing marginal returns of spending increasing amounts. Put differently, each increment of $x will produce successively smaller increases in p_x.

(c) There is a limit to p_x. Using terminology from Blattberg and Deighton's article, we refer to the maximum possible probability of success as the ceiling rate.

The equation used to generate the plots in Figure 5.5 is the following:

---

[3]Blattberg, R. C. & Deighton, J. (1996). *Manage Marketing by the Customer Equity Test.* Cambridge, MA: Harvard Business Review Press.

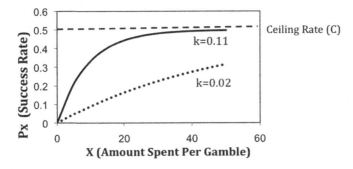

Figure 5.5 The exponential curve.

$$p_x = C * (1 - e^{\wedge}(-k * X)),$$

where

p_x is the success rate (probability of converting the customer);

C is the ceiling rate, taken as 0.5 in Figure 5.5;

X is the amount spent "per gamble" [in the case of acquisition, each prospect is a gamble];

$e = 2.71$ is a mathematical constant;

k = a parameter, of a characteristic that dictates the shape of the curve in Figure 5.5.

The solid curve in the figure is the relationship between the amount spent and the success rate when $k = 0.11$, while the dotted curve is the relationship for $k = 0.02$. Notice first that at higher levels of k, p_x shoots up quickly with the first few increases in X and then stabilizes to a value just below the ceiling rate. This suggests that the first few dollars are key in inducing conversion, and additional dollars help but not to a great degree. As k becomes smaller and smaller, however, the relationship becomes flatter. At very small k's, the relationship is almost linear, and every dollar seems to help as much as the other at least in the range of values plotted in the figure. The "k" parameter, therefore, helps us understand how a particular group of people responds to a particular marketing intervention. Note that different marketing interventions will have different k's, and the "k"

of the same intervention may vary as a function of what the intervention is used for. Put differently, for example, the p_x versus X plot might look different for telemarketing when it is used to convert a prospect to an entry-level customer than when it is used to convert an entry-level customer into a loyal customer.

Insight Box 5.4

MCV Insight

The more you spend on any particular marketing intervention, the greater are your success rates. However, the increases in success rates taper off beyond a certain spending level. For any particular customer level outcome, therefore, you should spend an optimal amount per customer. Anything less than that produces low success rates, and anything above that produces higher success rates — but does so inefficiently!

Before going further, we note that a manager should know what their p_x versus X plots look like, both in terms of its ceiling rate $[C]$ and the exponential parameter $[k]$. How does the manager estimate these two quantities? In their original article, Blattberg and Deighton suggest that the manager uses their expert judgment to estimate C, and then use one other combination of p_x and X (from a previous use of the same marketing intervention) and the equation above to estimate k. If the manager has a number of past instances of the same intervention — and hence a number of p_x versus X combinations — they can use regression analyses to find the best combination of C and k that explain these data. With both these approaches seem horribly complicated at first blush, we reassure the reader that they are mathematically extremely simple. The intuition is simply one of using past data to estimate the mathematical relationship, and the actual calculations can be entrusted to our capable undergraduate student, Mike the mathematician. For illustrative purposes, let's assume that Mike reports that $C = 0.50$ and $k = 0.05$.

The manager needs one more important piece of information: the expected benefit of upgrading the customer from one state to the other. Suppose we are looking at acquisition, and our goal is simply to move a prospect to buy a product that gives us a margin of $M once. Recall that the value of the gamble is EV (customer gamble) = $p_D * (V_2 - V_1) - D$. Using the present notation

$$EV = p_x * M - X$$

The manager who is selling a $200 margin product can now ask the question, what would happen if I spent $5 (i.e., $X = 5$) per prospect? Since Mike has helped identify the equation that links p_x with X, the manager can use a simple spreadsheet to calculate p_x (which turns out to be 0.11, or 11%) and therefore the value of the gamble [$0.11 * 200 - 5 = \$17.06$]. As shown in Figure 5.6, the manager can repeat the same calculations for $X = 10$, $X = 15$, and so on (this is easily done in a spreadsheet by copying formulae), and then determine the X at which the EV is the highest. In the example provided here, it turns out that the value of the acquisition gamble is the highest at $X = 30$. Thus, our analysis would suggest that if the manager's goal is to maximize value, they should spend $30 per prospect in the given set of circumstances. Of course, before making the final decision, the manager may also try to increase X in smaller

X (Spend)	Px (Success Rate)	EV (Value of Gamble)
0	0.00%	$0.00
5	11.03%	$17.06
10	19.63%	$29.25
15	26.33%	$37.66
20	31.55%	$43.10
25	35.62%	$46.24
30	38.79%	$47.58
35	41.26%	$47.53
40	43.19%	$46.38
45	44.69%	$44.39
50	45.86%	$41.73

Figure 5.6 Determining the optimal VOC gamble.

increments to get a more fine-tuned estimate. Alternatively, they could call Mike the mathematician to solve the problem analytically and get a more accurate answer.

We see that the relationship between value and X (the amount spent) is an inverted U-shaped function. When too little is spent, the success rates are relatively low. When too much is spent, the success rates are higher, but a lot has been spent in trying to push those success rates higher.

We offer two final comments on this analysis. First, at the risk of repetition, we have illustrated our Customer Gambles using acquisition as the desired outcome. However, the same exact approach will work for any other movement in the value ladder. Second, one concern raised about this approach can be paraphrased as "this is all very fine if I have good historic data, but how do I begin?" This is a very valid question, but it is not the end of the world. As Blattberg and Deighton have illustrated, it takes only one data point coupled with managerial judgment to estimate the exponential equation. And as more and more data become available over time, the manager could continually update the equation. These models are learning models — the more data one feeds them, the better their accuracy and predictive abilities become. All it takes is the commitment to make a start, and then the models grow and flourish as they feed off more and more data!

The three illustrations we have provided thus far deal with the customer as gamble analogy. We now turn to the measurement of VOC, the value of the customer.

Insight Box 5.5
MCV Insight No model is perfect to begin with. However, models learn with time as they are fed with more and more data. All it takes for a successful model-based approach to marketing a decision-making model is a commitment to start and to continually train and refine the models with new data!

5.3.4 *Scenario 4*

We introduced VOC with the simple illustration of a customer buying two bottles of shampoo annually forever, and came up with a dollar estimate of this customer. In this scenario, we will extend this example into more realistic situations.

Consider first the case of the same shampoo customer who "lives" for five years with cash flows of $100 accruing at the end of each year. Using the formula for the value of an annuity (with a discount rate of 10%) or a numerical spreadsheet, we can show that the value of this customer is:

$$\text{VOC}_{\text{5-years}} = \$379.07$$

Now suppose a marketing manager comes up with a proposal for an intervention (for simplicity, let us call it a lock-in program) that will increase the life of the customer from five years to seven years, all else held constant. The question is, is it worth it?

To answer that question, the first thing that the manager would need to do is to calculate the change in value that this movement along the value ladder will create. When the annuity formula is now applied, it reveals that

$$\text{VOC}_{\text{7-years}} = \$486.83$$

Therefore, the increase in value if the move along the value ladder can be successfully completed is 486.83 − 379.07 = $107.76. This is the value — to the organization — of moving the customer from one step to the other.

Now suppose the manager knows that the cost of the lock-in program is $20 for each customer who is presently in the "five year" category. Is it worth launching the program? Thinking of this problem in gamble terms, we can say that a $20 intervention has a $p\%$ probability of creating a $107.76 value increase. Therefore, the program will break even if $p * 107.76 = 20$, or $p = 18.6\%$. At any success level greater than this 18.6%, the value of the gamble is positive. The final question that remains to be answered is this: Will the program result in a 18.6% probability of success? The manager could make that assessment using expert judgment, historic data if available, or by conducting a limited market test of the lock-in program. A decision that previously no analytical basis to support if now seems relatively scientific and structured to make.

Insight Box 5.6

MCV Insight

Use lifetime value (VOC) calculations in conjunction with what-if scenarios to determine what the value of a certain customer outcome to the organization is, and therefore how much an organization should spend in trying to achieve that outcome.

Just like we showed the analysis for a lock-in program to extend the life of the customer, we could use a similar approach to assess growth programs (e.g., increasing volume and frequency of purchasing through cross-selling and up-selling) that result in increasing levels of contribution over the years, cost savings programs that also increase contribution, or even financing programs that may change the time course of revenues and costs from the customer. The structure is the same: compute the increase in value from moving from one step to another, estimate the cost per customer of the marketing intervention needed to achieve this outcome, and then estimate the minimum probability of success needed to make the transition a positive, valued one.

5.3.5 *Scenario 5*

In one of our consulting projects, one of us presented a simply VOC calculation to a manager. The customer returned a $100 contribution at the end of each year for a life of six years, and the discount rate was 10% yielding a VOC of $436. The manager found the assumptions too restrictive and was quick to reject the analysis. "How do we know that the growth rate is exactly zero each year," "couldn't the life be sometimes five years and sometimes seven?" We put ourselves in the shoes of the manager and saw the point — the excessive level of specification in the assumptions did not encourage belief in the results. However, there was a broader issue — we believe that managers are not used to thinking about people in dollar terms (much as they say they would love to). They are more naturally trained to think in terms of a specific action (say, a product launch, or a new marketing program) and then thinking about its likelihood of success. The mismatch between the VOC model and the mental model that managers use to make decisions also does not lend itself well to bolstering the credibility of the models. Thankfully, there is a joint solution to both problems.

Suppose we heard the manager out and then asked him, "In your estimate, how low or high could the life of the customer be? How low or high could the growth rates be?" Suppose the manager believes that the marketing program could result in a lifetime that was either five, six, or seven years, and a growth (of contribution) rate that was either –5%, 0%, or +5%. We now have nine (or more) possible combinations of possibilities as shown in Figure 5.7, and we can calculate the VOC for each combination separately. We could also ask the manager how likely he believes each outcome could be. For simplicity, we assume that the nine possible outcomes in the figure are normally distributed (although Mike the mathematician could help identify the actual distribution). For the nine outcomes, the mean $X = \$436$, and the standard distribution (SD) is $\$21.60$.

With this information, the manager is now able to answer the following question: If the effective cost of a successful customer is

Lifetime	Growth Rate		
	-5%	0%	+5%
5 Years	$346	$379	$415
6 Years	$390	$435	$487
7 Years	$427	$487	$556

Figure 5.7 Sensitivity analysis for a VOC calculation.

$500, what is the probability that this marketing effort is successful? Using the standard normal distribution, the *z*-value is 2.99 and the corresponding probability is 0.15%.[4] This is a very low probability of success, and hence the manager might then decide not to go ahead. However, if the cost were $400, the *z*-value is −1.67 and *p* = 95.25%. It is almost certain that this marketing effort would add overall value, and hence it would be a go! Again, note that in this illustration, we have allowed the life of the customer and the growth rate to vary, but we could repeat a similar analysis by allowing any number of variables to vary.

5.3.6 *Scenario 6*

> **Insight Box 5.7**
>
> **MCV Insight**
> Sensitivity analysis will allow you to convert estimates of customer value into the probability that a marketing intervention will result in positive value. This probability assessment is useful because it corresponds to the manner in which most managers think about making decisions.

In all of our examples thus far, we have assumed brand loyalty — the fact that people continue to purchase the same product over time. How might we be able to explicitly incorporate brand switching in our models?

Let us look at a specific stylized example, a customer of hair care services: Mandy who is a patron of your salon (let us call it salon A). You know the following about Mandy: (a) Salon A earns $100 as contribution from Mandy every year she uses them, (b) last year, she used Salon A, and (c) she has also shopped previously at Salon B. For simplicity, we assume that in a given year, Mandy spends her money in only one of the two salons and that all revenues accrue at the end of the year. What is the value of Mandy to Salon A?

---

[4]Keller, G. (2005). *Statistics for Management and Economics* (7th edn.). London, U.K.: Duxbury Press.

In order to answer this question, Salon A needs an important piece of information that is shown in the left panel of Figure 5.8 and is called a transition matrix (or a stochastic matrix). In the pure sciences, a transition matrix shows the probability that an object transitions from one state to another state over a period of time. In the world of customers, brands and value ladders, a transition matrix could refer to the probability with which customers who once bought a given brand (say A) either (a) stay with Brand A or (b) switch to Brand B in the next period. In Figure 5.8, for example, if customers bought Brand A this period, there is a 70% probability that they will buy Brand A again next period and a 30% chance that they will switch to Brand B. If however, if they buy Brand B this period, the chances are 50–50. Note that this transition matrix is an example of a stationary transition matrix; one in which the probabilities do not change with time. For the purposes of marketing analysis, stationary matrices are fine as long as they are updated from time to time.

There are a couple of different ways of estimating a transition matrix. The first approach is for Salon A to routinely poll their

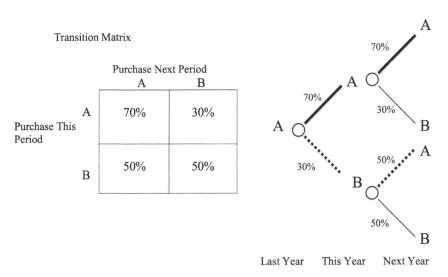

Figure 5.8 Value of customer under brand switching.

customers and ask them questions about where they spent their money over the years and then using that data to estimate the current probability of transition. The second approach is to use syndicated data sources that use panels and track their purchases in different product categories over time. In the domain of consumer-packaged goods, for example, grocery retailers will also have access to transition data by simply studying a given customers' history of purchases.

The manager now has all the information needed to estimate the VOC of Mandy. Recall that Mandy spent her money in Salon A last year. Therefore there is a 70% chance that she would spend her money there this year, and so the expected contribution this year is $0.7 * 100 = \$70$. Assuming a discount rate of 10%, the present value of the first year is $\$70/1.1 = \$63.63$.

What about the second year? The right panel of Figure 5.8 shows the likelihood of various alternative outcomes. Things get a bit trickier here, because there are now two separate and independent ways in which Mandy could be at Salon A: (a) A (last year) — A (this year) — A (next year), or (b) A (last year) — B (this year) — A (this year). These paths are indicated by the bold solid and bold dotted lines in the figure, respectively. The probability of path a occurring is (70% * 70%) 49%, while the probability of path b is (30% * 50%) 15%. But these two paths are independent, so the total probability of Mandy shopping at Salon A next year is simply 49% + 15%, or 64%, and the expected contribution is $0.64 * 100$, or $\$64$. Therefore, the present value of the second year is $\$64/1.1^2 = \$52.89$.

A similar approach could be used to compute the value arising from subsequent years. If we attempted to draw out years 3, 4, and 5 like we did the first two years, the decision tree diagram would get quite complicated fairly quickly. However, with the aid of a spreadsheet and matrix mathematics, our assistant Mike the mathematician should be able to run these computations for us relatively quickly!

But wait, this example only looked at two brands. In the real world, we have not just Brands A and B, but also C, D, E, and F. ... Thankfully, if our goal is to estimate the value of Mandy to Salon A, it does not matter how many brands there are in the market. Our transition matrix for this case would not measure transitions between A and B, but rather between A and not-A, that is, between A and any other brand. The rest of the analytics remains the same.

Another interesting analysis that could be conducted along similar lines is what we call the "value of loyalty" analysis. Recall that for Salon A, the probability of continuing with A in the next period was 70%. What would happen if this number were 60? Or 80%? The manager could conduct analyses like the one outlined above for different levels of loyalty and then come up with statements like the following: The value of Mandy to my salon would increase by $M if the loyalty rate went up from 70% to 80%. $M would then be the value of the increased loyalty — if the cost of increasing the loyalty rate exceeds $M per successful upgrade, then it is not worth increasing loyalty!

5.3.7 *Scenario 7*

In all the examples thus far, we have calculated the VOC — the value of a customer. However, we could apply the value idea to broader units of analysis; to groups of customers, or even to marketing interventions. In particular, we could quantify the value of a marketing intervention by quantifying the effects it has on customer value.

Let us consider a catalogue that sells apparel via a catalogue. The catalogue business is a fairly straightforward one.[5] The organization drops, say 1,000 catalogues to a mailing list purchased from a list vendor, who will charge the organization a per-address fee that

---

[5]See Muldoon, K. (1995). *Catalogue Marketing* (2nd edn.). London, U.K: Amacom, for some details on the business model.

increases as the level of specification increases. For instance, the per-address fee for "a list of 1,000 households in Toronto" is much lower than the fee for "a list of 1,000 addresses of households in Toronto that have two or more children and live south of Lawrence Avenue." Suppose each address costs $1, and the production and shipping cost of each catalogue is $4. The organization's data suggests that the return on prospecting (the percent of catalogues sent to a mailing list that result in an order; i.e., the success rate) is about 2%.

Once a customer buys from the catalogue, their address is added to a separate mailing list called a "house list." Members of the house list get a catalogue each month for five years, and the organization's data suggest that the rate of return from customers (the percent of catalogues sent to current customers that result in an order) is about 15%. While we can make this analysis complex by including multiple products and variants, we choose to stick to simplicity and work with the assumption that the net contribution earned by the organization per order is $50. The question that the manager is grappling with is this: Is the catalogue drop profitable? What is the value of a catalogue drop?

We start our analysis by first noting that the organization is trying to push customers along the following, simple value ladder with three steps:

Prospect → First time customer → Repeat purchaser

Our goal in this analysis is to treat the drop of 1,000 catalogue as a financial project, and to identify all cash flows that can be attributed to the catalogue drop. For starters, we look at the first year. The cost per catalogue is $ (4 + 1), or $5, and hence the total cost is $5,000. The number of orders received are 2% of 1,000, that is, 20, and hence the total contribution is 20 × 50 = $1,000. Therefore, for the year in which the catalogues are dropped, the organization ends up with a negative cash flow of $4,000, which we count in its full and undiscounted form.

However, in each of the subsequent years, the situation is different. Each year, the number of catalogues mailed out is 50 (customers) × 12 (months), and the total contribution earned is 50 (customers) × 12 (months) × 0.15 (customer rate of return) × $50 (per order) = $4,500. The total cost is 50 (customers) × 12 (months) × $4 (per catalogue, the address is already on file) = $2,400. Hence the annual positive cash flow is $2,100 [4,500 − 2,400], all attributable to the original drop of 1,000 catalogues. The net present value of the cash flows shown in the left panel of Figure 5.9 as a function of the discount rate is shown in the table in the right panel. Trial and error shows that unless the discount rate exceeds 44%, the catalogue drop is an extremely profitable endeavor from the value perspective.

Note that this analysis could be extended in a number of different ways. If the discount rate is known, the manager will be able to calculate the yield or return on investment for the catalogue drop. Suppose the discount rate is 20%. As the figure shows, the initial

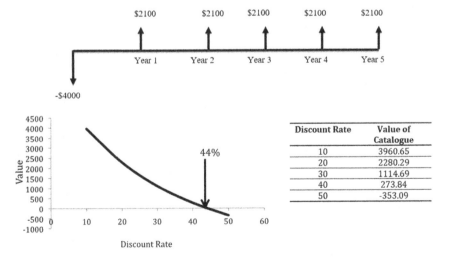

Figure 5.9 The value of a catalogue.

investment of \$5,000 creates a surplus value of \$2,280, for a five-year yield of 45.61%. Alternately, the manager may be able to use this analysis to decide whether it is worth borrowing money for a particular source to fund the catalogue program.

5.4 The Building Blocks of Customer Gambles: Utility of Analysis

In this chapter, we presented seven different scenarios in which we used the following building blocks for the analysis of customer value.

5.4.1 *Building Block 1: The Customer as a Gamble*

Moving people from any one step to the next step is like playing a gamble; the organization decides to introduce a particular intervention that, with a certain probability, moves the customer up the value ladder to the next step. A manager trying to move a customer from one step to another (where the value in the first step is V_1 and the value in the second step is V_2) spends \$$D$ to try and engineer this upgrade, and at that level of spending, the probability of success is p_D. The net expected value of this gamble can be written as follows:

$$\text{EV (customer gamble)} = p_D * (V_2 - V_1) - D$$

When we relate the gamble analogy to the customer value ladder, we think about each successive transition from one state to the next state as a gamble. The act of moving a prospect — someone who has been touched by your marketing communications — to your best possible customer can now be modeled as a series of gambles. However, we reiterate that unlike casino gambles where the player has no control on the outcome, the manager can actively influence the probability of success by choosing different marketing interventions, changing spends, and improving the effectiveness of marketing.

5.4.2 *Building Block 2: The Value of the Customer*

The prize for winning the customer gamble game is the incremental value that accrues from each transition. We use discounted cash flow analyses to capture customer value. Using the retailer metaphor, all costs incurred to attract the business of the client for the first time are used to compute the acquisition costs. All revenues and costs once the customer is "in the building" is counted under the value umbrella. The net VOC is $V - A$.

5.4.3 *Building Block 3: Sensitivity Analysis*

In Scenario 5, we used sensitivity analysis to convert a point estimate for the VOC into a probability estimate — the probability of a given marketing intervention creating positive value. This conversion is consistent with the mental model of most managers we spoke to; it not only includes all the uncertainties but also presents a decision tool that best reflects the manner in which managers think about problems. We used this approach with a VOC calculation, but it could also be used more generally.

5.4.4 *Building Block 4: Building Models That Learn*

When each of the nine scenarios is applied to real-world situations, it is easy to identify imperfections in the available data. However, as we have argued before, most of these models get better when they are fed with more and more data. Estimated become better, and predictive value improves. Another general concern that sometimes gets raised is this: "you're suggesting that we use historic data to make predictions about the future. But this may not be true." We absolutely agree, but that is why we also emphasize that it is critically important to update models regularly to ensure that trends and changes in the environment are picked up routinely before we get to a point in time where the model and the reality are long divorced from each other!

5.4.5 *Building Block 5: Mike the Mathematician and the ROI of Analysis*

The multiple references to "Mike the mathematician" are not meant to be facetious. An architect does not build houses, he gets carpenters and masons to do it; a designer does not make products, the workshop team does that; the creative director in an advertising agency does not make commercials, the production crew is responsible for those. We truly and genuinely believe that the manager's job is to provide the intuition, and to then outsource the mechanics of the mathematics to Mike. The computations are relatively cheap; the framework, logic, and intuition are worth their weight in gold. It is critically important that the underlying vision of any modeling is to help the form add value over time, and that is why we believe that it is general management that needs to build the vision and supply the intuition.

Across the seven stylized scenarios, the following are the kinds of questions that we have been able to answer:

(1) What is the acquisition cost of a customer in a given campaign?

(2) Is it worth spending money on a given marketing intervention to move customers from one step of the value ladder to the next?

(3) What is the return on marketing investment?

(4) What is the value of loyalty? Is it worth trying to increase loyalty rates?

(5) How can I compute the value of a marketing intervention?

(6) Should I borrow money at a specified interest rate to fund a new marketing activity?

(7) What is the probability that a given marketing intervention will create positive value?

(8) Which of three customer groups should I acquire? If I have acquired all three, which ones should I spend the marginal marketing dollars on?

(9) What is the optimum level that I should spend per customer (per gamble) in trying to move them along to the next level in the value ladder?

This is only an illustrative list of questions, and the reader has hopefully generated many additional questions that could be answered with approaches like the ones presented in this chapter. Most of these are questions that have had very little scientific basis for determining the answers to, and hence the utility of the simple models we have presented here should have become apparent.

5.5 What This All Means

In closing, we reiterate the value of the "one-step-at-a-time" approach. By studying successive transitions along a value ladder, we could design interventions that are specific and targeted. In previous approaches, these value ladder steps have been broken down into two coarse categories" acquisition and retention. We studied approaches for breaking down these coarse categories into finer steps. For instance, we were able to break down and model acquisition as:

Prospect → Respondent → Qualified Respondent → Customer. Likewise, we could break down retention into steps like Entry-level customer → Repeat purchaser → Loyal customer.

We offer specific prescriptive guidelines for the reader.

5.5.1 Guideline 1: Model the Effects of Any Marketing Intervention Using a Gamble

As might have become clear after a reading of this chapter, we believe that a simple gamble metaphor provides elegant simplicity with which to model customer value financially. As discussed in the earlier section, we encourage the manager — or his analyst — to outline with precision what the costs of the marketing intervention are, what the probability of success might be as a function of spends, and what additional value addition would happen should there be a successful move to the next higher level in the value ladder. Once this is done, the manager and the analyst could use many of the frameworks and tools described here to estimate quantities like the optimum spending, the value and ROI of specific marketing activities, and the probability that a given marketing campaign can result in increased value to the organization.

5.5.2 Guideline 2: Accuracy ≠ Utility

One quote that is often attributed to Confucius is "Do not use a cannonball to kill a mosquito." What does this mean in the present context? Rather than obsess about the accuracy of the models that they generate, we encourage managers to think about whether the model actually has utility. Models have utility if they truly help the manager in the decision-making process, and the correct benchmark for making this assessment is the manager's decision-making process in the absence of a model. Research has shown that even simplistic models — models that use correct variables that point the manager in the right direction without regard for the accuracy of their coefficients — significantly outperform armchair decision-making by managers.[6] We also remind the reader that the use of sensitivity analyses — and the development of models that learn as they are fed more data — will further add utility to the models as exemplified earlier.

5.5.3 Guideline 3: The Model is Merely a Crutch; the Manager is the Decision Maker. Effective Decision-Making = Model + Manager

Often times, practitioners and students who are exposed to the materials in this chapter believe that we are taking the extreme position that decision-making should be relegated to models. We would like to reiterate that this is not our position. Rather, we advocate the following: the manager uses the results of a model as a starting point, or an "anchor" and then makes adjustments, as they deem appropriate in order to make a final decision. Alternately, we would recommend a strategy first proposed by Blattberg and Hoch in 1990 — that the manager and model provide recommendations independently, and that the manager uses the average of the two outcomes as the final decision.[7] For instance, suppose that the

---

[6]Dawes, R. M. (1979). The Robust Beauty of Improper Linear Models in Decision Making. *American Psychologist*, 34(1979), 571–582.
[7]Blattberg, R. C. & Hoch, S. J. (1990). Database Models and Managerial Intuition: 50% Model + 50% Manager. *Management Science, 36*(8), 887–899.

manager wants to determine how much to spend on a particular acquisition intervention in order to maximize the profits from customers who are going to purchase just once. A model like the one provided in Scenario 3 might say that the optimal spending should be $30. However, the managers' judgment — independent of knowing what the model says — might be $36. We would then suggest that the manager use the average of the two, $33, on the intervention.

Why do we recommend this hybrid strategy in which we incorporate the elements of both the model's output as well as the manager? Like Blattberg and Hoch, we believe that each of these two sources has something unique to contribute to the decision-making process. Models are capable of tireless computational consistency, while managers are prone to making systematic computational errors given the many other things they have to do and given a whole slew of psychological factors that drive judgment and decision-making.[8] Models are impartial and do not tire, managers subconsciously tend to lean toward their own judgment of what is right over what the data tell them is right. However, models only know what managers tell it, and as the models of the world changes, the manager's role becomes even more critical. In addition, managers are privy to "special case" information about variables that may not be captured by the model. For instance, suppose that the data used to estimate the models in Scenario 3 were from an era of normal competition, but it is now a recession — or competition has launched new products aggressively — the relationship between spends and success rates may now have changed. The manager has access to intuitions about what these changes might look like, but the model will not.

---

[8]Plous, S. (1993). *The Psychology of Judgment and Decision Making*. New York: McGraw-Hill.

5.5.4 Guideline 4: The Structure and Logic is Priceless; for Everything Else, There is Mike the Mathematician

Our goal in this chapter was for readers to develop an appreciation for the kinds of models that could be used in managing customer value. The critical contribution of the manager in these efforts is not in running the data and doing the computations — it is in structuring the problems and supplying the logic behind the models. We started with this statement of our philosophy and would like to reiterate this philosophy as we close this chapter. Many of the analyses presented here could be done using a simple spreadsheet program, but as the complexity desired increases, the manager could get external help in using more sophisticated computational programs in solving and implementing these models.

Chapter 6

Behavior Change

Behavior: (1) The way in which someone conducts oneself or behaves. (2) Anything that an organism does involving action and response to stimulation.[1]

In Chapter 1, we made the case that success in our MCV framework involves moving our customers up the value ladder till they reach an appropriate point. At that appropriate point, the marginal value created for the customer is either zero (i.e., it makes no sense for the customer to move any further up) or the costs to create the marginal value exceed the benefits of the value. More generally, we made the case that it is important to move the customer up the value ladder by using tools such as promotions, product enhancements, additional services, advertising, or referrals. And in Chapter 5, we model the customer as a gamble — we said that a marketing intervention (any of the above examples) creates the likelihood that the customer moves up one step in the ladder.

But how do we move people up? In this chapter, we will unpack the specific behavioral and psychological factors that facilitate such a move. We emphasize that while Chapter 5 is a good way to model the outcome of a behavior change, the mechanics of the behavior change are best understood by understanding the psychology of the customer.

---

[1]Behavior. (n.d.). *Merriam-Webster.* Retrieved April 1, 2021, from http://www.merriam-webster.com/dictionary/behaviour

Keep in mind that every step in the value ladder represents an increased value to the customer. Therefore, it would be perfectly reasonable to believe that customers do not need to be "pushed" to move to the next step because it is clearly in their best interest to do so. In the domain of new product introductions, this belief was reflected in what Ralph Waldo Emerson referred to as the mouse-trap analogy. In particular, a popular paraphrase of a quote attributable to Emerson is — "build a better mousetrap and the world will beat a path to your door." This phrase essentially says that as long as a new product or a new offering clearly has greater value for the customer than the incumbent, they will naturally be attracted to it, make a purchase, or — in our language — move to the next step in the value ladder.

However, many writers in marketing, as well as researchers in the field of behavioral economics, have written about the fallacious nature of Emerson's observation. In particular, it has been demonstrated that people often do not do what is in their best interest. In the world of individual welfare, for example, people who know that they need to exercise more, get annual health checkups, save for retirement, or in general lead healthier lifestyles fail to do so despite being made aware of the many benefits of these activities. In the domain of marketing, the so-called "last mile problem" is a statement of the fact that many products and services that are clearly superior to incumbent products do not succeed in the marketplace because manufacturers fail to take into account the psychology of potential purchases. In particular, it has been shown that customers often do not make purchases even when they are aware of the superior nature of certain new products, as a result of which success rates for new products and initiatives are abysmally low.[2] In the domain of government, policy, and welfare, it has been shown repeatedly that a number of initiatives that are in the citizens' best interest do not

---

[2]Gourville, J. T. (2006). Eager Sellers and Stony Buyers: Understanding the Psychology of New-Product Adoption. *Harvard Business Review, 84*(6), 98–145.

succeed because citizens fail to embrace and adopt these programs or policies. For instance, a well-intentioned program in Canada called the Canada Learning Bond offered parents of low-income families $2,000 to educate their children. This was as close to a utopian product as possible. There was absolutely no string attached to receiving $2,000 (expect, of course, that they had to be spent on education). However, results showed that in the first few years, only about 16% of eligible Canadians availed of this offer.[3]

We now know that there are several reasons for why people do not do things that are in their best interest. In the language of a value ladder, there are four reasons for why customers do not naturally climb ladders on their own even though they may realize the value of doing so.

(1) **Change is difficult:** Research in behavioral economics shows support for a tendency for customers to maintain the *status quo.* For instance, consider the purchase of a new product such as an electric car. Even though customers might be well aware of the benefits of an electric vehicle, making the purchase entails giving up on the existing lifestyle. As a concrete example, customers are used to a network of gas stations where they could easily refill their petrol vehicle such that advance planning is not needed in the driving decision. However, taking an electric vehicle on a long drive requires that the customer plan ahead and fully charge the vehicle as they are not as confident of having easy access to recharging stations. This loss of a lifestyle looms larger than the potential gain from adopting the new product.

(2) **Small frictions have big effects:** In addition to the experienced loss in giving up the current product or the current benefit, the actual mechanics of change might impose costs on customers.

---

[3] Soman, D., Stein, J., & Wong, J. (2013). *Innovating for the Global South.* Toronto, Canada: University of Toronto Press.

Frictions in the process of making a change loom large and are often overvalued. For instance, the hassle cost of buying a new vehicle, shifting accounts to a different bank branch, canceling a magazine subscription, moving from one service provider to another, or getting accustomed to doing business on the internet as opposed to in-person are daunting and might deter customers from even wanting to make the change. Other frictions might include complicated processes, poor communication, or emotional barriers. For instance, many potential recipients of welfare benefits (like the Canada Learning Bond) do not accept payments they are entitled to because they feel a sense of shame or embarrassment. We will refer to these frictions as sludge later on in this chapter.

(3) **The benefit is not salient:** In some situations, the benefits of moving up a step in the ladder might be mathematically and economically clear customers, but are psychologically not as compelling. For example, a new product might offer a higher level of performance compared to the incumbent (see, e.g., the case studies highlighting economic benefit in Chapter 2). As a result of the greater levels of economic value created, the new product might have a higher price. In making the decision to move from one rung of a ladder to another, the customer might be blinded by the difference in out-of-pocket price and therefore not fully account for the value that arises from the new product. Also, in many cases the value is "invisible" — it takes the form of a reduction in ongoing costs, and hence is not very salient.

(4) **Delayed consequences but immediate costs:** Consider a customer contemplating a purchase of an energy-efficient appliance in their ongoing relationship with their utilities company. Such a purchase often entails an immediate cost of acquiring the new appliance, but an ongoing benefit of a reduction in energy bills over the next few years. Research in behavioral economics shows that people tend to overweigh the present and

discount the future. As a result, the value of the present price looms much larger than the positive gains from the future benefits.

In this chapter, we will take a deep dive into the science of behavioral economics. In particular, we will understand why so many organizations struggle with behavior change on the part of not just their customers, but also internal stakeholders (their own employees or agents). Our key point in this chapter is that managers in organizations often make unwarranted assumptions about how rational their customers are, and that it is important to remember that a marketplace is a collection of human beings who might diverge systematically from what managers believe them to be. We also provide a process by which organizations could use this science to design interventions to move customers up the value ladder.

6.1 Humans Are Not Econs

In 2008, the field of behavioral science and behavioral economics was made popular through the publication of a seminal book by Richard Thaler and Cass Sunstein called *Nudge*.[4] This book, as well as many others that followed it, made a series of eloquent arguments about the fact that marketplaces are a collection of humans, and therefore, a scientific understanding of human behavior is critical to success in understanding, and therefore, succeeding in commercial marketplaces.[5]

---

[4]Thaler, R. H. & Sunstein, C. R. (2008). *Nudge: Improving Decisions About Health, Wealth, and Happiness* (Updated edn.). New York: Penguin Books.
[5]Halpern, D. (2016). *Inside the Nudge Unit: How Small Changes Can Make a Big Difference*. London, U.K.: WH Allen; Soman, D. (2015). *The Last Mile: Creating Social and Economic Value from Behavioural Insights*. Toronto, Canada: Rotman-UTP Publishing.

We use terminology from the book *Nudge* to illustrate the basic principles of why an organization should care about the science of behavioral economics. In particular, we make a distinction between two kinds of entities. Econs are hypothetical creatures that live on the pages of economics textbooks. They are forward-looking, and they have infinite knowledge, as well as unlimited computing powers. They are patient, unemotional, and can process copious amounts of information with ease. Econs are also able to integrate information with the appropriate mathematical sophistication and are always looking to maximize outcomes. These robot-like creatures are the essence of the manner in which the field of microeconomics depicts the behavior of agents. In particular, econs try and maximize utility — a concept that primarily originates from the attributes of a product or service. In some narratives, these econs are also described as rational creatures.

In contrast, humans — real people — are very different. Unlike econs, humans often get overwhelmed by too much information and too many choices, make decisions based on emotion or gut feelings, are averse to making stressful and critical decisions, are impatient and myopic, and therefore often choose to maximize short-term happiness rather than long-term utility. Humans are also cognitive misers and lack the sophistication involved in complex decisions that might involve spending and consumption over periods of time (e.g., decisions such as how much to save for retirement, or what is the optimal sequence in which financial products should be consumed).

As might be apparent to the reader, there are stark differences between humans and econs. One notable difference has to do with the ability of these two entities to digest and act on information. Econs respond well to information and to instructions — when they have a complex decision to make, econs are best served by information and directions on how to optimally make that decision. Humans, on the other hand, do not respond well to copious amounts of information. Research has shown that the volume and nature of information matter to how humans react to it. In particular, giving people too much information can have a backfiring effect because humans ignore the information altogether. Likewise, information that is presented in dense textual formats is usually ignored relative to information that is provided in visually easy-to-read and sequential formats. Another difference relates to motivation — econs are inherently motivated to do things that are in their own best interest. Humans, on the other hand, might surprisingly be resistant to doing things that are good for them. For instance, it is unnecessary to try and persuade an econ to exercise routinely, to lead a healthy lifestyle, to eat a balanced diet, to not overwork or to save for retirement and for the nest egg. Unlike econs, humans often need to be persuaded to do these things. A third difference relates to the temporal orientation of decision-making. Econs can be infinitely forward-looking. They might be willing to sacrifice current consumption in order for long-term benefits (e.g., forgoing a cup of cappuccino from a fancy coffee shop in order to make a small contribution toward their nest egg) while humans are easily tempted by the immediate. In popular folklore about the field of behavioral science, econs are often referred to as rational why humans are described as irrational — as if it is a flaw in human decision-making.

Our own opinion of rationality and irrationality diverges from this popular depiction. In particular, we believe that the human brain was never designed to solve complex intertemporal and highly information-rich decision problems. The fact that humans do not comply with the basic laws of economics should come as no surprise. However, we are struck by the fact that many organizations and leaders within them seem to believe that their stakeholders (customers or employees) are more like econs than humans. We believe that last mile problems occurred in organizations because of this fundamental empathy gap.

> **Insight Box 6.1**
>
> **MCV Insight**
>
> Customers are not econs, they are humans. Design products and services assuming that they might not be motivated, that they will be confused by too much information and too many options, and that they might not always do what they want to do

In particular, last mile problems happen because organizations design products and services for econs when — in fact — their actual customer is human. For instance, when launching a financial product or a healthcare product, we tend to assume that all of our customers will be motivated enough that they will wade through masters of complex information, periodically update their knowledge about products and services, spend time with advisors to figure out investment or health strategies, or have the patience to deal with processes that might not be easy in order to open accounts or gym membership plans. However, research shows that many customers are not as motivated as we think they might be.

Therefore, our prescription for organizations is simple — design for humans rather than for econs! In particular, as we design products or services, we should assume that our target customers might not be as motivated as we believe they are. We might also assume that people might forget to do things or be discouraged by small frictions that they might encounter. Rather than trying to simply give people information that they may likely get overwhelmed by, we, as organizations need to think about how best we can make it easy for customers by giving them the right information at the right time, but also making our processes for consuming products and services as easy as they could be. In other words, we truly need to understand what it means to be human.

The question of what it means to be human has its roots in a large body of research in the field of behavioral economics/social and cognitive psychology, as well as sociology. Here, we will focus on four specific aspects of being human: the importance of context in decision-making, the role of procrastination, the use of heuristics in order to make complex decisions, and *status quo* and habits.

6.1.1 *Context Dependence*

It has long been assumed in the world of business and policy that customer preferences are invariant to context. However, this is the furthest from the truth. The origin of the importance of context and decision-making goes back to philosopher and psychologist William James, who wrote that human behavior arises from an interaction between the individual and the context in which decisions are made.[6] James believed that the very same individual could make dramatically different decisions as a function of the context.

Of course, the field of economics recognizes the role of context by acknowledging that the utility of products and services could change as a function of its form (form utility — that a piece of wood has a greater utility when it takes the shape of a chair or a desk than a log) and time (time utility — that a breakfast food has greater utility in the morning than in the middle of the night). However, research over the past few decades has shown that there are many other elements of context that could affect decisions. Nobel Laureate Richard Thaler highlighted the importance of context by talking about the importance of SIFs — supposedly irrelevant factors — on decisions.[7] SIFs could include aspects of timing (e.g., the time of the day, the day of the week, the season, the month, or even venue during a given week or a year when a choice is made); the physical features of the immediate environment (e.g., whether a decision was made at the office, at home, or a coffee shop; in the digital world or the physical world, in a brick-and-mortar store or a

---

[6]James, W. (1950). *The Principles of Psychology, Volume 1*. New York: Dover Publications.
[7]Thaler, R. H. (2015). *Misbehaving: The Story of Behavioural Economics*. New York: W. W. Norton & Company.

shopping app); the information and choice presentation (e.g., whether there were other options available in the physical surroundings, whether the information about options was presented side by side or one after the other, whether it was presented textually or visually); or the presence of social others at the time of decision-making (e.g., whether there were others present in the physical environment, the degree of crowding, whether those physical others were similar or dissimilar to the customer).

There are possibly an infinite number of contexts that might change the manner and the outcome of choices that a customer makes. One specific example of the importance of context was presented in *The Last Mile*. In a particular coffee shop, people were offered a choice between three sizes of coffee, 8, 10 and 12 ounces. In this case, the majority of customers tended to purchase the so-called compromise option, which is the 10-ounce option. However, when the coffee shop changed the sizes and customers now were offered a choice between 10, 12, and 14 ounces, the majority of the customers now chose the new compromise option that is the 12-ounce option. This study was done in a coffee shop that was housed in the atrium of a busy office building suggesting that the set of clientele was stable week after week. However, when people who had purchased the compromise option cup of coffee were asked as to why they made their choice, they suggested that "the smaller option has too little while the larger option has too much coffee" irrespective of which choice set they faced.

In this example, changing the assortment (an important element of context) significantly influenced the choices that people made. Interestingly, customers did not seem to be aware of the fact that context had changed their preferences. Examples like the compromise effects have been documented in different domains — stores often surround products by cheaper and lower quality products on the one side and more expensive and higher quality products on the other to make the compromised product look more attractive. Likewise, an example in the book *Predictably Irrational* shows that newspapers and magazines often include a decoy option — a subscription plan that is inferior to one of the other options but implicitly makes that other option look better than it would have otherwise.[8]

6.1.2 *Procrastination*

Research in the behavioral sciences is replete with demonstrations showing that customers who intend to make certain decisions or take certain actions end up not doing so. For example, respondents in a survey about purchasing retirement planning products said that they intended to open accounts and to start saving but were unable to do so because "life gets in the way." Likewise, there are a number of demonstrations of the fact that people who intend to purchase newer versions of products, save, spend more time with their families, learn new skills, develop healthy habits, or improve their diet and exercise regimens, but despite all good intentions, they are unable to actually get the job done.

A recent review and synthesis proposed that in any behavior-change challenge — conceptually, in any situation where we want to move a group of people from one rung of the value ladder to the next rung — there are three segments of customers.[9] Motivated enthusiasts are customers who agree with the need to move up one rung and get it done immediately. Diehard opponents, unlike motivated enthusiasts, however, might have a number of reasons for why they have absolutely no intention of moving up the rung — perhaps they do not see the value that they would get from moving up, or

---

[8]Ariely, D. (2008). *Predictably Irrational: The Hidden Forces That Shape Our Decisions.* New York: Harper Collins.
[9]Soman, D. & Ly, K. (2018). The Growing Market for Self-Control. *Rotman Magazine,* Winter, 36–41.

perhaps it genuinely does not make sense because they would not get any incremental value.

However, there is a third, potentially large, and significantly insidious segment called naïve intenders. These are customers who agree with the need to move up the ladder (e.g., purchase a new product, or increase their consumption and activity levels) but somehow never managed to get it done. Rather than dedicating efforts and resources to convince these people to move up the ladder, a better strategy might be to help these customers by making the process easy. Persuasion for this sub-segment is wasted because these customers are already persuaded, but simply face obstacles. Examples of interventions that might make it easy for people to act on their intentions might include auto-enrolling people into retirement plans, changing defaults on donation forms, introducing sludge-free methods of purchasing or changing consumption levels (for instance, Amazon's 1-Click shopping button), are generally making it more costless for people to complete transactions (for instance, by providing home delivery services or 24/7 omnichannel access).

6.1.3 *The Use of Heuristics in Making Choices*

> **Insight Box 6.2**
>
> **MCV Insight**
> There is usually a large and insidious segment of naïve intenders — customers that want to change behaviors and move up the ladder, but simply fail to do so. Persuading these customers is a waste, so effort should be focused on making things easy for them.

Nobel laureate Herbert Simon argued that human beings are cognitive misers. In particular, while people might be motivated to solve complex decision problems, they are limited by the cognitive bandwidth of their brains. Therefore, they often result in using rules of thumbs or mental shortcuts in making choices and decisions. These mental shortcuts are called heuristics.

When customers are confronted with decisions that require large amounts of complex information (e.g., purchasing high-ticket items or products that involve a lot of risk and uncertainty) and they do not have the motivation or the ability to process the information, they will look for simpler pieces of data (cues) that could help them make the right choice. For example, rather than making a detailed assessment of ambiguous content, a client might believe that a consulting firm that took a longer time to produce a report did a more thorough job than another consulting firm that took less time. This client would be using the duration heuristic — the belief that the longer one works on a project, the better is the quality of work. Another example of a well-documented heuristic is the so-called availability heuristic which suggests that instances of information that come more readily to the customer's mind are over vetted in their decision-making. For instance, customers are likely to believe that there are significantly larger numbers of deaths in automobile or plane accidents relative to natural causes, or even more mundane causes like flooding because instances of automobile or plane accidents are often published in newspapers and therefore come to mind more easily. This might have significant implications for how customers perceive risk and therefore purchase products that are related to their assessment of risk (for instance, insurance products or investment products).

Yet another cue to determine which product to purchase might be the "popularity cue." If a large number of other people are purchasing a particular product, then it must be good. In cases where product quality is difficult to assess or requires a lot of complex information processing, the popularity cue often drives decision-making. Infact, customers might make inferences on what to buy from what is available. For instance, products that have a large shelf display must be better, or restaurants that have a long line outside must have better food.

Another cognitive phenomenon that might have implications for taking a product to market is referred to as appraisal-based decision-making. Imagine that a customer is looking for a new pair of shoes, or perhaps a new computer. A well-reasoned and comprehensive decision would involve sifting through a large body of information on multiple attributes from all available options in each product category. Instead, the customer might base their judgment on salient cues and then seek in-depth information about a smaller subset of products. For instance, customers might make appraisals — snap judgments of products based on superficial cues such as how attractive they look or what their friends have said about those products and then evaluate those products in greater depth. Therefore, even when your product or service might be economically superior to the incumbent or in situations where it makes sense for a customer to move up one tank of the value ladder, it is important to ensure that the new product or new rung passes the appraisal test — that there is something simple and salient about the new product that can form the basis of a more thorough evaluation by the customer.

6.1.4 Status Quo *and Habits*

The idea of humans as cognitive misers carries forward to another simplifying decision rule. The *status quo* preference suggests that unless the current option is particularly bad, customers may not be motivated to switch to new products or services. On the flip side, habits simply mean that people continue by momentum to purchase products or services that worked well for them in the past because change is difficult and change is often aversive. Therefore, even when electric vehicles offer clear economic benefits and arguably some experiential benefits over petrol engine vehicles, the *status quo* bias of customer basis conspired to make it difficult for these products to succeed in the marketplace. In a different domain, research has shown that in the context of financial products and investment portfolios, many customers do not update their portfolios or rebalance their portfolios, even as new information becomes available to them.

This seems surprising, after all, as the customer has more information about the performance of financial securities, it would make sense to make changes to their financial portfolios. However, the *status quo* bias again rears its head and unless there is an absolute necessity to make a change, this causes most customers to make no changes even in the face of new information.

6.1.5 *Nudging, Choice Architecture, and Sludge*

Since research shows that customer decision-making depends on the context in which people make choices, we could also steer people toward choices by changing elements of the context. For example, we know that cognitive miserliness results in people sticking to the *status quo* or default option. In the domain of organ donations, research shows that countries that have an opt-in system in which a citizen has to actively take steps to become a registered organ donor has significantly lower consent rates than countries that have an opt-out system in which it is presumed that every citizen will be an organ donor. If this was the case, perhaps we could increase consent rates by simply changing the default option. In another example, research shows that customers of an insurance product who had paid for an annual doctor's visit fail to make that visit because the default option was that they needed to take some active steps in order to book an appointment. Changing the default by assigning people appointments and asking them to take active steps if in fact they could not make the appointment significantly increased the consumption of annual health checkups.

Likewise, knowing that customers might tend to forget to make contributions to their retirement product, and intervention whereby a financial services company sends a one-click reminder to its customers might increase donation rates. Knowing that one cue that customers might use to judge the popularity of a particular product or service is whether others in the population are purchasing that product or service. If a company decides to publicize which of their products are the most popular and what percent of the population consumes them — this increases the likelihood that the target customer will also make a purchase.

These are all examples of situations in which the organization has used a basic understanding of human behavior to change the context in which the decision has been made. That change in context can take the form of either a change of the features of a decision (what the default option is), additional low-cost elements of information (a reminder), or information about the consumption of others (which should be irrelevant to the utility for the target customer). These changes in context are SIFs that cause behavior change are often referred to as a nudge, and this approach to behavior change is called choice architecture.

However, other contextual factors can conspire with human tendencies like procrastination or the *status quo* bias to create the opposite effect — to make things particularly difficult and cumbersome for the customer. Imagine that a customer of an insurance company is trying to complete paperwork to move from an existing plan to a different plan. This customer has been meaning to change plans for a period of time but has procrastinated because other things have kept them busy. As they start completing the paperwork online, they realize that they now need to get a new password for the new product and that this password can only be delivered through regular surface mail for security reasons. This customer — having mustered up the motivation and self-control to get the job done — still fails at the last hurdle because they now need to wait for the new password to arrive in the mail. When it does eventually arrive, they might have lost the motivation to upgrade to the new insurance plan. This customer has just been the victim of sludge — the evil cousin of nudge.[10]

Sludge could arise from many sources but of three different types. The first source of sludge is simply difficult, complex, and inelegant processes. This is often a failure of customer experience (CX). Sometimes a process for upgrading insurance plans or health plans, or even changing credit cards to get better terms and conditions might involve multiple signatures, approvals, forms — several steps spread out over time. Each of these represent an opportunity for the customer to fall through the cracks of trying to upgrade. Standardized CX processes work really well if they are automated, but if there are exceptions and human interventions required, the greater is the potential for sludge.

A second source of sludge is communication. Sometimes communication is excessive while on other occasions, it is incomplete. Incomplete information can result in a flawed understanding of the value of the new product or of moving to the next rung in the value ladder. Too much information can run the risk of confusing the customer who then decides not to try and upgrade at all. A third source of sludge relates to emotions like embarrassment or stigma. In the Canada Learning Bond example discussed earlier, a number of recipients of the program decided not to enroll because they were embarrassed by the fact that they would be visibly in a queue for collecting welfare. Likewise, many people who should access mental wellness initiatives often do not do so even when programs are easily available to them because they might feel stigmatized. The manner in which the CX process was designed was perhaps operationally efficient but ended up creating emotional barriers that resulted in sludge and in customers dropping out.

---

[10]Soman, D. (2020). *Sludge: A Very Short Introduction.* Toronto, Canada: Behavioural Economics in Action at Rotman (BEAR) Report Series, available at http://www.rotman.utoronto.ca/bear

6.2 Approaches to Behavior Change

In order to better understand how behavior change can be influenced, we consider a simple stylized problem. Imagine that a customer is currently engaging in behavior A and the organization is interested in trying to move them to behavior B. Note that A and B could stand for all kinds of behavior-change situations. For instance, a client might not be paying their invoices on time and the organization is interested in getting them to do so (a problem of compliance). A potential customer might be currently purchasing products from a competitor and the organization is interested in getting them to purchase their products (a problem of brand switching). Similarly, a customer might currently be purchasing infrequently from the organization and the organization would like them to increase the frequency — or perhaps even the volume — of purchasing (the problem of increasing value). A potential customer might have expressed interest in a suite of products and services that they had never really gotten down to purchasing and consuming — in this case the firm might be interested in accelerating the consumption of certain products and services (the problem of accelerating consumption). More generally, we can liken behaviors A and B to different rungs in the value ladder and the organization's goal might be to upgrade people from A to B.

How do we solve this general problem of getting customers who are currently doing A to now do B? In *The Last Mile*, four approaches are illustrated through the hypothetical example of a lawyer, an economist, an advertiser, and a behavioral scientist walking into a bar. While they are in the bar, the bartender asks them about how they would get people currently choosing A to switch to B. The lawyer's approach is simple; they argue that customers might switch to B if A was impossible or very difficult to get. More generally, these strategies are referred to as restriction strategies. If the organization was a government, they could potentially simply ban option A or if it was a for-profit organization, they could withdraw product A from the marketplace or otherwise make it difficult to obtain product A by reducing distribution or increasing costs associated with using that product. The economist has a different approach to engineer this behavior change. The economist is familiar with a long tradition of research showing that incentives matter. Incentives could be both monetary (e.g., a discount, a coupon or other form of sales promotion for purchasing product B) or nonmonetary (e.g., the status awarded to some customers on achieving a certain level of consumption via loyalty programs, see earlier discussion in Chapter 4). However, recent research suggests that while promotions might have a significant effect in the short run, the withdrawal of those promotions might result in a return to the earlier behavior. Since our approach in MCV is to hopefully try and move the customer up the value ladder permanently, it might be risky to depend entirely on incentives because it would run the risk of the customer returning to the previous rung once the incentive has been withdrawn. A classic example of the short-run effectiveness but long-run futility of incentives is the well-documented post-promotion dip. This is the phenomena from supermarket sales data which shows that once a promotion on a particular product has been discontinued, sales levels dip below the historic average (largely because customers have stockpiled when the item was on deal).

The third person to respond to the bartender's question is the advertising executive. They are not interested in banning or offering incentives as much as they are in persuading the customer to switch to option B. Persuasion can be done through a number of different routes anchored at two extremes. The first relies on the use of information-heavy and logical appeals to make a case why product B is superior to product A. These are often referred to as informational advertising. Alternately, one could rely on imagery, hedonic aspects of the consumption of the product, or appeals to the emotional part of the customer to persuade them to choose product B. These are referred to as transformational appeals. The advertiser believes that behavior change can be achieved through simply choosing the appropriate appeal given the context in which the customer will make a decision.

Finally, it is the turn of the behavioral scientist. After reading the proceeding paragraphs, the reader of this book will know exactly what the behavioral scientist would recommend. Their preferred approach is the notion of choice architecture, the idea that we could create contexts in which we could steer people toward the right decision. Here is a formal definition of a nudge.[11]

A nudge is any aspect of the choice architecture that alters people's behavior in a predictable way without forbidding any options, or significantly changing their economic consequences. To count as a mere nudge, an intervention must be easy and cheap. Nudges are not mandates. Putting food at eye level to attract attention and hence to increase the likelihood of getting chosen counts as a nudge. The banning of junk food does not.

Our goal in highlighting these four approaches to behavior change is not claim that any one of them is superior to the others. Rather, we would like to highlight that each of these four might have a role to play and that we should think about these four as four different tools in our arsenal for engineering behavior change. Combinations of these four approaches could be used either simultaneously or sequentially to achieve the desired behavior change.

As an example of an organization that uses two approaches simultaneously, consider a fitness center that is trying to get people to exercise more. Their approach is to move people up the value ladder by increasing consumption rates and thereby hopefully improving the chances of renewing their annual memberships. This fitness center could nudge people to exercise more frequently by framing their annual membership as a series of monthly payments. For instance, rather than saying that they charge $1,200 a year, this facility could highlight the fact that customers are paying $100 per month for the privilege of using the center. This intervention uses a behavioral

---

[11]Thaler, R.H. & Sunstein, C.R. (2008), *Nudge: Improving Decisions about Health, Wealth and Happiness.* New Haven, U.S.A: Yale University Press.

phenomenon known as the sunk cost effect — when people are aware of how much they have prepaid for a product or service, they are more likely to consume that product or service. Simply reframing their annual membership as a monthly (or perhaps even a weekly) payment would remind their customers on an ongoing basis to use the fitness center. This is an example of an intervention that is based primarily on an economic consideration (the annual fees paid), but a nudge has been added on through the manner in which the payment has been presented. As another example of using multiple approaches in conjunction — but in this case, sequentially — a financial services product company was looking to increase the incidence of bank account opening amongst younger customers and to eventually convert those customers into consuming additional products and services. The bank found that it was relatively easy to get people to open accounts by offering an incentive; in this case, a gift that took the form of a MP3 player or a smartphone. However, they also learned that once the offer ended, customers did not do much with their bank accounts and generally lost interest. Therefore, it employed a strategy of following up incentives with an informational campaign and choice architecture that made it relatively easy to remind customers about making ongoing contributions and providing information about additional products and services. By using this cocktail of behavior-change approaches over time, the bank was able to gradually move people up the value ladder. On the contrary, simply providing them with an incentive to open an account would get a lot of people onto the first rung of the ladder, but most of them would unfortunately continue to remain there.

Table 6.1 provides a comparison between the four approaches to behavior change and provides additional guidance as to when each of these approaches are particularly helpful and when they are not.

Insight Box 6.3

MCV Insight

The four approaches to behavior change can be used in conjunction either simultaneously or sequentially for maximum impact.

Table 6.1 Four approaches to behavior change.

	Regulations (Bans, Compliance Rules, Mandates)
Useful when	Behavior has consequences that are a high risk to society or takes advantage of others (e.g., *crime, intentional fraud, pollution*) or against society's values or ethics (e.g., *racial discrimination, freedom of speech*).
	Third-party effects are present and the consequences of the behavior are not entirely absorbed by the individual or corporation.
	Establishing standards that enhances standard of living or protects individuals (e.g., *minimum wage requirements, product safety*).
	Enforcement is feasible and cost-effective.
Avoid when	Regulation is perceived as overly restrictive or intrusive.
	Individuals would likely respond with defiance or by undermining regulation.
When choice architecture can help	Enforcement is in place but may not be working effectively. Choice architecture may help increase compliance.
	Economic Incentives (Taxes, Penalties, Grants, Subsidies)
Useful when	Behavior is motivated by costs and benefits and hyperbolic discounting does not take effect (benefits are felt up front, losses are painful).
	Incentives are salient to the individual.
	Market is in line with the incentives and does not work against them. (e.g., Subsidies for energy-efficient products are in direct competition with cheaper products. "Green" taxes on computers must work against marketing efforts to sell the latest and greatest products.)

Avoid when	Behavior is motivated by fairness, altruism, or social norms (e.g., organ donations).
	Taxes and penalties create "licenses" to engage in behavior.
When choice architecture can help	Behavior is affected by cognitive influences (loss aversion, *status quo*, etc.). Choice architecture can help highlight incentives or reduce particular barriers to accessing incentives.

Information and Persuasion

Useful when	Combined with other policy tools.
	Encourages learning and can improve decision-making skills over time.
Avoid when	Information is presented in a complex manner.
	Message conflicts with what is being presented in the media or by other influencers such as peers.
When choice architecture can help	When information is overly complex, choice architecture can help improve information processing using nudge techniques such as salience and simplification.

Nudges and Choice Architecture

(Defaults, Simplification, Opt-In versus Opt-Out)

Useful when	Freedom of choice is important and individual preferences vary.
	Economic incentives or penalties are not appropriate.
	Behavior is affected by cognitive influences and individuals struggle with turning intentions into action.
	Increasing alignment with current regulations or incentives.
Avoid when	Context can be changed by businesses or other institutions in the marketplace. Additional regulation may be needed to set boundaries for market behavior. Or, incentives may need to be changed to improve alignment with policy goals.
	Intended outcome of the nudge may go against individual intentions.

6.3 A Process for Designing Interventions

Now that we have discussed the basic ideas of behavioral economics and talked about different approaches to behavior change, we would like to outline a process for how behavioral change interventions can be developed and used in order to move customers up a value ladder. The process that we outline below has been developed by The Behavioral Economics in Action at Rotman (BEAR) Research Centre at the University of Toronto.

Before describing the process, we would like to outline five considerations and caveats for the practicing manager:

(1) **Context always matters:** As we have repeatedly mentioned earlier in this chapter, the research on behavioral economics repeatedly emphasizes the idea that behavior is a function of context, and that supposedly irrelevant factors (SIF) might matter in influencing the outcomes of a particular intervention. This centrality on context has two implications. First, in trying to design an intervention to move customers up a value ladder, it is critically important to understand the context in which customers will be making those choices and to recognize that those contexts might change over time and across different groups of customers. Second, the success of interventions obviously hinges on the context in which that intervention was run. This implies that just because a particular intervention (a communication campaign, an incentive, or a choice architecture intervention) was successful elsewhere or for some other segment is no guarantee that it will succeed again.

We, therefore, recommend that practitioners think about past successes — whether in their own organization or based on work that they may have read in publications elsewhere — be considered as starting points or hypotheses in developing interventions rather than simply being treated as an off-the-shelf idea. In particular, we encourage managers to avoid the temptation of copying an intervention as is from another source and rather going through the process that we document here to increase the likelihood that it would be appropriate in the particular context.[12]

In Chapter 11, we present a detailed glossary of behavioral economics' phenomena and terms that the practicing manager might use as a starting point in designing their own intervention.

(2) **Heterogeneity and variability across customers:** A further corollary of the point we made earlier is the fact that the same intervention might affect different groups of customers in different ways. Some of these differences across customers might be due to demographic and individual differences — for instance, an appeal that hinges on safety and security for one's family will obviously only be effective for customers with families or certain products might only appeal to certain age groups. In addition, differences and variability could also arise due to differences in context. For instance, the same group of customers might be influenced by certain interventions at different times of the day or different times of the year — for instance, interventions that promote efficient usage of time (time management) are often more effective during work days when there is a lot more activity to be managed than during weekends and during most of the year but not during the summer when people have lower levels of activity.

(3) **Use of third-party observers:** Heterogeneity across customers simply implies that no one person will be able to support any behavior frictions or bottlenecks other people might experience. For instance, going back to the example of sludge that we discussed earlier, the fact that one had to wait for a new password might be seen as a friction for people who are relatively

---

[12]Soman, D. & Yeung, C. (2021). *The Behaviorally Informed Organization*. Toronto, Canada: Rotman-UTP Publishing.

more disorganized but not so much of a friction for well-organized customers. In a situation like this, a very organized customer might simply not appreciate difficulties faced by others. It is therefore important that practitioners use neutral third-party observers to make judgments about what aspects of the decision context might provide frictions and which aspects might help people make better choices.

(4) **Three tools of the choice architect:** Based on our discussion of human behavior, we encourage practitioners to think about three kinds of behavior tools that they could use to help engineer behavior change. The first is a frame. Just as the same exact painting might have different visual appeal in a wooden versus a metallic frame, the same information or decision could have different impacts as a function of how the information or choice is framed. A second tool is a prod — just as cattle often need to be prodded in order to move along, humans — who are susceptible to the *status quo* bias and to cognitive limitations — often also need to be prodded to re-examine decisions and to make new ones. Prods could take the form of reminders, changes in default, or even small frictions such as decision points that get the customer to pause and re-evaluate the product or service that they are consuming. The third tool is a lock. As discussed earlier, customers are often unwilling to make a behavior change now, but conceptually agreed to doing so in the future. Therefore, one strategy to engineer behavior change is to get customers to pre-commit to making a change in the future, and then creating a lock to ensure that they follow through on that pre-commitment. This lock could take multiple forms that include reminders, public commitments, contracts, or social pressure.

(5) **Motivation and friction:** Changing behavior from A to B can often be compared conceptually through fluid that flows in a pipeline from A to B. Engineering tells us that two things are required for a good flow of fluid. One, that there is a pressure

differential across A and B causing the fluid to flow in that direction, and two, that the pipe is clean and free of friction. In the language of behavioral economics, this implies that people need to be motivated to make the behavior change and that the process of making the behavior change should be friction free. The process that we describe below focuses on both of these elements.

Figure 6.1 captures the eight-stage process for designing behavioral intervention. The first stage in the process relates to identifying the desired outcomes. In the language of our value ladder, it will be helpful for the manager

> **Insight Box 6.4**
>
> **MCV Insight**
> Behavior change = Motivation + Reduced Friction. Make sure people understand why they need to move up the ladder, then make it very easy to do so.

to precisely articulate which rung of the ladder the customer is currently at and what ladder they would like the customer to move to. The second stage involves a careful landscape analysis — an understanding of the context in which the behavior change will happen. In trying to document the context, it is important to identify who the various stakeholders are, what actions are involved in the behavior change, and what are the existing touchpoints that the customer

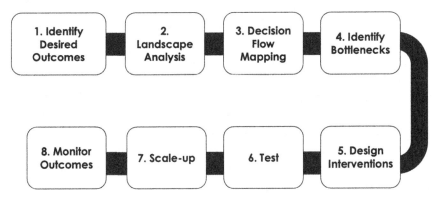

Figure 6.1 A process for designing behavior change interventions.

encounters in that interaction with the organization? This will allow the manager to ask questions such as — which stakeholders' actions are most critical? How influenceable are each of the stakeholders? What are the frictions to the actions that might enable behavior change? What are the touchpoints that could be altered or added in order to engineer the behavior change?

The third stage involves a detailed mapping of the decision flow. What are the various steps through which people go through in order to make the behavior change? For instance, the decision to open a retirement account in itself could have multiple stages — need recognition, accessing the relevant information, making choices as to which is the most appropriate account for one's given needs, and then actually completing the paperwork to open an account. What are the touchpoints that the customer encounters during each of these stages and what is the role of each of the touch-points? Might the touchpoints be contributing to the friction that customers might experience? Do customers have enough of a motivation to go through each of these stages? A careful mapping of these processes will further provide the practicing manager with a richer picture of the context, the actors, and the frictions that the customer might experience.

We note that the term decision mapping is also often used in the design community and would like to caution readers that the mapping that we speak about differs from the mapping done by designers in one important way. In particular, designers in the CX/UX world tend to draw maps to represent what customers actually do. In the behavioral science world, it is also important to draw a map to illustrate what customers "should do" in order to move to the next rung of the ladder. Comparing the "should do" with the "actually do" maps will shed light on parts of the process that people tend to get stuck at.

The fourth stage involves an identification of the bottlenecks that customers might experience in traversing through the decision flow that has been documented in the previous stage. This stage is important because it relies on a combination of behavioral science as well as imperative data to make judgments about who is getting stuck where. The glossary provided in Chapter 11 is one approach to thinking about which behavioral factors might play a role in creating a friction.

However, it is also important for the practicing manager to get as much data on transition rates between different stages of the pipeline as they can. For instance, what is the likelihood that somebody who is in the first stage actually moves to the second stage? While this data might be laborious to collect in the physical world, it is particularly easy in the digital world. For instance, a manager in an online bank has access to copious information about click streams — the specific paths that people take through their websites — and can easily identify frictions and bottlenecks using simple statistical techniques.

The fifth stage involves the actual design of the intervention. Once the manager has an understanding of what the friction is and therefore what the underlying psychology causing it is, they can either modify an existing touchpoint (simplify the exposition, add in reminders, reframe the information) or add in a new touchpoint (a text message reminder, a follow-up communication) to solve for the friction. Once interventions have been designed, they will then need to be tested (Step 6). In the world of behavioral economics, testing usually refers to an experiment or a randomized control trial comparing two worlds — one in which the extinct touchpoint or product is used with a second world in which the reframed/intervention is present. Doing an experiment rather than simply asking people questions allows the manager to see if the intervention actually had an effect on people's behavior rather than assessing whether customers believe that they had an effect on its behavior.

At the conclusion of a successful pilot, the manager might choose to scale up the intervention to all customers who are currently at that given rank in the value ladder. Alternately, they might prioritize customers as a function of their potential value and only roll out the intervention to some customers meeting certain criteria. It could also be the case that the experiment reveals the role of heterogeneity, the fact that different subgroups of customers react differently to the intervention. In this case, the organization could choose to customize interventions as a function of which subgroup the customer actually belongs to. As the interventions are rolled out, it is critically important to monitor the outcomes (Step 8) as this allows the organization to take any corrective action or to fine-tune interventions over time.

We have provided here a relatively simple description of the BEAR process and a further analysis is beyond the scope of the current book. However, we recommend the interested consult the center's website for additional materials: https://www.rotman.utoronto.ca/BEAR.

As is evident from the proceeding paragraphs, a critical aspect of the behavioral approach to moving people up the value ladder is the need for evidence because the success of interventions depends so critically on contextual factors, some of which might not even be visible (because they're seemingly irrelevant), the only way in which a manager can be assured of the success is by continuously testing the intervention and adapting it as a function of the learning. This test-learn-adapt approach is a hallmark of the new wave of behavioral scientists' approach to managing customer value.

6.4 What This All Means

In closing, we reiterate some of the fundamental changes that the field of behavioral economics has brought to the practice of managing customer value. Consistent with our approach in this framework, the behavioral approach also advocates for breaking down complex behavior changes into specific ones. For instance, rather than defining behavior change challenge as "increasing the loyalty of our customers," the behavioral approach will advocate breaking down improvement of loyalty into smaller steps. Second, the empirical approach of behavioral economics pushes the practice of customer value management into an empirically driven discipline. Rather than relying on used cases that have worked well elsewhere, or on theory to help us figure out how best to move people up the value ladder, the behavioral approach emphasizes that we should use used cases and theory as starting points or hypotheses, but continuously test, learn from the tests, and adapt interventions. Third, for the behavioral approach to be successful, not only does an organization need a good understanding of human behavior and the ability to collect evidence quickly, but it also needs to be able to react to what it has learned. This calls for agility in practice.

6.4.1 Guideline 1: Be Very Clear in What Behavior Change You Are Trying to Articulate

We reiterate our position that it is important to ensure that the behavior change challenge is defined at a very precise level: Who is the target of your behavior change? What are they currently doing that you would like them to do differently? Why is that behavior change important for the organization? Clearly articulating the responses to these questions will give the manager a clear roadmap on why the behavior change is necessary and what the organization can do to engineer it.

6.4.2 Guideline 2: Motivation and Friction

Just as water can be made to flow through a pipeline by creating a pressure differential and ensuring that there is no friction in the pipes, customers can be made to change behavior by ensuring that they have enough motivation to do so and that the proverbial pipes (the process that they need to go through to change) is also friction free. If there is friction in the process — for example, if upgrading an insurance product requires the filling out of complex forms, approvals, and updates to online accounts — the level of motivation needed to make that change will be much higher and customers might simply give up. Therefore, an easy starting point for all of our customer-facing processes is to audit each one of them to ensure that it is as friction free as possible.

6.4.3 Guideline 3: Reduce the Sludge

Making processes friction free is important because sludge — friction in the system — can come from multiple sources and can come insidiously. Sludge is a bit like having weeds in the backyard. Sometimes people do not deliberately plant weeds, but unless the backyard is tended to all the time, weeds will grow. Sludge is a lot like that in organizations. Even if the organization is not deliberately trying to confuse its customers, sludge creeps in because of legacy systems, failure to appreciate changes in customers, and the way in which they prefer to communicate with the organization, and changes in the competitive landscape.

6.4.4 Guideline 4: Behavioral Science Isn't a Silver Bullet, But It Is Critical in Enabling Behavior Change

One of the strengths of behavioral economics in an organization is that it applies to every single part of the organization. Behavior change challenges crop up in customer value management, in sales, in human resources, in product design, and indeed in the decision-making of the C-suite. However, because it is applicable broadly, it is sometimes easy to dismiss the importance because it is so diffused across the organization. There is often also a misconception that behavioral economics in itself can offer a solution independent of other behavior change techniques. This is furthest from the truth. Suppose that if a customer-facing process is truly sludgy and difficult, no amount of behavioral science is going to successfully get people to navigate through that process. Put differently, the success of behavioral science intervention critically depends on other parts of the organization being aligned with it. We will explore some of these ideas in greater depth in Chapter 10.

6.4.5 Guideline 5: Context is Everything

At the risk of being extremely repetitive, we would like to leave the practicing manager with the reminder that context is the heart of effective marketing. The same intervention that has worked well elsewhere might not work well now and at this present time because of differences in context. Likewise, the same intervention that might work on certain sub-segments of the population might not work well for all sub-segments. It is critically important for the practicing manager to avoid the temptation of using the concept of scaling up to mean doing the same thing for all customers. That would be a mistake.

6.4.6 Guideline 6: Data ≠ Evidence

In a science that relies so much on collecting evidence to build good solutions to move people up a value chain, it is critically important to remember that data is not the same as evidence. Data can be used to illustrate what is going on, while evidence also informs the manager as to why that thing is going on.

For example, if a manager launches a new approach for moving people up the value ladder, data might simply tell us about what percent of people moved up and what their reaction to the intervention was, but only a control experiment — evidence — would tell us if this percent of people who moved up did so because of the intervention or perhaps because something else had changed in the context.

Acknowledgements

Some of the materials from this chapter have been developed in partnership with the Behavioural Economics in Action at Rotman [BEAR] Research Centre at the University of Toronto. We are grateful to the BEAR team, particularly to Nina Mazar, Melanie Kim, Bing Feng, Liz Kang, and Kim Ly for their contributions to the MCV book project.

Chapter 7

The Data Revolution

Data: (2) Information in digital form that can be transmitted or processed.[1]

In Chapter 1, we talked about the changing landscape since the first edition of this book was written. Much of this change has to do with the rapid penetration of internet adoption globally surpassing 50% in 2018.[2] Thanks to advancements in smartphones, much of the world skipped the desktop computer phase of internet adoption, jumping directly to smartphones. Today smartphones represent about half of entire web traffic. For example, in many parts of the world such as Africa and Asia, 60% to 70% of people access the internet via smartphones versus about 30% that use a desktop to access the internet. Smartphones have fundamentally changed how people connect to the internet by bringing affordable computing power to the palm of our hands. Nowadays you can buy a smartphone for a few dollars. To date, the biggest barrier to adoption remains the high cost of data. But that's starting to change, as in the last decade data costs have dropped drastically. Much of this rapid decline is driven by increasing competition amongst telecom providers. In India, for example, in September 2016, new entrant to the

---

[1]Data. (n.d.). *Merriam-Webster*. Retrieved March 19, 2021, from http://www.merriam-webster.com/dictionary/data
[2]Internet Milestone Reached, as More Than 50 Per Cent Go Online. (2008, December 7). *UN News*. Retrieved April 5, 2021, from https://news.un.org/en/story/2018/12/1027991

telecom market Reliance Jio brought a 4G LTE service in India by launching a free internet campaign. In a matter of seven months Reliance Jio signed up 100M customers, dramatically accelerating uptake of smartphone LTE adoption in India. Reliance Jio's aggressive free internet campaign to drive market share not only drove down India's cost of data by forcing competitors to slash price, but it also advanced India's internet adoptions by bringing online millions of new users.

With more people going online, there is a significant increase in volumes of data flowing through smartphone devices. With rapid advancements in smartphone technology, they are also considered to be the most essential and highly personal devices for many people. Recent studies demonstrate the impact of smartphones on our daily lives as they have become the first and last thing we interact with each and every day.

We have become increasingly dependent on our phones. We rely on our phone to wake us up, tell us what's going on in the world, connect us with our loved ones, manage our personal finances, navigate us from our homes to our jobs, manage our social connections, report the latest breaking news, be the first to tell us about new restaurant openings, help us make purchases, manage our health information, entertain us, and help us go to sleep. Smartphones have replaced Samsonites and photo albums as the single medium to our most personal information. But what truly sets smartphones apart from all other technology is that unlike stationary devices such as laptops, mobile devices follow us everywhere we go. Meaning, mobile devices not only store and process personal information but they can collect and process raw contextual data about our surrounding environment and our corresponding behavioral activities. This gives rise to a new type of data known as contextual, the idea that our hardware and software will be able to understand the context of our surroundings. Back when the first edition of this book was written, the concept of contextual data did not exist, at least not to the extent it does today. Contextual data has fundamentally changed the landscape of data analysis and given rise to new corners around user data protection and privacy considerations.

7.1 Personal Data

Before digital photos and documents became a norm, unwanted documents could be destroyed by simply throwing them into a shredder without concerns of seeing them resurface in a different form at some point into the future. But as more personal data is transmitted through digital means, retaining control of the ever-growing digital footprint has become nearly impossible. There are four factors that have fueled the rapid expansion of our digital footprint.

7.1.1 *Advancements in Technology*

In just the last decade, technology has revolutionized our daily lives. The introduction of innovative tools and services have brought access to information and resources within our fingertips. The most profound change is how easy and fast communication has become. Gone are the days of writing a letter, sending a fax, finding a payphone, or buying long distance calling cards. Nowadays all is needed is a reliable internet connection to jump on a video call to connect with loved ones regardless of where you might be in the world. Similarly social media has enabled new ways of connecting and communicating with friends, family, strangers, organizations, and businesses.

Online banking is another notable advancement in technology. Gone are days of walking into a bank, waiting in line just to withdraw and transfer money to someone. Companies such as Venmo and PayPal have made it easy to send and receive money. Banking apps have streamlined check depositing and bill payment. Mobile payment technologies such as Apple Pay and Google Pay have replaced the need for cash and cards. Technology has also made it possible for anyone with a credit card to access and purchase goods and services from any part of the world.

Thanks to Amazon and its Prime program, buying goods online once considered cumbersome with long wait times are now just a click away with one-day delivery. Items once considered off limits for online shopping such as fresh groceries and medicine are now everyday normal. The rise of the gig economy can be credited to companies such as Airbnb, Uber, and DoorDash having found ways to commoditize trust. Before these companies even existed, trust was based on brand. I doubt 10 years ago any of our readers would have agreed to vacation at a complete stranger's home when there were brand-name hotel chains with price options to meet any budget requirements.

Finally, data personalization combined with voice assistive technologies have increased productivity and created an equal level playing field for anyone with access to computing. It's much easier to ask Siri to set alarms, play music, turn lights on and off, search for things, and to place phone calls. In many parts of the world with low literacy rates, voice technology has fundamentally changed how people interact with their devices. For example, in India, 60% of mobile users are interacting with voice assistants on their smartphones.[3]

We can dedicate an entire chapter to how technology has made it easier to meet and date people, to travel, to learn new skills, to stream our favorite shows, and to capture memorable moments. The point is, many of these advancements are made possible by access to users' data.

---

[3] Ok Google: How Is Voice Making Technology More Accessible in India. (2020, October). *Google*. Retrieved March 19, 2021, from https://www.thinkwithgoogle.com/intl/en-apac/country/india/ok-google-how-is-voice-making-technology-more-accessible-in-india/

7.1.2 *Data Currency*

Much of this innovation is funded by consumer data that is shared with companies. Broadly speaking, this is done in two ways:

(1) By collecting, processing, and analyzing usage data, companies and app developers are able to make continuous improvements to their services and features. Technology has made it easier for companies to gather usage and behavioral data of their consumers' engagement with their products online or in app versus in store. Digitally, the retailer is able to track what consumers are searching for, their browsing behavior, what they click on, how they comparison shop, what attributes they care about, what filters they use, how reviews impact their decision, and finally what they choose to purchase. The richness of digital data is many times more advantageous in identifying and driving improvements to product offerings than the data retained by a physical retailer.

Retailers such as Everlane[4] understand the value of digital data so much so that they launched their retail business in 2011 as a direct-to-consumer online platform. Once they established their brand, built a strong customer following, and a rich database of customer behavior, the company launched its first physical retail shop in 2017. Even with physical stores the company heavily relies on its digital platform to improve its products and services as all customers are required to have an account as the physical shop only carries limited supplies and samples for customers to try the merchandise. This intentional focus on digital has helped Everlane grow to one of the top retailers in the United States. The ability to harness rich data to improve product offering is ultimately a competitive advantage for companies such as Everlane.

---

[4]Everlane Landing Page. (2021, March). *Everlane.* Retrieved March 19, 2021, from http://www.everlane.com/

(2) Data monetization is another means of funding advancements in technology. Facebook, Snapchat, Google, and Twitter wouldn't be here today if it weren't for their ability to monetize their platforms. Think about the number of services that you use on a daily basis that offer utility for free. But this is not free, as there is always an exchange where the data collected provides utility for these companies. It allows them to improve their marketing spend by narrowly targeting offers and driving higher returns. Platforms such as YouTube allow anyone to stream any type of content from the comfort of their homes. But it is also a platform that has redefined learning by democratizing what it means to be an expert. The top two categories of videos on YouTube are "product reviews" and "Ho tos."[5] Seventy percent of millennial YouTube users have used YouTube to learn how to do something new or learn more about something they're interested in.[6] YouTube also serves ads to its viewers that are highly customized based on the viewer's personalized ad profile,[7] as an agglomeration of the viewer's online activity and behavior across Google's products. It is the sale of this ad inventory that allows YouTube to grow and expand its reach as a platform that encourages anyone to become a CS professor, a makeup artist, or a tech reviewer. Access to knowledge has never been more accessible and the means to have a platform to share knowledge has never been easier.

---

[5]Three Ways Digital Video Has Upended TV as We Know It. (2018, July). *Think with Google.* Retrieved March 19, 2021, from https://www.thinkwithgoogle.com/marketing-strategies/video/online-video-shopping/

[6]Thirteen Most Popular Types of Videos on YouTube. (2020, March 7). *Impact.* Retrieved March 19, 2021, from https://www.impactplus.com/blog/most-popular-types-of-videos-on-youtube-infographic

[7]Google Ad Personalisation Landing Page. (2021, May). *Google.* Retrieved March 19, 2021, from https://adssettings.google.com/u/0/authenticated

7.1.3 *Value Exchange*

This brings us to the notion of value exchange. Without often realizing it or thinking much about it, information such as credit card data, home address, location, contact, photos, and messages are shared with apps numerous times in a given day. This information is exchanged for access to unique services offered by apps that have significantly improved how we go about dealing with mundane day-to-day activities. Granting access to location can be considered a low price to pay for not having to carry around a road atlas in the car or sharing access to contacts beats having to manually look up phone numbers in a phonebook. The exchange between personal data and technology can unlock new features that many people consider valuable. However, what has become less clear is exactly how much data is needed to unlock value. It might be easily justifiable to share location data all the time with an app that allows you to track your young children's whereabouts or to share access to all your SMS data for an app whose sole purpose is to deliver and send SMSes. But how do you quantify how much location data a social media app needs to tag photos with location information, or how much photos access does a chat app need to share photos with friends and family?

There is no doubt that the app ecosystem and the underlying technological innovation that has proliferated in the last decade would not be possible without access to context-based data made possible by the popularity of smartphones. But there remains the question of exactly how much is enough to unlock magical experiences? This book will not attempt to solve this question, but it is the underlying question fueling discussions on user privacy and data protection laws.

7.1.4 *Cloud Computing*

As mentioned in Chapter 1, thanks to Moore's Law, an axiom of microprocessor development usually holding that processing power doubles every 18 months especially relative to cost or size,[8] the cost of recording, storing, organizing, and analyzing data have diminished in recent years. This has enabled companies to further move analytical operations to the cloud and invest in developing data science and machine learning technologies.

Many companies leverage machine learning models to enhance how users interact with their products. For example, advances in machine learning and cloud computing have enabled Google Translate to significantly improve the quality of translation for over 100 languages.[9] Spotify, a top on-demand music streaming service relies on machine learning models to compare similar customer profiles and curate the perfect playlist and recommendation for its users.

One of our flagship features is called Discover Weekly. Every Monday, we give you a list of 50 tracks that you haven't heard before that we think you're going to like. The ML engine that's the main basis of it, and it's advanced some since, had actually been around at Spotify a bit before Discover Weekly was there, just powering our Discover page — David Murgatroyd, Machine Learning Leader at Spotify.[10]

Amazon uses machine learning models all over its service value chain. It applies models to form product recommendations based on correlations between products. The recommendation algorithm

---

[8] "Moore's law." (n.d.). *Merriam-Webster.* Retrieved March 19, 2021, from http://www.merriam-webster.com/dictionary/mooreslaw

[9] *Recent Advances in Google Translate.* (2020, June 8). *Google AI Blog.* Retrieved March 20, 2021, from https://ai.googleblog.com/2020/06/recent-advances-in-google-translate.html

[10] How Spotify Uses Machine Learning Models to Recommend You the Music You Like. (2020, May 1). *Great Learning Power Ahead.* Retrieved March 20, 2021, from https://www.mygreatlearning.com/blog/3-machine-learning-models-spotify-uses-to-recommend-music-youll-like/#:~:text=Spotify%20uses%20a%20combination%20of,features%20is%20called%20Discover%20Weekly.&text=Spotify%20uses%20three%20forms%20of%20recommendation%20models%20to%20power%20Discover%20Weekly

reviews the customer's actions such as recent purchase history, wish list, and items added to the cart and for each action generates a list of related items. It also constantly redefines and optimizes its delivery services by applying artificial intelligence models to predict how many units of a specific product customers will buy, which then factors into where the product is stocked so it is as close as possible to the people who will buy them.[11]

Our personal data has provoked the rapid expansion in technology, which in turn has helped significantly improve our livelihood. But there are real privacy concerns with the increasing amount of data that exists across multiple devices, in the cloud, and in the hands of countless developers and companies.

7.2 Digital Privacy

Privacy meant very different things 10 years ago. For many, privacy meant ensuring the latest anti-virus software was installed on computers, it meant adding screen covers to Blackberries and laptops, it meant password-enabling phones and computers. Today digital privacy has a more complex interpretation. Digital privacy is about transparency, control, and data reduction.

7.2.1 *Transparency*

In a recent study by PwC, 39% of consumers cited transparency about a company's use of consumer data and transparency about

---

[11]How Amazon Leverages Artificial Intelligence to Optimize Delivery. (2019, October 22). *Feedvisor.* Retrieved March 20, 2021, from https://feedvisor.com/resources/amazon-shipping-fba/how-amazon-leverages-artificial-intelligence-to-optimize-delivery/

whether and how their data is shared as crucial policies.[12] Yet a longitude study sponsored by Verizon in the United States found that 45% of 18–24-year-olds would share their data in exchange for a more personalized and intuitive experience.[13] This provides an opportunity for companies to provide their customers greater transparency into how collection and use of their data will help deliver value through a more personalized product and service experience. Clearly communicating to customers how their data is being used will go a long way in building trust and willingness to share data.

7.2.2 *Control*

Insight Box 7.1
MCV Insight Do not assume your customers understand why you need access to their data. Be honest, clear, and transparent about why you need access to their data and how you plan to use their data.

Once consumers agree to share their data, they want to know that they have control over how their data is being used. According to a study conducted by Pew Research, 81% of Americans feel they have little to no control over data collected about them.[14] This is an alarming metric, but companies can help reduce consumer anxiety by ensuring their customers have ways to control what data is being shared. For example, if a customer wishes to end their relationship with a company, they should be able

[12]Consumers Trust Your Tech Even Less than You Think. (2020). *PWC Consumer Intelligence Report*. Retrieved March 20, 2021, from https://www.pwc.com/us/en/services/consulting/library/consumer-intelligence-series/trusted-tech.html#a-tipping-point

[13]What Customer Experience Do Consumers Really Want. (June 11, 2019). *Verizon*. Retrieved March 28, 2021, from https://www.verizon.com/about/news/what-customer-experience-do-consumers-really-want

[14]Americans and Privacy: Concerned, Confused and Feeling Lack of Control over Their Personal Information. (November 15, 2019). *Pew Research Center*. Retrieved March 28, 2021, from https://www.pewresearch.org/internet/2019/11/15/americans-and-privacy-concerned-confused-and-feeling-lack-of-control-over-their-personal-information/

to retain control of the data that has been shared through simple steps. In fact, companies should encourage their customers to request data deletion of their private and personal information and provide easy and simple steps for customers to initiate.

7.2.3 *Data Reduction*

As advances in data analytics have progressed, there is less need for companies to collect exuberant amounts of data about their customers. Companies should reduce their reliance on personally identifiable information and avoid using uniquely identifiable IDs to track customers. Customers agreeing to share their data is a privilege and companies should treat their data with respect by being strategic about what and how much is collected, minimizing how long the data is stored for, and enforcing strict guidelines on data deletion practices.

Recent high-profile data breaches have heightened consumers and regulators distress about data privacy. In 2014, Yahoo was the victim of the biggest data breach in history where, according to the company, state-sponsored actors compromised names, phone numbers, email addresses, and dates of birth of 500 million users. Then again in 2016, Yahoo disclosed another breach from 2013 compromising personal information of 3 billion user accounts.[15] Similarly Equifax, one of the largest credit bureaus in the United States, in 2017 announced that a vulnerability in their website resulted in data breach exposing about 147 million consumers. The breach compromised personal information including Social Security numbers and drivers' license numbers.[16] With the volume of personal and private data managed by companies all over the world, there are policy

---

[15] All 3 Billion Yahoo Accounts Were Affected by 2013 Attack. (October 3, 2017). *New York Times*. Retrieved March 27, 2021, from https://www.nytimes.com/2017/10/03/technology/yahoo-hack-3-billion-users.html
[16] Equifax Data Breach FAQ. (February 12, 2020). *CSO Online*. Retrieved March 27, 2021, from https://www.nytimes.com/2017/10/03/technology/yahoo-hack-3-billion-users.html

efforts aimed at reducing access to the data, limiting storage practices, and enforcing stricter guidelines in sharing data.

The most extreme measure is enforced by the European Union (EU) known as the General Data Protection Regulation (GDPR). To date, GDPR is the toughest privacy and security law in the world and though it was passed in the EU, it imposes obligations on companies all over the world as long as they collect data related to people in the EU. GDPR sets rules on how companies should process data such that it ensures privacy and protection of personal data, and assigns powers to regulators to require accountability and to impose heavy fines. Since its enforcement in 2018, data protection agencies at state levels in the United States have begun to impose privacy policies. Most recently California introduced the California Consumer Privacy Act (CCPA),[17] which empowers residents of California to know the types of personal information collected about them and gives them the right not to agree to the sales of their personal data.

The sentiment and landscape around data privacy and protection is changing. More than any other time in history, there has never been a greater need for companies to provide transparency, control, and data minimization practices. Regulations often lag the industries they are meant to protect, and thus the responsibility must fall on companies to implement and abide by strong data privacy practices.

7.3 Harnessing Customer Data

Privacy needs to be respected by any organization in order to win long-term trust and extract maximum consumer value. Through transparency and control, the onus is on companies to justify the value their consumers will gain from sharing their data and to

---

[17]California Consumer Protection Act. (2021). *Office of the Attorney General.* Retrieved March 27, 2021, from https://oag.ca.gov/privacy/ccpa

Attract	Serve	Grow	Nurture

• Awareness
• Relevance
• Consideration
• Understanding
	• Trial & initial
	  purchase
	• Post-purchase
	• Replacement or
	  repurchase
		• Loyalty
		• Share of wallet
		• Share of household
		• Propensity
			• Attitudinal loyalty
			• Advocacy
			• Retention

Figure 7.1 Four phases of value creation.

respect the data by only using what they need to deliver the expected value. Under no circumstance should companies mine or harness data that the consumer did not opt into sharing. Access to the data unlocks opportunities for companies to deliver innovation and better customized experiences for their consumers. This data will help companies move customers up the value ladder by improving acquisition, service delivery, growth, and loyalty. This process can be outlined in four phases: attract, serve, grow, and nurture as shown in Figure 7.1.

7.3.1 *Attract Phase*

The attract phase includes programs that identify prospects with a high propensity to purchase one of the company's products or services, and a multitouch communications campaign to entice the prospect to consider and then shop (at which point the prospect crosses into the serve phase). An example of this would be a high-end fashion retailer analyzing customer transactional data and discovering that a high percentage of their beauty salon customers also buy their premium cosmetics products as well. This retailer would then display cosmetic-focused marketing in the salon, send personalized discount offers via direct email, followed by an invitation to a private after-hours champagne reception to view the new spring line-up. We refer to this practice as proactive prospect management. Traditionally such proactive prospect campaigns were direct mail incentives and as a result very expensive. With a big-ticket or high-margin service, the cost can usually be justified if the prospect volumes are fairly limited. Using direct mail, mass marketers have accurately determined, is too expensive to attract the large volume of prospects and customers they need, so they stick with less targeted mass marketing and advertising. However, the advent of a new and cheaper communication media that can be directed at individual prospects — namely outbound email and direct social media outreach — greatly changes the economics of "mass direct marketing," which is already changing the ways mass marketers move from a mass to a more targeted, directed, or customer intelligent approach. The following points highlight some of the discrete activities involved:

(a) A Prospect Intelligence capability as an extension of a company's Customer Intelligence (CI) system. Within this, a full Prospect Record is created in a database at the time a prospect is first identified by name, address, or some other unique identifying data. The record is then enriched over time as more is learned about the prospect and their preferences. Prospects are generally identified in two ways: (1) through the purchase of a targeted outreach; or (2) by eliciting prospects to identify themselves and volunteer their contact information, often in exchange for an offer to receive product information. These latter prospects are often known as opt-ins or warm prospects. With the intelligence the firm generates on the prospect, it can personalize its marketing and sales efforts toward him based on his preferences. The objective here is to stimulate his purchase motivators and we refer to this process as Proactive Prospect Management. In contrast to this, many companies diligently collect personal information from opt-ins or do outbound outreach campaigns to purchased lists and then *wait passively* to see if the prospect eventually buys something.

(b) Companies who have integrated their Prospect Intelligence system with their CI system, or who have skilled CI analysts, will segment and prioritize their prospect database to identify the prospects they believe have the highest probability to become customers. The analysis used to determine these potential customers is called propensity modeling. The process asks the question, "Which of our prospects appear to have the highest propensity (or likelihood) to buy our products or services based on some characteristics or preferences that we can identify about them?" As it is rare to have a large amount of detailed personal or preferences data about a prospect, propensity modeling often involves overlaying existing data about other prospects, customers, or the general population to try to create a "best guess" as to the characteristics of the prospect. A simple example of this is to overlay Government of Canada census data such as household income by matching prospect postal codes to the average income level by postal code. While this will not reveal the actual household income of a prospect, it will provide an indication whether or not he or she is within the range of income levels of people who most frequently purchase your products. An advanced capability in this area is a company's ability to recognize a prospect when they interact with one of the company's Customer Interaction Channels (e.g., retail store, website, call center, app). If a front-line agent is able to recognize the prospect and record this information to a Prospect Intelligence system, the company can measure the effectiveness of its attract activities in delivering qualified prospects to the serve channels. This is often a challenging capability to implement, particularly in retail store environments where front-line agents are trained to present products or services with minimal efforts to identify shoppers as existing

Insight Box 7.2
MCV Insight
Do not confuse customer research with CI. Both are valuable: if information about a customer is not appended to their profile, it is not CI.

customers or known prospects. While electronic collection of this type of information directly from the store is ideal, simpler mechanisms can also be created to capture this data — for example, special offers that require a prospect to present a coded letter or coupon to the front-line agent who then forwards it to the company (or the company's agency) for tracking purposes or, more recently, QR codes can be used to map prospects. This mechanism allows the company to track which prospects actually become shoppers and customers and help to tie successful results to a company's propensity modeling efforts.

7.3.2 Serve Phase

Below are some examples of Customer Intelligent activities within the Serve phase:

- The company has a defined customer experience process within sales activities. It is designed based upon CI of customer preferences and is institutionalized through rigorous deployment across various retail and/or service delivery channels and locations. When it comes to sales and marketing effectiveness, this is one of the greatest "moments of truth" between the company and its prospective customer. This is where the customer decides if the company is going to deliver on its promises and/or "surprise and delight" the customer with a great experience that compels them to make the purchase.
- Another good habit is the extension of the customer experience to the delivery of services and/or the post-purchase support of customers in the ongoing use and enjoyment of products.

A good example of this is the quality of the experience a customer receives when he returns to the retailer to service his new computer, or to have an unexpected defect rectified. This is a defining moment in the development of the relationship with a newly acquired customer and will set the tone for the next three to four years of ownership. Recognizing and treating it accordingly will have a big influence over whether that customer will become a loyal and "growable" customer or one that will be lost at the time of computer replacement.

- A third capability is the ability to capture both transactional data (e.g., number of purchases last month) as well as personal profile and preference data that can be gleaned through the shopping interaction in a central CI system for future use and analysis. These additional data might include the number of household members, upcoming trigger events for the purchase of a complimentary product, etc.

- The ability to recognize shoppers as existing customers or known prospects, and access their customer records in order to tailor the sales experience to their profile, preferences, and previous purchases or contacts. This can include identifying mechanisms such as loyalty cards.

- As an extension of the above capability, the next level of development is the ability to support front-line agents in their management of the customer sales experience. This is achieved by providing the agent with recommended treatments and tactics that have been identified as those most likely to stimulate the desired purchase response from a customer or prospect. Such capabilities are currently fairly widespread in call center and digital applications where the front-line agents are interfacing with systems integrated to the CI system, or, in the case of transactional websites, where the front-line agent is in such a system. This capability is called Intelligent Customer Interaction Channels, which will be covered in more detail in the following section.

As the reader can see from the broad range of experiences and capabilities, covered in the Serve phase, it is much more comprehensive than the purchase cycle approach that many companies take to defining firm–customer interactions. Taking this broader perspective of customer experiences across marketing, sales and customer service interactions offer companies a chance to positively influence customer behavior. As an example of a firm that has developed superior customer insights capabilities in the serve phase, consider a hypothetical hotel firm, SS Hotels. This chain of hotels has created a very successful customer loyalty program that offers benefits based upon the purchase behavior of customers once they sign up for the program. They first gather valuable data about their prospects/customers and then continually add new insights about these customers into their database as the relationship continues. They gather or generate the four key types of data: transactional, behavioral, attitudinal, and inferred. The stated demographic data, while limited in scope, includes fundamentals including customer's age, gender, area of residence, profession, and contact information. The transactional data (what they have bought and when) is recorded each time a guest stays at their hotel or purchases other services. Behavioral data (when, how, and in which channel they buy) are tracked with great detail via their call center, website, app, and at each hotel location. Finally, attitudinal data, the most elusive to gather for most marketers, are gathered with great efficiency at the time of program registration, during interactions with front-line agents at the hotel or call center, and via customer satisfaction surveys. SS Hotels convert their CI into a series of strategic Serve tactics executed across the firm. Beginning with the call center, they offer exclusive reservation lines and unique promotional phone numbers for their high-value customers — their platinum members. Agents are trained to bring a holistic approach to the customer's total travel plans offering greater convenience for the customer and incremental sales for the firm. Based upon a customer's past activities while staying at a hotel property (such as skiing, spa, or golfing), customized emails are sent with offers that match the customer's preferences. A dedicated website has been built for platinum members; this site customizes content and offers based upon the customer's profile and preferences after sign-in. Front desk and hotel staff are automatically notified of the guests that have preferred status in the hotel. Customized in-room treatments such as type of pillow, proximity to elevator, floor preference, and type of newspaper are only a request away, and special requests are often extended to restaurants as well. Finally online feedback forms and post-stay customer satisfaction survey data are appended to platinum member customer files to help staff meet future customer expectations.

7.3.3 *Grow Phase*

Insight Box 7.3
MCV Insight
Creating a description of your "average customer" is not advised. Averages contain the characteristics of everyone, but rarely describe any of your actual customers.

The Grow phase is related to activities targeted at increasing the revenue and profitability from existing customers through the stimulation of behaviors like increasing the frequency of consumption, basket sizes (through cross-selling and up-selling), and share of market (through referrals). Companies that routinely interact with customers on the phone via a call center, or through email, websites, or apps have inherent advantages when it comes to creating cross and upsell opportunities when a customer begins an interaction with them. These companies can leverage this routine contact very well, harnessing their CI to target special offers on additional services to those who called in with inquiries or concerns about their existing service, or to activate or inquire about additional services. If highly successful, these call center activities could be tracked and measured for the new revenue they generate.

To illustrate the potential to harness CI in this area, we present a hypothetical vehicle manufacturer. This firm goes to market through a network of independent dealers, which is typical throughout their industry. As such it relies on its dealers to sell its products to end customers and concentrates on its role as a manufacturer and distributor to provide the products, related logistics, and some level of mass advertising to drive traffic to dealers. In its accessories and merchandise business, it provides merchandising recommendations to the dealers, which are based on both retail best practices and some level of customer and market research. All these efforts are fundamentally right and have had a positive impact on the business. However, these are still largely at the discretion of the dealer and the company has not institutionalized a superior customer experience related to the shopping and buying process for accessories and merchandise across its dealer network. As is very common in such dealer networks, you will see some dealers excel at selling accessories and merchandise and some having very dusty collections at the back of their showrooms, and few sales from them.

Interestingly, this vehicle manufacturer can show a positive correlation between the amount of customer spend on branded accessories and merchandise and customer loyalty and repurchase rates of the primary big-ticket product. This provides an opportunity for both direct and indirect revenue growth from customer insights efforts to specifically and directly target customers with tailored offers on branded accessories and merchandise. This has the potential to create a very powerful virtuous cycle illustrated in Figure 7.2. This sequence illustrates the direct and indirect benefits that a Grow strategy can have in truly entrenching a customer with a company, making them a reliable revenue base and one that is very cost effective to serve from a marketing and sales standpoint. Examples of carefully stimulated customer behaviors such as this demonstrate why data-driven efforts are such a powerful tool for increasing sales and marketing effectiveness — driving more revenue and profit from every dollar spent on customer marketing and handling.

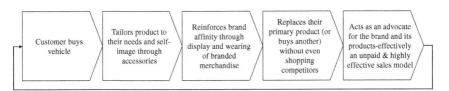

Figure 7.2 The virtuous cycle.

7.3.4 *Nurture Phase*

Insight Box 7.4
MCV Insight
Take every interaction with your customer as an opportunity to update their profile.

This phase can be considered a destination or end objective of the activities taken throughout the other three relationship development phases of Attract, Serve, and Grow as it generally follows those phases chronologically. It also represents the ultimate behaviors and attitudes that the marketer has tried to instil in the customer through these earlier phases. These behaviors and attitudes are commonly referred to as "Customer Loyalty," reflecting:

- A predisposition, or default behavior, on the part of the customer to favor the firm with all of his business in the relevant category.
- A strong affinity to the company, its brand, and products/ services that create self-barriers to defection.
- An unprovoked tendency to promote the company and its products/ services in a very positive way to friends and family (sometimes referred to as advocacy).
- A sense that the company should also recognize his strong patronage and advocacy.

These four points above represent our working definition of customer loyalty, a term with many different meanings and definitions. We use the above behaviors and attitudes to distinguish real or attitudinal customer loyalty from less sincere forms of purchase behavior. For instance, we should not confuse repurchase with loyalty. To illustrate the difference, think of a product category that requires a fairly involved level of consideration when shopping and choosing between alternatives — for example, a mobile device such as an iPhone. When the time comes to replace a mobile phone, many manufacturers strive to get to the customer with a loyalty offer as an inducement for the customer to stay with their brand. For a customer who does not have the time or inclination to go through the often-onerous shopping process, this may be enough to cause him to simply replace his current unit with a new similar model. But ask that customer why he bought it and his answer could be "I don't know — they're all the same — but they offered me a discount to replace my old phone, so it was the easiest option." We trust the reader would agree with our assessment that this is hardly the ringing endorsement of a real "loyalist"! This will not cause many other people to run to the manufacturer that sold the customer the phone and demand a demonstration of this wonderful device. But this customer will feature in the company's loyalty measures (usually reported industry-wide as the number of owners who replaced their mobile phones with one of the same brand). This distinction between attitudinal and behavioral loyalty is captured in Figure 7.3.

A company cannot become passive with customers who have entered the Nurture phase. On the contrary, a very deliberate set of Programs, Experiences, and Tactics (PETs) should be created to ensure that these valuable customers and advocates are maintained and their loyalty nurtured and strengthened. Nurture PETs should reflect the specific preferences of customers — particularly those reflecting the last of the above=described attitudes — that of an expectation of "recognition" by the company for their patronage and support.

Loyalty programs could facilitate Nurture activities in two ways. First, the existence of the loyalty card — or at least the unique customer identifier that the card represents — means that these

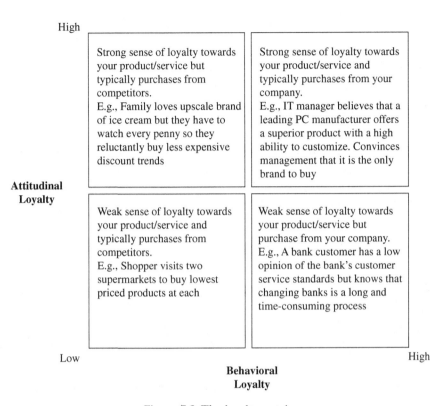

Figure 7.3 The loyalty matrix.

companies can systematically capture and track a customer's purchases and other transactions (like call center inquiries or responses to an outbound email). Companies must justify to their customers *why* they are requesting detailed profile information. If a company can be transparent with their data use and can demonstrate the connection between the information a customer gives them and the customization of future products and services based upon the customer's stated preferences, customers will be satisfied and these companies will have very rich data on them. These data greatly facilitate the analysis required to identify truly loyal and valuable customers from the overall customer base. Good programs also include a tiered element of program members/customers that enables the company to offer additional, special benefits to customers who meet the profile or the behaviors and attitudes of someone in the Nurture phase.

These benefits can include dedicated service channels, pre-launch announcements, and offers on new products and services, rewards for referrals, and personalized offers and gifts on special — personal — occasions. In addition, if there is a point-collection aspect to the loyalty program, Nurture phase members may enjoy an accelerated point accumulation benefit, which further entrenches their self-barriers to defection, as this non-cash but very valuable "discount" is not available to them from competitive companies who are targeting them for acquisition.

To illustrate how a program could be used to nurture, we present the example of a niche product retailer who developed the ability to establish entrenched customer loyalty with their high-value customers. Their nurturing is rooted in a card-based loyalty program that enjoys very high usage rates among their customer base, complemented by "surprise and delight" retention tactics. There are no points associated with their program, rather the card offers exclusive discounts on a rotating group of products. An overwhelming majority of cardholders use their card at point of sale *every* time they shop at one of the retail stores. As a result, the company has close to perfect transactional data about their customers. By customer and by store, they are able to track frequency of purchase, combinations of products in the customer's basket, average basket size, and total monthly spend by the customer. By separating their customer base into tiered-value segments, they are able to target and tailor their approach according to the behavior and profit generating potential of the different tiers. This also enables them to create a distinct Nurture program for their most loyal and profitable customers.

How does this company act upon these capabilities to nurture these customers? The key to their success seems to be empowerment at the store level through a combination of centrally developed

> **Insight Box 7.5**
>
> **MCV Insight**
>
> Print on your customer's invoice a description of the next product or service you think they should buy. Use CI to predict what that next product should be.

retention tools, regional managers who visit stores frequently, and a steady flow of CI. Every month retail locations receive a list that identifies their best customers. The head office also supplies the stores with a range of printed promotional items that can be sent to these customers in varying combinations based upon their historical shopping preferences. These include new product announcements, coupons, thank you cards, holiday cards, and invitations to open houses. Several times a year, each retail location will open its doors after hours for its best customers to preview new products over a glass of wine. These invitation-only events reinforce the company's appreciation of their customers' business and sends a clear message that these customers are at an exclusive level. Further, the top echelon of customers receives gifts and flowers at their home on key holidays as an ultimate demonstration of appreciation. The retailer also frequently offers reward programs based upon a minimum number of purchases over a given period of time. Make "x" purchases within "y" weeks and you could win "z." They then contact customers who are close to the value of purchases necessary to be entered and invite them to a store to shop before the deadline. Customer shopping behavior is then tracked before and after these programs to identify the level of incremental spending and successful programs are repeated. Additional Nurture tactics include printing the savings a customer has received on the bottom of their receipt to reinforce the benefits of shopping at that firm with every visit. Also, high-value customers are provided with elevated levels of service for problem resolution through the call centers.

While this niche retailer has not broken into the level of one-to-one personalization, they are approaching an advanced level of customer Nurture programs, experiences, and tactics.

7.4 Core Customer Intelligence Capabilities

Insight Box 7.6
MCV Insight
The more your company becomes customer intelligent, the less it should rely on traditional mass media approaches and broad segmentation.

Previously, in this chapter, we identified four elements of the core CI capabilities. Based on our research, companies that did well on the strategy and objective setting element had a defined strategy to leverage the CI it had, a strategic mandate to balance mass marketing and merchandising efforts with more customer intelligent capabilities and tactics, and a proportionate approach between its acquisition marketing (Attract phase) efforts versus its customer retention activities (Serve, Grow, and Nurture phases). These companies had some form of metrics and measurement systems in place so that they could track results and demonstrate the relationship between their strategy and resulting activities (e.g., that sales results or customer satisfaction/loyalty measures could be linked back to specific actions). This is an essential feedback mechanism that enables marketers to see what customers do and do not respond to in order to quickly adjust programs as needed. It is particularly essential in the early phases of CI development as there is a critical need for early wins to validate efforts, build organizational momentum, and create a knowledge base that can be used to create business cases for additional programs and capabilities.

Insight Box 7.7
MCV Insight
A successful deployment of CI should not add to your marketing budget. Your budget should instead be reallocated to make your marketing dollars work harder.

We also identified some of the skills required within the Core Customer Intelligence Capability of Customer Experience Delivery Process. These include the following:

- The discipline of envisioning and documenting in great detail the movements and activities of customers and front-line agents as they interact in the sales process. This could include a point-of-sale interaction, an inquiry into a call center, a post-purchase service interaction, or a resolution of a customer concern.
- The ability to understand the relevant preferences at play in the customer's mind during the above interactions, ensuring these preferences are being met and points of customer dissatisfaction avoided.
- A training capability that addresses the significant challenges in modifying the behavior of potentially thousands of front-line agents, who may or may not be direct employees of the firm.
- IT and communication systems that can support front-line agents by delivering the required information and prompts needed to execute the customer experience process in real time, with a customer in front of them.
- The ability to design front-line agents' roles with the appropriate definition of needed skills and personal attributes, objectives, metrics and measurement systems, and motivational mechanisms, including compensation tied to objectives and career paths. In the case where front-line agents are employees of independent dealers or channel partners, the ability to influence the activities and behavior of required skills in how channel partnerships are defined and compensated.
- An extension of these skills to the use of website as a Customer Interaction Channel, and the extent to which websites are designed to take a customer or prospect through a natural and value-adding process — as opposed to just making information available to them and requiring them to do the work of finding what they are looking for.

The key capabilities and competencies required for CI are straightforward. A robust database infrastructure that enables easy, real-time access to all customer data contained within the Customer Records is essential. Likewise, a "single view of the customer" database design that aggregates all key customer data that the firm holds or has access to into a single, master customer record is needed. Tools that allow data analysts and marketing personnel to do quick, real-time data queries and data visualization (e.g., charts and tables) will aid the decision-maker to make timely decisions. Integration of the customer database platform with core firm operating and transactional systems enables seamless and accurate data capture into customer records. Data management and quality processes ensure the matching of data to the appropriate customer record and the flagging of suspect records for treatment. Dedicated and skilled data analytic human resources charged with creating and disseminating "real" CI throughout the organization are also central to this effort, ensuring accurate measurement of customer activities and providing thought leadership on opportunities.

The last capability — Intelligent Customer Interaction Channels — represents the communication mechanisms that link the CI of the organization with the customer experience delivery processes. This capability makes CI actionable by delivering the right information to the front-line agent at the right time to facilitate the delivery of a superior customer experience. This capability is driven more by technology than the previous three, as it requires the ability to flow information to and from a variety of customer interaction channels in real-time. Table 7.1 gives examples to illustrate what we mean by "Intelligent Customer Interaction Channels." As the table suggests, intelligent customer interaction channels enable companies to design increasingly detailed customer experience processes, including those that allow for real-time personalization of the experience to the specific customer, based on the profile of that customer held in the CI database. Without this "intelligence aid," it would be impossible for front-line agents to be able to remember all the permutations of personalized customer experiences, even if they were able to look up a customer's record. Making

Table 7.1 Intelligent versus passive customer interaction channel.

Customer Interaction Channel	"Passive" Channel Traits	"Intelligent" Channel Capabilities
Retail store location or service deliver point	• Front-line agent has no access to previous customer transactions or profile to facilitate customer handling • Front-line agent cannot record any information gathered about customer for further use	• Front-line agent can bring up customer profile to aid in serving customer and matching new products to previous purchases • Front-line agent can capture and record observed customer behaviors, motivators, and preferences for future use by any interaction channel/front-line agent • Front-line agent is prompted on special targeted offers or promotions that can be offered to the specific customer to stimulate purchase
Customer support call center	• Front line receives call and uses a variety of reference tools to identify customer and resolve their issue or inquiry • Front line cannot access customer records to better understand and serve the customer — resulting in need to ask customer more questions • Nature and result of customer issue or query is not captured in a coded format in customer records	• System recognizes incoming phone number and refers to customer record to call routing instructions in real time • Customer is routed to a customer service representative they have spoken with before • Customer service representative has a relevant subset of the customer record in front of them by the time they pick up the customer's call • System routes the customer service representative through an appropriate call handling process, automatically delivering to the customer service representative necessary information and data, and capturing customer response and observations

(Continued)

Table 7.1 (*Continued*)

Customer Interaction Channel	"Passive" Channel Traits	"Intelligent" Channel Capabilities
	• Front-line agent is not enabled to tailor marketing opportunities after resolution of issue	• System prompts customer service representative with a relevant and personalized offer to make to the customer once original issue is resolved
Customer website or app	• Website only makes information available to customer on a self-serve basis • Site cannot hold any customer information to enable recognition of customer information at next visit and build upon previous interactions • Site is designed to serve all potential needs of the public including both customers and other unrelated users	• Website is structured to facilitate user navigation based on defined customer experiences processes for most common user needs • Website allows for creation of a user profile, and for existing customers allows this to link to existing records • Site allows users to save information for future access and remembers user preferences to enable automated site personalization

the customer experience seem natural and personalized is not possible without some form of intelligence and process support for front-line agents. Companies that show high degrees of capability on this element show the following specific capabilities.

- Multiple interaction channels enabled access and write to customer records in real time during a customer interaction.
- Channels that reference a common customer record, in order to benefit from the knowledge of past customer interactions in different locations and channels.
- Website and app functionality that delivers a personalized customer experience, as opposed to just being a repository of generic firm information.
- The ability to deliver actionable intelligence, beyond customer profile information to front-line agents, effectively "loading their lips" with targeted and personalized experiences and offers.

7.5 What This All Means

Many of the underlying principles of CI go back more than a century (and probably even longer). The challenge today is to understand and be able to institutionalize these capabilities that existed in a small enterprise — and exist even today at the level of service agents and their customers and make them work in a large enterprise. Companies have generally found it very difficult to both shift their organizational mindset from a product emphasis to a customer-centric model, and successfully manage the more technical, IT-intensive creation of new capabilities. Furthermore, the growth of the modern enterprise has led to data privacy concerns, increase in regulations, and new ways for malicious actors to breach and compromise personal data. Today marketers need to balance innovation and marketing that is based on CI against the backdrop of privacy standards. Based on the framework we presented in this chapter and on our research, we offer eight specific guidelines for managers on how to best manage the process of introducing and growing CI in an organization.

7.5.1 Guideline 1: Respect User Data by Being Transparent, Giving Controls and Minimizing Data Access to What You Need

Building a CI infrastructure that is founded on strong privacy standards and practices is a fundamental requirement. Companies should be honest and transparent about why they need access to data, who they plan to share the data with, and how the data will be used to bring more value for the customer. Customers should feel empowered and in control of their personal data. With transparency, marketers should be prepared to give their customers controls to decide if they want to share the data, how much data they're willing to share, and at what frequencies. The more granular the controls the more customers will be empowered. Accessing less data and only the data that is needed to deliver the expected value is the most effective means of institutionalizing a privacy forward organization and building trust with customers. We advise marketers to think about alternative ways of achieving their goals that do not require access to customers' data and only request access where there are no other alternatives. Once access has been granted, marketers should be diligent to minimize access and storage to preserve customers' privacy.

7.5.2 Guideline 2: Create a "Bottom-Up" Strategy Based on Vision, Objectives, Metrics, and Internal Marketing

Creating, institutionalizing, and making use of a Customer Intelligent approach to sales, marketing, and customer handling is a highly involved and frequently transformational endeavor for any firm. For product companies, it requires adopting a completely different perspective about how the firm goes to market — from "here are my fabulous products for you to buy," to "how do we deliver maximum value to our target customers?" Service firms benefit from already having this perspective to some extent. But for all firms, it will take a concerted effort over months and years to fully institutionalize CI practices into their operating model, so a strategy that can be shared across the firm is a necessity.

We strongly believe that such a strategy should take weeks, not months to create, and should err on the side of being high level and visionary rather than being a laundry list of specific initiatives and projects. This strategy must articulate a vision that describes the superior customer experiences that the firm will deliver to its customers across all firm-customer touchpoints in the future, ideally within the next two to five years. This vision should be aspirational — every employee and front-line agent, putting themselves in their customer's shoes, should see how it will be compelling to customers and a source of competitive strength. The firm's objectives for creating this new customer approach should be explicitly stated: "We are going to increase our market share/repeat sales/improve sales per customer/ etc. by $X\%/Y\%/Z\%$/etc. by delivering a superior customer experience. ..." And, as illustrated here, these objectives should be expressed in terms of the business performance metrics on which functions, groups, and individuals will be measured.

With a well-crafted overarching strategy that is supported by senior-level management, active marketing of the Customer Insights strategy will stimulate the many involved areas of the organization to start creating their own Customer Insights strategies to contribute to achieving the customer vision. This bottom-up approach to defining and implementing the dozens of capability-building projects and new customer-touching programs, experiences, and tactics will help focus efforts on impacting the customer experience across multiple customer touchpoints. This is favorable to creating a situation where operating units sustain existing practices while waiting for the silver bullet from a central, corporate CI group that may be disconnected from the front-line realities of the business.

7.5.3 Guideline 3: Start from the Customer Experience — and Work Backwards

One of the greatest sources of frustration, failure, and negativity toward the concept of harnessing CI is the database-first approach many companies have adopted in their early attempts to build Customer Insights capabilities. Over the last 20 years, many smart companies who understood the benefits of CI embarked down the path of building the "mother of all databases" and layered on the latest, greatest "CRM solution" (according to the software provider and/or their IT consultants). These projects frequently ran into millions of dollars and when they were finally delivered (typically a year late and 30%–50% over budget), they were greeted by an ambivalent reaction at best from the key marketing and sales groups in the firm. Why? Frequently they were the result of a top-down strategy to implement CRM. Rather than beginning by asking, "What will improve the customer experience and drive greater revenues for the firm?" their first question revolved around the best type of technology to implement.

What these companies failed to do was to initiate change in the critical area first — the customer experience. They effectively put the cart before the horse, thinking that if they built a database (or hopefully a more comprehensive CI capability), their marketers would be able to use it in many wonderful ways to change the customer experience. There are really two key lessons to learn and remember from this (a) when building capabilities in the form of tools or systems, make sure you involve the ultimate users of these tools as early as possible in their development; (b) if you do not know exactly what you want to achieve with your capabilities, you will be forced to build overly broad and/or flexible tools that will be either unnecessarily expensive or not sufficiently focused to be effective — or both.

7.5.4 Guideline 4: Start Small — Grab the Low-Hanging Fruit

Despite the goal of creating the superior total customer experience as articulated by the firm's CI strategy, organizations should not become too fixated with trying to achieve perfection. Many of our interviews with managers tasked with implementing CRM efforts highlighted frustrations with the rejection of large-scale business cases to build large-scale CI capabilities. However, some companies understand that there is no need to wait to have the finely honed, end-to-end, major customer experiences developed. They are already getting out there and taking advantage of some of the obvious opportunities first. We support this by saying: follow your instincts — grab the low-hanging fruit! There are several reasons for balancing this incremental approach with the more transformational approach of the firm's overall CI strategy.

First, most companies can quickly identify through the customer experience mapping process some obvious areas of customer dissatisfaction and missed marketing opportunities. Many of these can be simple to correct and can have immediate impact on customer behaviors, values, and attitudes. A second reason for building incrementally is to manage employee expectations within your organization. If employees can see the impact of this new approach early in the process, they will be more likely to embrace the future changes that will be required for them. In this way, a small initiative that produces tangible results quickly can be much more powerful from an organizational behavior point of view than the impact from a large initiative that will not be seen for a year or two. This process of "getting points on the board" helps create the quick feedback and gratification that all people need from their work: the firm to start building a knowledge base of customer responses to various programs, experiences, and tactics. This is an essential resource for any firm committed to harnessing CI. It creates a fact base that marketers can draw upon as they try to predict and anticipate how certain actions will influence customer behaviors and attitudes. In other words, a "virtuous cycle" can be created by successful small CI initiatives that will accelerate a firm's CI development and create a significant and growing competitive advantage.

7.5.5 Guideline 5: Balance Capability Building with Execution

A theme that emerged in our research was a frustration around the inability to move beyond a current state of CI development. Often this took the shape of business cases to build CI Programs that could not get approval due to the funding that would be required to build the necessary supporting capabilities. Another theme that we have touched on several times in this chapter is representative of the opposite issue — companies who have invested in and developed significant CI capabilities only to find that little changes when it comes to bottom-line results.

Let us illustrate a recommended strategy to balance capabilities and execution. The principal rule is to build only the CI capabilities that you have identified a need for in the support of the customer experiences you plan on delivering. Conversely, do not build a lot of other future capabilities at the same time that will bog this down. The responsible approach would then strike the right balance between short-term requirements and ensure that IT-based capabilities will be designed to accommodate future extensions. To accomplish this, marketers must truly partner with their IT resources — and ensure that they understand the longer-term customer vision. With this, they can help select the technical approaches and standards that will help avoid creating capabilities that cannot be extended or scaled as your requirements advance.

7.5.6 Guideline 6: Identify and Coordinate Core Capabilities

In our earlier discussion, we defined four core CI capabilities that underlie a firm's ability to effectively harness CI. These core capabilities are applicable and fundamental to delivering any CI-enabled program, experience or tactic, regardless of the type of customer interaction involved. Because these capabilities need to reach across the organization, a coordinated approach to their development and deployment should be used to optimize investment and ensure their consistency and quality across customer experiences. While this might sound like a contradiction to the need for a bottom-up strategic approach, one area where a top-down strategy is beneficial is in the definition and development of these core capabilities. This will require some form of cross-firm CI integrating mechanism — such as a small, central group charged with core capability development. Another approach is establishing a steering committee with the same function but composed of representatives of all functions responsible for customer-touching activities.

The two core capabilities to which this approach is most applicable are the CI and intelligent customer interaction channel capabilities. Both of these involve significant technology investments and well-articulated functional specifications defining how front-line agents and other marketing, sales, and customer handling personnel will use them. The creation of these specifications must be led by someone outside of IT who has a sharp focus on business performance, but they should be supported by knowledgeable IT resources.

The core capability of customer experience delivery process design is less about IT systems, and more about expertise in the areas of workflow process design, customer behaviors, and front-line agent capabilities, as these are specialized skill sets. For many companies, it may make economic sense to have a small central group of these experts who serve all functional groups as in-house consultants.

This will also have the benefits of creating another integrating mechanism that will facilitate experience sharing across all functional groups and enable the development of a stronger knowledge base of customer response.

7.5.7 Guideline 7: Focus on Customer Needs, Expectations, Interests, and Motivations (NEIMs)

It is easy for companies who have been diligently collecting customer data for years to get so "buried under data" that they cannot transform it into real CI. This was a common complaint we heard in our research — "We have so much data that we do not know what to do with it!" Companies may bemoan the recent privacy legislation that can inhibit their ability to buy customer data from third-party data sources. But we believe that these obstacles can be overcome by taking a better approach to CI generation: decide what you truly want to know about your customer and prospects at the CI level, and then go gather the data you need to generate this.

This approach is greatly facilitated by the process of mapping out current and planned customer experiences and desired customer behaviors. This exercise will quickly reveal what NEIMs you need to understand and address in order to effectively influence customer behavior. Focusing on these NEIMs will help to make your CI efforts more actionable and effective. It will also help to structure a prioritized customer data collection strategy through which the firm gathers only the most necessary customer data. As a result, data collection may actually be less intrusive and demanding on customers and prospects.

By contrast, companies who take a data-centric view to CI often end up tasking a team of data miners (often expensive outside consultants with little familiarity with the firm's customer experiences) to sift through the mountain of data in search of nuggets of marketing gold. While this "boil the ocean" approach can be successful, it is very time-consuming and frequently reveals trends or insights which are interesting but likely not very actionable for marketing purposes. We believe a targeted, NEIMs-based approach will help companies gain a much better understanding of not only who buys what, but more importantly, "Why do they buy?" and "What role our actions have in their purchase decisions?"

7.5.8 Guideline 8: Continuously Spread the "Religion" of Customer-Centricity

Moving toward a more customer intelligent and customer-centric approach to the business is a major transformation for many products. Many of the world's leading marketers have made bold statements over the last decade that customer-centricity was their future — and some have made sufficient progress in this transformation. But many others have failed to significantly change their approaches and organizational behaviors, and their claims to being customer-centric are still unfulfilled promises to consumers and equity analysts.

Marketing, sales, and customer service leaders must take leading roles in spreading the "religion" of being a customer-centric organization. They must constantly refer to the customer vision of the firm's CI strategy and challenge their employees, peers, and others in the organizations about how their efforts and activities are contributing toward the customer vision. Great CEOs know to focus on a few key themes and keep reinforcing them in all communications. Great marketers need to do the same on the theme of harnessing CI to drive marketing and sales effectiveness and competitive advantage.

The greatest obstacle that CI leaders will face are the people we refer to as "Palm trees." When management makes a statement that change is underway, many people compare the statement to an oncoming storm. There will be a lot of wind and noise, but if they simply bend and sway with the storm, while keeping their roots firmly planted where they are, eventually the storm will pass and they can resume their previous posture. Palm trees are dangerous. They appear to share your enthusiasm and be working toward change, but they are not emotionally committed. To truly move toward customer-centricity, you must stimulate emotional commitment as well as behavioral change within a firm's ranks.

Acknowledgments

Some of the material in this chapter is adapted from a monograph *Harnessing Customer Intelligence* (2005) by M. Ryhorski, R. Wilson, J. Slow an D. Soman. We thank Ryhorski, Wilson and Slow for their contributions to the MCV project.

Chapter 8

The Digital and Social Marketplace

Digital: Composed of data in the form of especially binary digits.

Social: Marked by or passed in pleasant companionship with friends or associates. Of or relating to human society. The interaction of the individual and the group; or the welfare of human beings as members of society.[1]

In Chapter 1, we made the point that the biggest difference in the business environment since the time the first edition of this book was written is the advent of the internet — both through network desktop computers, as well as mobile devices. The internet has had massive implications for not just the way in which business has been done, but also how marketplaces as a whole have reacted through changes in customer behaviors. More generally, the advent of digital technology — the representation of information in electronic bits — has had implications not only for communication, but also for products, pricing, and distribution strategy. In Chapter 7, we studied one implication of the growth of the internet, namely the explosion of data, its implications for the capabilities of an organization to better understand the customer and customize products and

---

[1]Digital. (n.d.). *Merriam-Webster.* Retrieved April 1, 2021, from http://www.merriamwebster.com/dictionary/digital; Social. (n.d.). *Merriam-Webster.* Retrieved April 1, 2021, from http://www.merriamwebster.com/dictionary/social

services; and on the flip side, the dangers associated with privacy concerns of customer data.

In this chapter, we will ask and answer the following questions: Why is the internet fundamentally different? What effects does it have on basic customer decision-making processes? How do these changes in processes affect marketplaces and the manner in which buyers and sellers — or two agents in any marketplace, interact with each other? What do we mean by a digital and a social marketing strategy?

The internet is a different playing field. We begin our discussion on the internet and its effects on organizations by using a sporting metaphor. Consider the sport of tennis. Legendary players John McEnroe, Serena Williams, Boris Becker, Venus Williams, Martina Hingis, Pete Sampras, and Novak Djokovic between them have amassed many Grand Prix titles, but have something else in common. None of them have ever won a French Open Championship. This is because many of these players learnt, and therefore specialized in playing tennis on hard court or grass surfaces. Changing surface to clay has an effect on the outcome of one's game, because the strategies and tactics needed to do well on clay (or more generally a different condition) are different from those on a hard court. As one of these tennis legends that remarked in an interview [loosely paraphrased], "My mistake was that I brought my hard court game on to Roland Garros and did not pay the surface enough respect."

Success of any strategy or tactic be it in sport or in organizations always depends on context and the nature of conditions. The internet presents one such example of a playing field that is fundamentally different from the brick-and-mortar world. Research and marketing and economics are replete with examples of why the internet is so fundamentally different, but in this chapter we will focus on three major differences.

First, the internet dramatically reduces search costs for information. This information could include product attributes, price, reviews, or even information about similar products in a given category or domain. Second, the internet creates close to zero marginal costs for the production of information. Any content can be digitized (music, movies, books, maps) and reproduced almost costlessly. Third, there is a very low cost of transportation of information. To put this differently, geography might become irrelevant in many situations because information could be transmitted over large distances instantaneously rendering prior geographical constraints irrelevant. There are other differences, for example, the internet creates a low cost of tracking behavior resulting in implications for personalized advertising and communication, and therefore privacy concerns; and lower costs of verification creating a market for reputation systems, recommendations, and endorsements. We have already discussed the implications of these two differences in previous chapters and hence we'll not discuss them in-depth here.

Taken collectively, the three factors create an interesting pattern of marketplace effects. These include, but are not restricted to the following:

- Price dispersion
- Different distribution of preferences into superstars and long tails
- Matching of two-sided markets — also known as platforms
- Move to streaming and on-demand services and bundles
- Growth of big-box online retailers like Amazon
- Changes in market definition and the scope of competition
- Agglomeration versus dispersion in marketplaces

In this chapter, we will explore some of these phenomena. We will focus on the effect that digitization will have on that so-called 4P's — products, pricing, promotion, and place (distribution).

8.1 Reduced Search Cost and the Death of Distance

Search costs refer to the costs associated with gathering information about products and services. Consider a customer that is interested in purchasing a technology product and needs to make price comparisons across stores and brands. In a brick-and-mortar world, the search cost of collecting all this information would entail the costs associated with transportation (i.e., the cost of visiting different stores), the cost of collecting, collating, and sorting all the information; and the costs associated with interpreting and using that information.

Some forms of information that customers seek will cost more to search for than other forms. In seminal research, Nelson identified three categories of attributes — search attributes, experience attributes, and credence attributes.[2] Search attributes are those that could be learnt and interpreted during a search process well before a choice is made. In the context of a technology product, its specific observable features like description, size, price, or speed of processor can all be learnt simply by searching for the appropriate information.

An experience attribute can only be understood after consumption. (Recall our discussion in Chapter 2 on experiential value.) The ease of using the technology product, how convenient it is to carry around, the durability of the product and its fit with one's lifestyle are all experience attributes. Finally, credence attributes are those that the customer might never truly understand even after choice or usage. A classic example of a credence attribute is the safety performance of a vehicle, or the quality of a dental procedure.

Of these three types of attributes, search attributes are very easy to collect information on in the online world. Price comparisons, tabulated comparisons of products across a number of attributes, or

---

[2]Nelson, P. (1970). Information and Consumer Behaviour. *Journal of Political Economy*, *78*(1970), 311–329.

even a comprehensive list of products that match one's criteria are relatively costless to do online compared to a brick-and-mortar world. However, experience and credence attributes might not be as easy to search online — indeed, they

---

Insight Box 8.1

MCV Insight

The internet reduces the cost of searching — but not for all kinds of attributes. The greater the instances of experience or credence attributes in a product, the less of an advantage does it get online.

---

might be as easy or as difficult online as they are offline. Internet businesses have attempted to overcome the lack of advantage in the experience attributes space through the use of recommendations, reviews, and ratings. That said, the overall conclusion is that the online world reduces the cost of a search, but not in the same way for all attributes — it dramatically reduces search costs and to some degree experience costs but might have no effect on credence costs.

Given that price, information might be particularly easy to search for online, so we might expect that the widespread use of the internet should reduce prices. It should also reduce price dispersion and enable wider media consumption. In reality, the evidence is not as clear if this actually happens.[3] For one, the gains that might accrue from reduced search cost of prices might be offset by the fact that the customer is now exposed to many more options — including options that are expensive and that they may not have had access to in the past. Organizations might also be making a search more difficult. In particular, it is possible that they increase the cost of a price search for the lowest quality products, while making it easier to find higher quality products.

Another way in which the internet is different has to do with a lower relevance of distance. Because a customer sitting in their

---

[3]See, for example, Bakos, Y. J. (1997). Reducing Buyer Search Costs: Implications for Electronic Marketplaces. *Management Science, 43*(12), 1676–1692; Orlov, E. (2011). How Does the Internet Influence Price Dispersion? Evidence from the Airline Industry. *The Journal of Industrial Economics, 59*(1), 21–37.

basement in a house in Toronto can access any marketplace any-where in the world, the internet should theoretically convert all of our marketplaces into global marketplaces. The customer in Toronto should be able to access a store in Cape Town, South Africa, and purchase a product. In fact, if the product can be digitized, then the cost of transporting that product to the customer's home in Toronto is also negligible. In reality, many products cannot be digi-tized, and hence there is a constraint on the reach of the internet as a marketplace.

That said, there are many goods for which the marginal cost of distribution does approach zero. Examples over the past decade include books, music, movies, and other informational products. In 1997, journalist Frances Cairncross famously wrote that the internet would cause the death of distance[4] — the internet means that individ-uals that were previously isolated can now be plugged into a big global marketplace. Similarly, Friedman wrote about the world becoming flat and that the internet and other information and communication technologies will level the playing field across geographies.[5] A corollary of Friedman's claim was that there would be no advantage to location for either customers or for organizations. In a similar vein Marshall McLuhan, the famous University of Toronto sociologist, wrote about a global village in which information is avail-able everywhere across the world in the same form and that it would result in a global culture, which is distinct from the local flavors of culture that we see across geographies.[6] This might mean that a pro-fessor teaching the Managing Customer Value course could have students from absolutely anywhere in the world or that communities of customers from across the globe could interact with each other on

---

[4]Cairncross, F. (1997). *The Death of Distance: How the Communications Revolution Will Change Our Lives.* Boston, MA: Harvard Business School Press.
[5]Friedman, T. L. (2005). *The World Is Flat: A Brief History of the Twenty-First Century.* New York: Farrar, Straus and Giroux.
[6]McLuhan, M. & Powers, B. R. (1989). *The Global Village: Transformations in World Life and Media in the 21st Century.* New York: Oxford University Press.

forums that cater to special interest groups such as music, sports, or other tastes and preferences.

Yet, though the theory suggests that online activity has significantly increased over the past decade, it is also simultaneously true that the people generating this online activity live offline. In that way, offline activities have an important bearing on what is communicated online and therefore who is interested in that communication. Geography matters because the internet has different characteristics across locations. There are also elements of government policy (copyright policy, privacy policy, or taxes) that might influence the communication and therefore impose a constraint on the idea of a global village. Trust is also easier to gain locally — people tend to trust organizations, brands, and stores that they can kick the proverbial tires of, and hence see in the real world. Finally, social networks also tend to be disproportionately local — while it is in theory possible to develop a social network from people all across the world, evidence suggests that people are more likely to take existing offline social networks online. Therefore, rather than utilizing the full power of the internet to make the world flat, customers seem to be simply using it as a digital mechanism to augment existing social relationships by adding a digital means of interaction.

8.2 Digital Advertising

Advertising serves two purposes — it informs potential customers about the product, and it persuades potential customers to make a purchase. Digital advertising has the same two purposes. There are two forms of digital advertisements. Search ads only appear to those who are already searching for your product or service, while display ads are paid placements that appear based on various targeting parameters, but independent of search. Display advertising includes banners on websites, multimedia on video platforms, and display ads on social media feeds such as Facebook. There are two additional types of ads — classified ads (such as online job boards or Craigslist) and sponsored stories where advertisers will pay a media organization to put a story up on their website that the advertiser typically has written. In addition, there is another kind of online marketing communication called "earned media" or "viral content." This is not advertising per se, but is defined by any content that an organization puts up and hopes that people share it, talk about it, or otherwise report on it. In traditional marketing this would be referred to as "word of mouth."

Search ads — such as the ones that are triggered by specific searches on engines like Google or Bing — tend to be informative. An online search is a statement of intent when a potential customer reveals what they are looking for, and the advertisement provides information about relevant products and services. In contrast, multimedia display ads tend to be sometimes informative, and often persuasive by using multimedia to convince people that this is an exciting product and something that they should grasp. Advertising, whether informative or persuasive, has both immediate and long-term benefits. Therefore, in the digital advertising world, the pricing of advertising is sometimes very much about immediate benefits, and sometimes it's about long-term benefits.

Pricing of online advertisements is called "cost per click" or CPC. Every time someone clicks on an ad, the advertiser pays the website that showed the ad; hence the name cost per click. Cost per action pricing is similar — every time somebody clicks and then buys a product, the advertiser pays the media site. Those are both immediate benefits of seeing the ad. There's also a long-term benefit in terms of brand building or getting people to know your product and become familiar with it. Those forms of advertising are priced differently.

Most display advertising is priced instead by a method called CPM or "cost per thousand"; in other words, cost per 1,000 impressions of the ad seen. In this method, the advertiser pays some amount to the media site as a function of every 1,000 ads displayed.

What makes all these types of online advertising different from offline advertising is that online advertising allows and emphasizes targeting. Search advertising targets as a function of what a customer types into a search box. Display advertising uses a different series of tools. Display advertisers typically use tracking devices, sometimes called "cookies." There are a variety of other techniques involved in grouping people based on their interests inferred from their past web-surfing behavior and using the results to predict what kind of ad is going to be most effective for each customer.

There are four different types of players in this market. First, we have the search engines, which are a type of media player that provide ads in response to that statement of intent. They also provide algorithmic links or organic search results that are not advertising, but they are part of what keeps people coming back to those search engines. Second, there are media sites. These, in many ways, are like old media, magazines, newspapers, TV, radio, in the sense that people go to consume the content and see the ads. Third, there are aggregators for the media sites, and they are increasingly important in the online world. A fourth important set of actors are the measurement agencies. How do you know if people have seen your ads, and how do you know if your ad's working? Organizations rely on a measurement agency to assess how the ad is working. These include companies such as ComScore, Nielsen, and DynamicLogic.

8.3 Customer Behavior Online: It's Different

As one of the key activities in our framework involved moving customers up a value ladder, it is critical to understand whether customer behavior in an online world is the same as in an offline world. In particular, when customers make decisions online, are they using the same decision-making model that they would in a

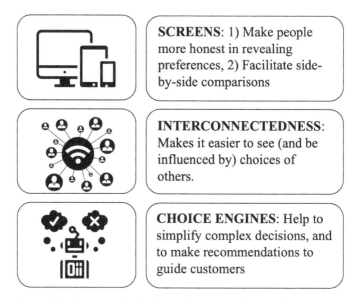

SCREENS: 1) Make people more honest in revealing preferences, 2) Facilitate side-by-side comparisons

INTERCONNECTEDNESS: Makes it easier to see (and be influenced by) choices of others.

CHOICE ENGINES: Help to simplify complex decisions, and to make recommendations to guide customers

Figure 8.1 Customer behavior online is fundamentally different.

bricks-and-mortar environment, or does the online environment fundamentally change how they make decisions?

Research shows that decision-making in the online world is not simply a digitization of decision-making in the bricks-and-mortar world.[7] In fact, it is a completely different playing field with different sets of rules. What is so different about online? There are three drivers of the differences — Screens, Interconnectedness, and Choice Engines (see Figure 8.1 for an overview).

Research shows that customers are much more honest in front of a screen. When people are asked questions about various habits like smoking or exercising, they are much more honest when the format of the question is a text on a screen rather than a human voice. Likewise, insurance customers are more likely to report

[7]See Kim, M., An, J., & Soman, D. (2016). *Financial Behaviour Online: It's Different!* Toronto, Canada: Behavioural Economics in Action at Rotman (BEAR) Report Series. http://www.rotman.utoronto.ca/bear

truthfully when answering questions on a screen rather than speaking with an insurance agent. Other research shows similar effects of screens on bringing out honesty in people from admitting poor academic performance, to reporting drinking habits, or to reporting the number of sexual partners they have.

Screens also allow people to express their true preferences in shopping behaviors. Researchers looked at data from a pizza delivery restaurant that introduced an online, web-based pizza delivery system to complement their phone-based and walk-in delivery and take-out orders. It turned out that when people order pizza online, they're more likely to make unusual and high-calorie orders. More specifically, the average item in an order had 3% more calories and 14% more special instructions. Online orders also had unique combinations of calorie-rich toppings. Online shoppers did not have to feel embarrassed about revealing their true preferences about their diet habits or their pizza desires, and also did not need to worry about making orders as simple as possible just so that you don't get judged for being difficult.

Another feature of screens is that it displays information differently. Online shopping sites allow for the side-by-side simultaneous comparison of options on multiple features, including price. In contrast, the physical world usually entails a sequential comparison of options with information sequentially being unfolded. In the physical world, a customer might first consider how much they like the product, and then decide whether they are willing to pay. In the online format though, where the price is more salient from the beginning, the customer is more likely to think in terms of trade-offs between the product and the price.

The second driver of differences in behavior is connectivity and the resulting interconnectedness. When people are always connected to the internet (including the time spent with mobile devices), they have instant access to all sorts of interesting information — including other people's behavior. Booksellers and movie streaming sites provide aggregate-level preferences in the form of "bestseller" or "top 10" lists. Shopping sites will provide information on what "people like you also purchased" or "what people who purchased what you just purchased also bought." Social media sites and apps connected to social media accounts are really good at sharing all this information about people who are in your social network, information about where they checked in, the kind of brands they like, what kind of music they're listening to. This mere knowledge of what other people are doing actually influences choice, particularly when the customer does not have strong or well-articulated preferences. Another feature of the connected world is the fact that individuals can actively seek out feedback from others in real time. Apps allow the modern-day customer to post a photo of a product they are contemplating purchasing, and to solicit feedback from their social circle on whether or not they should indeed make the purchase.

The fact that a potential customer is likely to make choices based on what others choose is widely documented (see, for example, Chapter 6). Investors tend to enter the market more when other people are entering the market, and they're also likely to choose to invest in certain stocks, depending on what kind of stocks the people around them have indicated interest in. Given this, an organization could give people a reference point for complex decisions. For instance, a pension fund could give customers on a given step of the ladder information about what "others like you typically do" to encourage movement to the next step of the ladder.

The third driver of difference are choice engines. Choice engines are tools that will help customers make decisions. These could take the form of calculators (e.g., a mortgage calculator that helps a customer choose the most appropriate mortgage) or recommendation engines that can match the customers' preferences with the most relevant products (e.g., iTunes Genius, which curates different playlists that you might be interested in or Netflix recommended TV shows based on your past history). Other choice engines allow customers to input cutoffs or criteria that gradually reduce the choice set over time. Finally, there are other advanced technology solutions that fundamentally change how we do things. For instance, Robo-advisors are financial advisors that operate 100% online using technology and algorithms to help customers build and manage their portfolios.

The point here is that the consumer online is different, or consumer behavior online is different. With these unique features that we talked about, the decision-making in the online environment is fundamentally different from decision-making in the offline world.

Insight Box 8.2
MCV Insight
Customer behavior online is fundamentally different from offline behavior. They are more likely to be influenced by the behavior of others online.

8.4 Superstars and Long Tails

The fact that the cost of communication online is very low and that customers have easy access to the choices made by others creates an interesting set of phenomena that we will refer to as superstars and long tails.

Imagine that a corner bookstore in the brick-and-mortar world is looking to stock a shelf with a limited capacity with popular books. Their goal, of course, is to maximize sales and therefore profits. Further, imagine that the retailer has data on the relative popularity of several authors. For argument's sake, let us imagine that Alpha is the most popular author followed by Beta, while Gamma and Zeta have limited appeal. This retailer will try to purchase as many units of the most popular Alpha, fill up any remaining shelf space with Beta, and will likely not have any space to stock the less popular authors. In short, in a real physical world marked by capacity constraints, it is easy for people with mainstream preferences to find products that match their taste while it is particularly difficult for people with relatively rare or niche preferences to find products of their choosing.

Now imagine that instead of a brick-and-mortar retailer, we are looking at an online retailer that has a large warehouse in a remote part of the world. For argument's sake, let us also imagine that the shipping costs and time taken to deliver products to the customer are small. In a world like this, the retailer has every incentive to stock as many different authors and in sufficient quantities to meet the needs of all customers over a large geographic base. After all, if they do not have capacity constraints, they could easily stock Gamma and Zeta books, knowing that they could ship these costlessly to any customer in the world that wants them. Businesses that operate in this online retail model, therefore, have every incentive to stock a broader range of products. This discussion is valid not only for books, but for absolutely any product that can be warehoused and shipped.

We will refer to products like Gamma and Zeta Coolers as members of the long tail. The long tail refers to a set of products that individually do not have high sales in any particular geographic territory, but in aggregate might represent a large potential opportunity. For instance, it is easy to see any blockbuster movie in a theater anywhere in the world, but it is not easy to find theaters that might show specialized art or indie films. However, on online platforms like Netflix and Amazon Prime, it is equally easy to see the blockbuster film as it is to watch the indie movie.

Now consider two kinds of customers. For the sake of argument, we will refer to the first customer as a *weak-preference* customer. This customer might have a general preference for the kind of products that they are looking to consume but do not have a specific strong preference for exactly which one. They may likely look for validation and social proof from others. With the internet, this customer is more easily going to be able to see the choices of others and allow those choices to influence their own preferences. For example, in the domain of books, the weak-preference customer might simply consult Amazon's bestseller list' or in the domain of movies, they might simply accept Netflix's recommendations on which movie to see next. In choosing vacation destinations, this customer might be largely influenced by the vacation photographs that their friends and family members posted on Instagram. As a result, this customer's decisions in the online space will be guided toward products that already have a lot of online presence. In other words, the rich get richer online in the context of weak-preference customers. This is the phenomena of the superstar.

Now consider a second set of customers, the *offbeats*. The offbeat customer has a strong preference, but it is significantly different from the mainstream. While the majority of the world might prefer to drink Coke, the offbeat customer might prefer Dr Pepper. While the majority of the world might prefer a vacation in the Caribbean, the offbeat customer might choose to go to Peru' and while the majority of the world might prefer reading books that are on the *New York Times* bestseller list, the offbeat customer might prefer a rare genre of books. Given that the internet store (unlike the brick-and-mortar store) will now carry all of these offbeat products, and the visibility of other people's choices in the internet might now reinforce the offbeat preference of these customers, rather than question whether they are alone in the world, these customers might find other people from all across the globe that might share their interests. As a result, we might expect to see a dramatic increase in user-generated content, products created by some customers for potentially widespread consumption. Examples of these today include YouTube videos, customer-suggested prototypes, blogs, vlogs, and yet other examples of customer creativity online. A key enabler of this tendency for user-generated content is the ability to find others who might have the same offbeat preferences as oneself. Collectively, the growth of these offbeat communities worldwide has resulted in the long tail phenomena.

> **Insight Box 8.3**
>
> **MCV Insight**
>
> In addition to creating superstars, the online economy also supports offbeat preferences. There is a lot of value to be made in niche and offbeat products and services.

Indeed, the potential for generating profits from the long tail is so high that business journalist Chris Anderson remarked, "Forget squeezing millions from a few megahits at the top of the charts. The future of entertainment is in the millions of niche markets at the shallow end of the bitstream."[8]

In order to maximize the value from this long tail, Anderson has three simple prescriptions. First, it is important to make everything available. Rather than using the brick-and-mortar rule of allocating scarce resources to popular products, the online retailer should simply stock absolutely everything that might be available in the marketplace. The second prescription is to reduce prices dramatically. Rather than using the offline prices as a reference point for making pricing decisions, it would be prudent to use the digital costs in a cost plus approach. Third, help the customer find the product — the presence of an overwhelmingly large series of options can be confusing unless the retailer actively helps the person from finding the right product. This can be done through facilitating easy search recommendation engines and the creation of offbeat communities, where users could guide each other towards finding the appropriate digital product.

Put differently, if you imagine two worlds that are otherwise identical in terms of customer tastes and preferences, as well as availability of product assortments, but are different in one other aspect — the first one is purely brick and mortar (left panel of Figure 8.2) while the second one is purely digital (right panel), what differences might we expect to see across these two worlds? The proceeding analysis suggests two vital differences. In the online

---

[8]Anderson, C. (2004). The Long Tail. *Wired Magazine, 12*(10), 170–177.

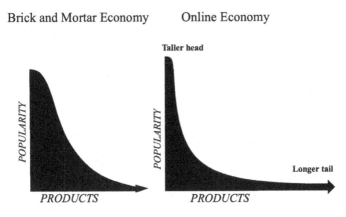

Figure 8.2 Superstars and long tails.

world, there are superstars, whose popularity and revenues are significantly greater than the ones in the brick-and-mortar world. Second, the online world has long tails. This suggests that it is important to be either amongst the most mainstream, or to create a niche and to engage with the right niche audiences in the online world.

8.5 Building a Social Strategy

We would like to start off by highlighting the difference between a digital and a social strategy. A digital strategy refers to the use of tools to digitize existing approaches to managing customer value. For instance, using the internet as a distribution channel (i.e., setting up a virtual store) or as a means of delivering advertising (e.g., search or display advertising) fall under the purview of digital strategies. A social strategy, on the other hand, relies on the consumer's need to establish relationships with other people and to strengthen those relationships. Creating platforms for people to engage with each other in online communities, or creating opportunities for people to share ideas and recommendations fall under the purview of social strategy.

Insight Box 8.4
MCV Insight
Digital and social strategies are fundamentally different. A social strategy relies on the social needs of customers to accomplish a value creating objective.

As a seminal article from Piskorski reminds us, it is important to remember that "people's main goal on social platforms is to connect with other people, and not with companies."[9] This is central to the design of a social strategy. This article further identifies two dimensions of social strategy. First, what is the social impact? What is the social goal that your social strategy is trying to help your consumers accomplish? Second, what's the business impact or the strategy of helping them achieve that goal?

We think about two kinds of social impact. We think about the ability of your social strategy to help consumers establish relationships with other consumers, or to help them strengthen already existing relationships. Likewise, you could think about two kinds of business impact. One is to help you reduce your cost of producing content, or it could be to increase a consumer's willingness to pay for products and services. These two dimensions result in four possible quadrants. For instance, Yelp acquires valuable content by helping people write reviews. They don't need to write their own reviews, reducing the cost of content that is posted on Yelp, but their approach also allows people to meet each other and to establish those relationships. Likewise, companies like Uber Eats or DoorDash use social strategy to increase revenue by strengthening friendships by encouraging gifts of meals via their app, and also decreases costs of acquiring new customers by encouraging referrals.

A template for writing a social strategy is presented in Table 8.1.

---

[9]Piskorski, M. J. (2011, November). Social Strategies That Work. *Harvard Business Review, 89*(11), 116–122.

Table 8.1 A template for a social strategy.

Overall goal of social strategy	Reduce costs, increase revenue
Target product	The product or service the strategy is written for
Mechanism to achieve goal	The specific cost reduction or revenue-increasing mechanism. For example, shifting to cheaper channels, crowdsourcing content, up-selling, cross-selling, etc.
Social benefit to customer	Meeting new people, strengthening existing relationships, developing a reputation
Mechanism for social benefit	Specific social goal mechanism. For example, participating in forums, demonstrating expertise, seeking likes, etc.

8.6 What This All Means

The internet and mobility and the growth of technology has changed the landscape on which organizations operate. While the basic principles of managing customer value remain unchanged, the mechanics by which they can be achieved might change. In particular, the fact that the internet reduces search costs and could potentially make geography less relevant opens up new opportunities for organizations. Our goal in this chapter was to highlight some of the key differences and point to opportunities that the digital and social worlds create.

8.6.1 Guideline 1: Customer Behavior Online is Fundamentally Different

It is often believed that the online world might simply be the digital equivalent of the brick-and-mortar world. Building on our understanding of the psychology of behavior change and three specific properties of the online world (screens, interconnectedness, and search engines), we suggest that customers online make decisions using fundamentally different processes. In addition to the fact that they can access and compare information about alternatives differently, they are also more likely to be influenced by the choices of others. In thinking about customer value in an online world, we encourage organizations to think of a few guiding questions: (a) What capabilities does the internet give me that I did not have before? What new product, pricing, promotion, and distribution opportunities do I now have? (b) How can I use the choices of others to influence customer behavior? (c) How can I use technology and choice engines to make things as easy and seamless for my customers as I possibly can?

8.6.2 Guideline 2: Digital Advertising Comes in Many Shapes and Sizes

Rather than thinking about "digital advertising" as one category, we encourage organizations to adopt a more nuanced perspective. What is the goal of the advertising? What are the desired short-term and long-term effects? Answers to these questions will allow the manager to then determine what form of digital advertising (search, display, or classified) might be the most appropriate.

8.6.3 Guideline 3: The Mobile Internet Offers Additional Capabilities

When the internet is available to people on mobile devices, it provides additional opportunities for both creating value to customers and increasing the value of customers. The mobile internet is particularly useful in situations in which both location and timing are relevant to value creations. For instance, a particular restaurant might add value to a customer only if they are in physical proximity at mealtime. Likewise, a plumber will add value to a homeowner if they are available to visit the home at a time when there is a need for their services. Mobile app-based platforms allow for the matching of demand and supply at the right geography and the right time. If organizations are in service businesses where matching is critical, they will benefit from a platform model. While a detailed analysis of the mobile economy, platforms, and the resulting gig economy is outside the scope of the present book, we refer interested readers to additional resources.[10]

8.6.4 Guideline 4: Digital ≠ Social

In our conversations with many practitioners and students, we have heard the terms "digital" and "social" often used interchangeably. However, we would like to reiterate the difference. A digital strategy refers to the use of tools to digitize existing approaches to managing customer value. In contrast, a social strategy — on the other hand — relies on the consumer's need to establish relationships with other people and to strengthen those relationships. We encourage organizations to articulate both their digital and social strategies. The template from Table 8.1 is a useful starting point for articulating a social strategy.

Acknowledgements

We thank Professor Avi Goldfarb and research associates Melanie Kim and Jessica An for many insights and materials that have formed the basis of this chapter.

---

[10]Prassl, J. (2018). *Humans as a Service: The Promise and Perils of Work in the Gig Economy*. Oxford, UK: Oxford University Press.

PART 3

Chapter 9

Pricing and Customer Psychology

Price: (1) *Archaic*: value, worth. (2) (a) The quantity of one thing that is exchanged or demanded in barter or sale for another. (b) The amount of money given or set as consideration for the sale of a specified thing. (3) The terms for the sake of which something is done or undertaken as (a) an amount sufficient to bribe one and (b) a reward for the apprehension or death of a person. (4) The cost at which something is obtained.[1]

When we embarked on the journey of managing customer value one step at a time, we noted that the framework we were presenting is orthogonal to the traditional marketing models of the 4P's (product, promotion, price, and place) that Philip Kotler first talked about.[2] In particular, we noted that products and services, promotions, and distribution management serve as vehicles by which we could move customers from one step to another. In keeping with this spirit, we allude to various elements of these P's (product, promotion, and channels of distribution) as we evolve the discussion of the MCV framework.

Pricing, though, has a special role to play in our framework; it is the only one of the 4P's that gets a separate chapter of its own in this book. Its centrality to the concept of value is not a surprise, with

---

[1]Price. (n.d.). *Merriam-Webster*. Retrieved April 1, 2021, from http://www.merriam-webster.com/dictionary/price
[2]Kotler, P. (2002). *Marketing Management*. New York: Prentice Hall.

even the *Merriam-Webster* dictionary acknowledging the deep connection between the words "price" and "value." Just why is pricing so
central to the value concept?

(1) Figure 9.1 illustrates the concept of a value spectrum. In the con-
     text of any instrument that adds value to a customer (a product,
     a service, a new process), the value spectrum is a range of quan-
     tifiable dollar values that goes from a low of the incremental
     costs required to add value, to a high of the economic VTC, the
     value to the customer. Any price in this range creates a positive
     surplus for both the customer [Customer surplus = VTC − Price]
     and the organization [Organization surplus = Price − Incremental
     cost]. We also remind the reader that we emphasized the impor-
     tance of creating VTC, but at the same time ensuring that
     customers create for the organization. Given the need to strike
     the right balance between VTC and VOC, choosing an optimal
     price point from the value spectrum becomes a critically
     important activity.

(2) Pricing has traditionally been treated as an application
     of microeconomics to marketing. In particular, a standard
     demand curve approach is used in conjunction with fixed and
     variable cost information to determine the optimal price at
     which profits are maximized. In their book, Dolan and Simon
     refer to this as "Power Pricing."[3] While this analysis is useful, it
     produces results that are static; that is, results that make sense
     in the context of a single shot transaction. One of the central
     premises of our framework is to move customer value manage-
     ment away from the management of transactions, to the
     management of relationships over time. The implication for
     pricing is clear — we need to think about prices not as a static
     concept but as a dynamic concept.

---

[3]Dolan, R. J. & Simon, H. (1996). *Power Pricing: How Managing Price Transforms the
Bottom Line.* New York: The Free Press.

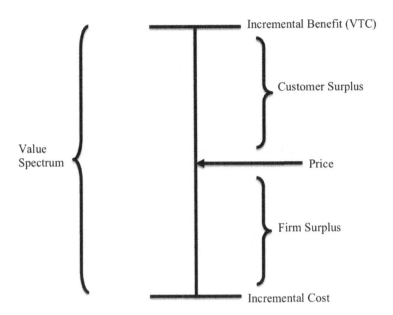

Figure 9.1 The value spectrum.

(3) The pricing decision is probably the most cross-disciplinary decision that an organization could ever make. While there are a number of considerations and inputs into pricing, the four that loom the largest are: (a) an analysis of the costs of delivering the product or service; (b) an appreciation of the economic value it creates for the customer (VTC); (c) a detailed understanding of the demand structure as a function of the price, and as a function of different groups of customers; and (d) a set of insights about how customers will psychologically respond to prices and price changes.

In this chapter, we will tackle this important decision in the following manner. We will first present a simple framework for thinking about the role of these four considerations in the pricing decision. Next, we will outline each of these considerations in detail. Third, we will tackle one important question that will arise from this discussion: How can the manager think about pricing products differently for different groups of customers? This involves a discussion of what is known as "price discrimination." During this discussion, we will also answer the question, Now that I know the four critical inputs into the pricing decision, how do I know which approach to use? Can I use all approaches in conjunction? Fourth, we study the effects of pricing on consumption. Finally, we will examine how prices should change over time and conclude with a series of guidelines on pricing strategy.

9.1 Pricing and the Value Spectrum

Setting the price for a new product or service is a science as much as an art. It calls on a good understanding of the economics of the business as well as the psychology of the customer. It calls for an appreciation of not only how the product is made, but also what the product does for the customer. It is based on objective analysis, but is often truly a subjective decision.

The building blocks of the pricing decision have been encapsulated in Figure 9.2, which builds on the value spectrum discussed earlier to indicate the acceptable range of prices, as well as a list of factors that need to be considered in setting the final price.

To illustrate how this framework works, imagine that an organization XY sells a machine tool (or a consulting service) and that their customers are manufacturing organizations. While there are several comparable machines, XY's creates value because it has a higher capacity and works at a greater speed than the machines made by the competition. For the sake of simplicity, assume that fixed costs are $1,000,000 and the direct cost (material and labor) of each unit produced is $1,000. What price should this organization charge for this machine tool? Remember that the difference between the price and the direct (or variable) cost is the contribution — and it goes toward covering fixed costs and toward the bottom line.

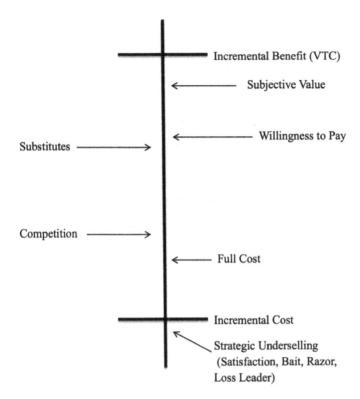

Figure 9.2 Inputs into the pricing decision.

(1) *The Variable Cost*: This is the very minimum that the organization should theoretically be charging in order to stay in business. In this scenario, the organization will still incur fixed costs and will have to

Insight Box 9.1

MCV Insight
Pricing is a crucial decision for the management of customer value — it divides the value spectrum and allows the organization to maintain a healthy balance between VTC and the value of the customer (VOC).

forget about profits. If they charge any lower than this, they will lose dollars on every unit they sell and that is economically infeasible. The variable cost therefore represents the lowest price that they should charge. In some cases, the organization might want to be more conservative and use the full cost (including overheads allocated to each unit of production) as the lowest price. These data are all available in-house through the organization's internal accounting.

(2) *The Economic Value to the Customer.* Now let's look at the equation from the customer's side. If they use XY's machine tool rather than the competitor's, they can complete the same job more quickly and efficiently. The XY product has real positive economic consequences for their customers. By doing some marketing research on how their customers do their business, the organization will be able to estimate the dollar impact of using their machine tool *vis-à-vis* the competitive product they currently use. In particular, XY could ask — What are the benefits that my product offers and what are they worth? And what are the additional costs of operating my product? The net of these is called the economic VTC — and it represents the highest price they should logically charge. No customer will be willing to pay you anything more than the economic value. We provided examples of the economic value created by a product in Chapter 2 when we discussed the examples of Coal Inc. and TH Corporation. For the sake of illustration in the present example, let us assume that the value of each machine to the customer is $2,000.

(3) *The Value Spectrum Is Your Pricing Zone.* Now that the organization has a pricing zone ranging from the variable cost to the economic value to customer (here, $1,000 — $2,000), what other factors should they think about in setting the final price. Why should they not simply charge a $2,000 price? The answers are intuitively obvious — while the organization's research tells it that their product delivers value, their customers may neither know, nor trust the analysis used to generate this estimate. Also, value to customer is often realized over a period of time — for example, the value due to increased efficiency is detected only when the next financial statement is released — while the price

is paid up front. And finally, the customer's perception of value is driven by psychological factors.[4] For instances, research shows that tangible objects are valued more than intangible services (try selling a pure service for a hefty price tag), and bigger objects are valued more than smaller objects (which is probably why software manufacturers package a small computer disk in a large box). A number of additional factors then come into play.

(4) *The Price of Competitors and Substitutes*: While the product has a value of $2,000, that price point might be hard to sell when all of the competitors price it at $1,200. XY's sales team then needs to convince the buyer of the value of the product. Data on competitor pricing can be gathered through simple market research.

(5) *The Subjective Value*: The customer's perception of value might not be the same as the economic value (VTC) that XY estimated based on its own research. Because of psychological biases we mentioned earlier, it may be lower. But suitable marketing interventions could make the subjective value in line with — or perhaps even greater than the economic value. For instance, customers might get added value because of the superior brand name of XY Corporation, its reputation, its after-sales service, or because they have a good relationship with the organization in other product categories.

(6) *The Willingness to Pay*: This is a subjective assessment on the customer's part — their evaluation of the value of the target product as well as all the factors listed above. Data on willingness to pay and subjective value could be gathered through market research or estimated by the organization's salespeople.

Once XY Corporation has the value spectrum and estimates of all of these quantities, they now need to sit down and figure out how much they will actually charge. Here are a few questions that

---

[4]Liu, M. & Soman, D. (2008). Behavioral Pricing. In *Handbook of Consumer Psychology* (pp. 659–682). London, U.K.: Routledge/Psychology Press.

will guide them to which part of the spectrum you can slide the price to.

(1) *How transparent is their value?* If the economic value arising from the product is large and salient, XY can slide the price toward the top of the spectrum. For instance, if the organization has evidence in support of the superior performance and a case study of how their product resulted in savings, they can do a compelling job of selling their value proposition. However, if the value (VTC) is not easy to detect (e.g., it occurs in the future, and it comes as a trickle of small savings rather than an immediately observable increase), they might need to stick to the lower end of the spectrum at least till such time that they can demonstrate the value.

(2) *What is the potential for future sales?* If XY knows that they have a good product, and that the customer might purchase more/ other products in the future, it might make sense to start at the low end of the spectrum as an entry point. As time progresses and as the relationship with the customer deepens and the value of the products is established, they could start to slide up the spectrum. Of course, the price increases need to be coupled with increases in service quality. However, our research suggests that once an organization has established a reputation with their products and services, it is easier for them to put a price on subsequent service. The extreme version of this strategy is strategic underselling, where an organization might sell a product under cost in order to keep a customer satisfied, in order to build a better relationship, or as a "loss leader" in the hope that they will buy other, high contribution products in the future.[5]

---

[5]Dreze, X., Hoch, S. J., & Purk, M. E. (1996). *Turning Traffic into Transactions: Innovative Strategies to Protect and Grow Gm/Hbc Sales Through Category Management.* American Greetings Research Council. Cleveland, USA.

(3) *How many competitors exist, and how stable are their prices?* If there are a large number of competitors, all of whose prices are in a narrow band and stay relatively stable over time (e.g., gasoline), it is difficult to justify a premium. In contrast, when competitors are few, and when prices jump around a lot (e.g., airline seats), customers do not have a good anchor for what the price "should" be and it is safer to move up the spectrum.

> **Insight Box 9.2**
>
> **MCV Insight**
>
> "Pricing Myopia" occurs when organizations try and set pricing decisions for products individually, ignoring the effect of certain prices on the possible purchase of other products. Sometimes it makes sense to sell one product below cost if it increases the probability that the customer might buy a second, higher margin product.

(4) *How do customers make subjective value judgments?* If tangible products are valued more, a change in packaging that enhances tangibility might allow an organization to slide up the thermometer. Similarly, rendering a service more tangible, adding support and additional features to it, and making its value known can allow the organization to slide up. Finally, it is critically important to manage the perception of the costs to produce a product. Whether a product adds value or not, customer psychology tends to view a price increase as unfair if it is not justified by a greater cost. Likewise, in the days in which music was distributed on CD's, many customers feel ripped off when they pay $20 for a music CD, knowing that it only costs a few cents to manufacture it. So it is important for an organization to clearly communicate its fixed costs, and the better they can do that, the higher they can slide on the pricing thermometer.

(5) *How creative are you with your pricing schemes?* Let's go back to our machine tool example. Suppose that XY Corporation has done its best to convince the customer about the $2,000 value of the product, but s/he remains unconvinced. Rather than walking

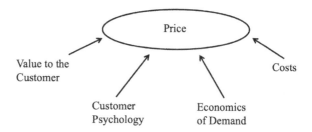

Figure 9.3 Elements of the pricing decision.

off without a sale, an XY salesperson could propose the following two-part pricing plan: "I will sell you the product at full cost,
but we will agree on a mechanism for measuring the dollar
impact of our product on your bottom line. At the end of six
months, we will split this value 50–50." While this proposal is
somewhat unusual in a seller-specifies-price world, it reduces
the risk for the customer, it gives the organization the incentive
to produce excellent products and to deliver excellent service,
and it eventually lets the organization shift up the value ladder
with their pricing!

The discussion above captures all the basic elements of the
pricing decision. In particular, we identify four elements that are
critical to the pricing decision — the value to customers, the cost
of the product or service, the demand curve and willingness to
pay, and customer psychology (Figure 9.3). In the rest of this chapter, we explore each of the components of the pricing decision in
depth.

9.2 Pricing on the Basis of Customer Value (VTC)

The philosophy behind pricing on the basis of customer value VTC
is simple — if an organization can document the value it creates
for their customers, it should be able to charge customers a price

up to that value estimate. The central question therefore is, how an organization can calculate VTC, the value it creates for its customers.

The conceptual underpinnings to this question have already been covered in Chapter 2. In essence, in order to calculate the VTC created for a specific customer, an organization should follow these steps:

- Identify the competing product of service that the customer currently uses.
- Make a comprehensive list of all ways in which the performance of the organization's product is different from the current product.
- Categorize these differences into positive differentiation (where the organizations product is superior to the competition) and negative differentiation (when the competitor's product is superior).
- Monetize as many of the positive and negative differentiation items as possible.
- Compute the base value: the costs that the customer would save if they did not need to purchase the competing product.
- Calculate VTC as base value + positive differentiation value — negative differentiation value.

We illustrate this calculation with some hypothetical data for the example of XY Corporation selling a machine tool to a manufacturer of automobile spare parts. Suppose that the machine tool in question is a milling machine, a machine used for shaping a metal rod that is the end product of the customer. The customer currently uses machines made by AB Corporation but now needs to make a decision on a new set of machines to order for an upcoming addition to their manufacturing facility.

After a series of tests, the team at XY Corporation knows that their machine differs from the AB machine in a number of ways.

First, it operates at a faster speed than the AB machine without any reduction in the quality standards of the output. In particular, in a given hour, the XY machine on an average can produce 20% more units than the AB machine which produces 100 units. Second, because it uses a newer technology, the XY machine reduces wastage significantly. The average utilization ratio (the percent of metal that the machine actually converts into the final product) for the AB machine is 65%, while for the XY product it is 85%. Third, the XY machine needs to be inspected and maintained once every 10-hour shift, while the AB machines need no maintenance. And finally, the XY machine needs an operator that has a higher level of skill, and hence costs more. The top panel of Figure 9.4 gives additional data on the costs associated with these two machines. XY's management also know that they enjoy a superior brand reputation and that the customers of their own customers might place a value on the knowledge that the manufacturing process uses XY machines.

The manager at XY can identify three sources of positive differentiation: (a) the fact that their machine produces more output in a given time, (b) that it uses less raw materials in producing this output, and (c) that XY has a superior brand reputation and hence the ability to possibly increase the quality perceptions of the customers'

	AB	XY
Purchase Price	$50,000	??
Life of Tool	9000 hours	9000 hours
Output per Hour	100	120
Contribution from product	$2 / unit	$2 / unit
	100/0.65	120/0.85
Input Needed per Hour	=153.85	=141.17
Raw Material Cost	$1 / unit	$1 / unit
Total Raw Material cost	153.85	141.12
Operator Cost	$10 / hour	$7 / hour
Inspection Cost (per 10 hours)	$200	$0
Working hours per day	10	10
Working days per year	300	300

Calculations per Day (10 hour Shift)

Positive Differentiation

1) Increased Contribution	$(120 - 100) \times 2 \times 10 =$	$400
2) Reduced Raw Material	$(153.85 - 141.12) \times 1 \times 10 =$	$127.30
		$527.30

Negative Differentiation

1) Inspection Cost	$200	$200
2) Increased Operator Cost	$(10 - 7) \times 10 =$	$30
		$230

Per Year Net Differentiation Value	$(527.30 - 230) \times 300 =$	$89214

Calculations Over Lifetime of Machine

	Now	Year 1	Year 2	Year 3
Base Value	50000			
Differentiation Value		89214	89214	89214
Discounted Value (i=15%)	50000	77577.39	67458.60	58659.65
VTC	253695.65			

Figure 9.4 Calculating the value to the customer.

products. There are two sources of negative differentiation: (a) the inspection and maintenance that are needed for XY's machine, and (b) the higher costs associated with the skilled labor. Of these five points of differentiation, the manager will not be able to monetize the superior brand reputation (although, over time they may be able to measure the effects of this enhanced quality perception on their customers' sales). The manager can monetize each of the remaining sources first for every 10-hour shift, then for the year, and then over the lifetime of the machines. The exact calculations are shown in the bottom panel of Figure 9.4. Given that the value-creating properties of the XY machine sustain over the course of three years, the manager should find the net present value of the resulting cash flows. The numbers tell us that the VTC of the XY machine is approximately $253,700.

There are several interesting insights arising from this analysis. The first has to do with the accuracy of this calculation. We note that we used average data in making this estimate, and we were unable to monetize all the differentiation factors. Note, however the claim that we made very early on in this book — when we conduct marketing analytics, our objective is not necessarily to be accurate. Rather, it is to provide a guideline or crutch in making an important marketing decision. In that spirit, we would encourage the reader to monetize as many of the benefits they can, and possible end up with a conservative estimate of the VTC. When they attempt to sell a product to their customer who might then say that the price based on VTC is too high, the conservative calculation allows the salesperson to say, "But we haven't even included the enhanced sales you might get due to brand reputation into the calculation!"

The second insight arising from this calculation is an important one. In order to illustrate it, let us suppose that XY Corporation has two different customers. Customer SA operates in a part of the world where labor and raw materials are cheap, while Customer RE's unit costs on these dimensions are high. It is easy to see, therefore, that the VTC of the new machine would be large for RE, and probably not very significant for SA. If we believe in the philosophy of value-based pricing, should we charge a lower price to SA than to RE? This practice is called price discrimination.[6] Would it be possible to do this, and what conditions would need to be met for this price discrimination to be successful? In essence, the same exact product or service could create a different level of value for different customers.

Insight Box 9.3
MCV Insight
The exact same product and service may create different economic value for different customers. Therefore, if you base your prices on value, you could charge different prices to these customers.

Third, we note that the VTC of $253,700 is significantly larger than the reference price of the competitor's' product, $50,000. In fact, the VTC is over five times the price of the competitor's price. A prospective customer might be thinking, "Yes I understand that the XY machine is better on speed, wastage, and reputation. But it needs maintenance and skilled labor. I don't see how I can pay above $250,000 for this machine when the competitor only charges me $50,000." Herein lies the key challenge for organizations wanting to practice value-based pricing — the value is not easy to see, and a considerable amount of resources need to be devoted to customer education. Selling in this already-tough circumstance might get even tougher when some customers are very likely to show disbelief in the data. One customer could argue that while the average utilization ratio is 65%, "our processes are superior and hence we already achieve close to 80%." Another might claim that the actual maintenance costs are higher than projected. In circumstances like these, a series of detailed spreadsheets and scenario analyses are the salesperson's best tools for success. Also, as discussed earlier, a two-part pricing approach might help in reducing some of the risks to the customer because — as we

---

[6]Monroe, K. B. (2003). *Pricing: Making Profitable Decisions.* Boston: McGraw-Hill Irwin.

can see from Figure 9.4 — a significant part of the VTC will only accrue in the second half of the lifetime of the machine.

9.3 Cost and Activity-Based Pricing

Cost-based pricing is the simplest form of pricing. In essence, the seller identifies the per unit cost of a product and then adds in a markup in the form of a percentage that serves as a contribution. Cost-based pricing has been around for a very long time — it makes a lot of intuitive sense to customers, it is easy to implement, and it is easy for all parties to understand and embrace.

What is the cost of a particular product? Readers are no doubt familiar with the concepts of fixed costs, variable costs, direct costs, marginal costs, and full costs.[7] However, fixed and variable costs are never as cleanly and crisply demarcated as accounting textbooks make them out to be. In the field of manufacturing, where direct costs account for a large proportion of all costs, the direct cost of a product (or the COGS — cost of goods sold) is often used as the basis of pricing.

While cost-based pricing obviously has the advantages of simplicity, it has recently lost its stature as the preferred method of pricing. The primary driver of this is the fact that the proportion of service (intangibles) in most product categories has grown, and the traditional practices of accounting are not as adept at handling per unit costs of services. Consider, for example, a very simple business model of an organization called PaperPusher, the seller of office supplies to various corporations. Many years ago, this seller pretty much sold a few types of supplies using a cost-plus pricing approach. Customers ordered supplies once a month, and PaperPusher would deliver all of their requirements in bulk within a week of receiving

---

[7]Eldenburg, L. & Wolcott, S. K. (2004). *Cost Management: Measuring, Monitoring, and Motivating Performance*. Hoboken, NJ: Wiley.

their orders. For the sake of illustration, suppose PaperPusher purchased $100 worth of products from a manufacturer, they would sell it for $110 to their customer. The 10% markup would go to cover their costs of distribution and selling, and whatever remained would go towards their bottom line. Note that PaperPusher was a pure services organization — while they did transport paper and pens, all their products — that is, their value-added component on these products — were completely intangible. In accounting terms, all the costs associated with transportation, inventory carrying, selling, and order processing were all lumped into selling, general and administrative expenses (S,G, & A).

As the years passed, the number of items demanded by customers also increased and consequently PaperPusher was compelled to carry more and more lines of products. This was accompanied by increased competition. Instead of just a standard letter-sized paper, customers now wanted legal, A4, and A5 as well as tabloid sizes in a variety of white shades, thicknesses, and finishes. This added to the costs of managing these different lines of products. Customers also became more demanding. One customer asked for delivery every week, another wanted just-in time delivery, a third wanted advice in addition to delivery, and a fourth said that they would like it if PaperPusher sorted their order out by departments, and then delivered the relevant subset of their orders directly to the respective department. As is apparent, customers did not hesitate to ask for these additional services — the pricing structure (where they simply paid a flat 10% markup no matter what services they demanded and got) actually encouraged them to make increasing demands. On the flip side, PaperPusher had absolutely no incentives to offer these services because they earned no revenue and only added to costs. However, customers could threaten to switch to its competition if they did not get these additional services, but — of course — none of the competitors would have high levels of enthusiasm to provide these services. All of this makes for what we call a poorly coordinated supply chain!

There was a second problem, as illustrated by this hypothetical conversation between a PaperPusher salesperson and a customer:

- *Salesperson*: Providing just-in-time delivery is possible, but it costs us to provide this service.
- *Customer*: Understood. But we're happy to cover these costs. How much does it cost you to provide just in time?

Unless PaperPusher uses activity-based costing (ABC), they will be unable to work out the costs of services like: (a) just-in time deliveries, (b) an extra delivery run, (c) advice, (d) breaking bulk (i.e., opening the bulk packaging) and delivering parts of the order directly to various departments. The philosophy behind ABC was introduced in Chapter 2 (see Figure 2.4), and the interested reader is referred to a book and an article by Kaplan and his colleagues for a more detailed treatment of the procedures underlying ABC.[8] Figure 9.5 lists some basic issues to keep in mind for organizations that use ABC in their pricing decisions.

ABC has evoked a lot of discussion, debate, and controversy.[9] In his pioneering work on the subject, Kaplan argues that ABC produces cost estimates that are more accurate than traditional average costing approaches. Like others, we believe that this conclusion is debatable.[10]

---

[8] Cooper, R. & Kaplan, R. S. (1992). Activity-Based Systems: Measuring the Cost of Resource Usage. *Accounting Horizons, 6*(3), 1–13; Cooper, R. & Kaplan, R. (1988). *Measure Costs Right: Make the Right Decision.* Cambridge, MA: Harvard Business School Reprint; Johnson, H. T. & Kaplan, R. (1991). *Relevance Lost: The Rise and Fall of Management Accounting.* Cambridge, MA: Harvard Business Press.

[9] Chenhall. R. H. & Smith, K. L. (1998). The Relationship between Strategic priorities, Management Techniques and Management Accounting: An Empirical Investigation Using a System Approach. *Accounting, Organizations and Society, 23*(3), 234–264; Englewood, C., Young, S. M., Borthick, A. F., & Roth, H. P. (1995). Accounting for Time: Re-Engineering Business Processes to Improve Responsiveness. *Readings in Management Accounting, 23*(3): 234–264; Jacobs, F. & Maiga, A. (2008). Extent of ABC Use and Its Consequences. *Contemporary Accounting Research, 25*(2): 533–566.

[10] Itmer, C. D., Lanen, W. N., & Larcker, D. F. (2002). The Association between Activity-Based Costing and Manufacturing. *Journal of Accounting Research, 40*(3): 711–726; Jacobs, F. & Maiga, A. (2008). Extent of ABC Use and Its Consequences. *Contemporary Accounting Research, 25*(2): 533–566.

1. Identify activities needed to serve customers

2. Understand the drivers of the costs of these activities

3. Use time and motion studies to assign S, G & A costs to these activities

4. Compute a per unit activity cost

5. Update activity costs periodically

Figure 9.5. Guidelines in using activity-based costing.

The process of estimating an activity-based cost involves a number of subjective assessments (e.g., what is the central driver of the cost), and hence the final determination of the cost varies as a function of the team making these judgments as well as the context in which the judgments are made. That said, we do believe that ABC has two important contributions to make. First, it helps the organization identify (and perhaps critically evaluate the need for) large pools of S, G, & A costs. Second, and of more relevance to this discussion, ABC can help the organization differentiate between customers of different quality. The objective behind using an ABC approach for customer management is not because it gives accurate cost estimates, but because it allows the manager to differentiate across customers as a function of their quality.

Insight Box 9.4

MCV Insight

Activity-based pricing allows the organization to charge prices for services and ultimately results in a well-coordinated supply chain. Customers that demand greater amounts of service are charged a higher price.

Just how does ABC do this? The end product of an ABC exercise is the cost of conducting activities. For instance, PaperPusher may be able to quantify the cost of activities like "breaking bulk (per occasion)," "additional delivery (per delivery)," or "providing advice (per hour spent in doing this)." Similarly, a retail bank could quantify the cost associated with clearing a check (per check), speaking with a teller (per minute), or preparing a bank draft (per draft). PaperPusher can now identify the two or three biggest activity costs and use them in a number of different ways. They could create a pricing structure in which there is a base price (pretty much like the original cost-plus model) and an additional service charge — which we call activity-based price — to cover the key activities. An alternate approach is to present prices as a function of behaviors, say in the form of a table (see Figure 9.6). Note that in this example, the additional price for adding each successive delivery remains constant, reflecting a relatively constant incremental cost for each delivery. However, the increased price for breaking bulk into a number of smaller units is not linear. In this case, the increase in cost is the highest for a jump from one unit to two units, and then drops off to a lower incremental unity for each additional unit.

This approach would not only help them cover the cost of delivering the additional service, but also has an incentive value. In particular, the organization now had the incentive to provide high-quality services because they know that they will get paid for it. The customer has the motivation to critically examine whether they truly need the service before shooting off a request for, say, breaking

Product: Bulk pack of Inkjet Printer Paper

20 Cartons, 2500 sheets each

		Deliveries Per Month			
		1	2	3	4
Number of Break Down Units	1	$750	$800	$850	$900
	2	$875	$925	$975	$1,025
	3	$950	$1,000	$1,050	$1,100
	4	$1,025	$1,075	$1,125	$1,175
	5	$1,100	$1,150	$1,200	$1,250

Figure 9.6 Hypothetical pricing schedule for paperpushers.

bulk and supplying the departments directly. The customer might perhaps be able to organize their own internal systems more efficiently such that their costs of breaking bulk and distributing internally are lower than the activity-based price charged by PaperPusher. In this manner, the activity-based pricing creates the incentives for customers to be more efficient. The incentive value is particularly high when a table is used to communicate pricing, because the customer can visually see the effects of changing their behavior on the price they pay for the product. Alternately, the customer might decide that they would rather pay PaperPusher to break bulk for them, in which case they will be assured of getting high-quality service from a motivated supplier. For the supply chain as a whole, activity-based pricing increases the coordination and aligns the incentives of all parties, resulting in greater efficiencies. In the end, customers end up paying different amounts for the same tangible product because they consume different levels of service.

Note that activity-based pricing and value-based pricing share the same end consequence — those different customers end up paying different prices. The reader might ask — When should I use activity-based pricing and when should I use value-based pricing? Our response is captured in Figure 9.7 and summarized by the following heuristic:

Insight Box 9.5

MCV Insight
Whether you use activity- or value-based pricing depends on the locus of the variance across your customers. If there is a large variance in the activities you need to do to satisfy the needs of customers, use activity-based pricing. If there is a large variance in the benefit your customers get, use value-based pricing.

Look at the locus of the variance across your customers. If there is a large variance in the activities you need to do to satisfy the needs of customers, use activity-based pricing. If there is a large variance in the benefit your customers get from your products and services, use value-based pricing.

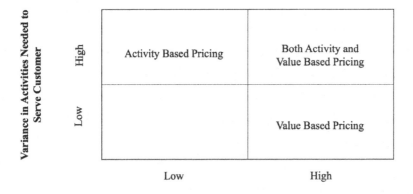

Figure 9.7 Activity-based and value-based pricing.

9.4 The Economics of Pricing

Any economic treatment of the pricing decision is hinged on the demand curve — the relationship between the price charged for a product and the demand for the product in the marketplace. Most microeconomics textbooks give a fairly comprehensive treatment of the demand curve, as well as of related concepts like demand elasticity, price sensitivity, and different functional forms of the demand function.[11] We will not get into any of those details here, but instead focus on a simple form of the demand curve shown in Figure 9.8 — a downward sloping, linear demand curve. Note that the plot in this figure is different from what the reader might see in an economics textbook. We have price on the horizontal axis and demand on the vertical axis (economists usually draw it the other way around). Why? Because in the context of customer value and marketing, price is the variable that is in the

---

[11] Nordhaus, W. & Samuelson, P. (2004). *Microeconomics.* Boston: McGraw-Hill Irvin.

organization's control — it is the decision variable — and demand typically responds to the price.

What is the behavioral intuition behind the demand curve? To illustrate, let us think about three hypothetical customers A, B, and C looking to purchase a flight ticket. C needs to travel on business to sign an important contract, and given that the value of the trip is high to this customer, he is willing to pay a high price (p_C) for this trip. A, however, does not really need to travel, and hence is willing to pay only p_A for this trip. B's willingness to pay is somewhat in the middle.

How do customers estimate their willingness to pay? Following research in the area of mental accounting, we believe that willingness to pay is captured by the following simple paramorphic process.[12] Customers first assess the value or utility of the product, then assign a dollar value to this utility, and finally adjust the dollar value as a function of the price of substitutes and complements. The resulting adjusted dollar value is what we will refer to as their "willingness to pay." In Figure 9.8, we can think about point A as — there are D_A people willing to pay p_A for the product. Likewise, there are D_B people willing to pay pB for it (where $D_B < D_A$). As we've discussed earlier in the case of value-based pricing, we expect that customers will vary in their willingness to pay for the same exact product. And the decision rule that customers follow is simple: if the price is lower than or equal to the willingness to pay, they will purchase the product; otherwise they will not.

If the organization gives away the product for free, a large number of people — anyone that can come up with a conceivable use for it — might choose to consume it. As prices increase, an increasing number of people will find that the price now exceeds

---

[12]A paramorphic process says that customers behave as if they follow the process; Soman, D. (2001). Effects of Payment Mechanism on Spending Behavior: The Role of Rehearsal and Immediacy of Payments. *Journal of Consumer Research*, 27(4), 460–474. https://doi.org/10.1086/319621

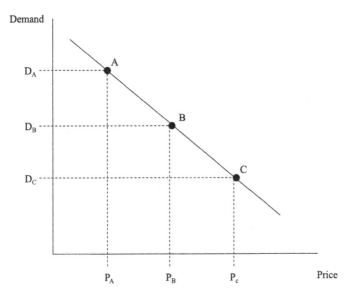

Figure 9.8 The demand curve.

their willingness to pay, and hence they drop out from the demand of the product. This explains why the demand curve is downward sloping.

The relationship between price and demand can be expressed by the following equation:

$$D \text{ (Demand)} = A \text{ (constant)} - b \text{ (slope)} * p \text{ (price)}$$

Similarly, the profit accruing to the organization can be expressed by:

Profit = Contribution * Demand − Fixed costs, or
Π (Profit) $= (p - v) * D - F$ (Fixed cost)

How does this pair of equations help us determine the optimal price that maximizes profits? Substituting the first equation into the second gives us:

$$\Pi = (p - v) * (A - b * p) - F = p * A - b * p^2 - v * A + b * v * p$$

This equation can be optimized analytically, and it can be shown that profits are maximized when $p* = (A - b * v)/2b$. However, a much more intuitive and easy approach is to use the formulae to (a) estimate demand at various levels of price, (b) calculate profits at each of these price points, and (c) estimate the price at which profits are the highest. An example of this approach is shown in Figure 9.9, where we have used the following data:

$$A = 40, \quad b = 5, \quad F = 500, \quad v = 3.$$

As the right-hand panel of the figure shows, the relationship between profit and price is an inverted U-shaped curve. The intuition behind this is simple — when prices are very low, demand is high but the organization does not make a very large contribution on each unit sold. Conversely, when the prices are high, demand is low but this is more than made up by the large per unit contribution of the product. Therefore, for every simple demand structure that can be represented by Figure 9.8, there is exactly one price which yields the highest profits.

Several caveats are in order here. First, in order for this pricing approach to work, the organization should be able to identify fixed and variable costs crisply and clearly. This is often not very easy to do. Likewise, this approach requires the organization to have a good

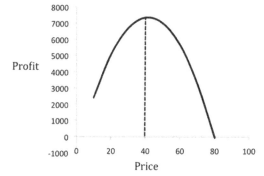

Price	Demand	Profit
10	350	2400
20	300	5050
30	250	6700
40	200	7350
50	150	7000
60	100	5650
70	50	3300

Figure 9.9 Pricing to maximize profit.

1. Expert judgment

2. Customer Surveys

   → Direct price responses

   → Conjoint analysis

3. Price experiments

4. Analysis of historical market data

Figure 9.10 Four approaches to estimating demand curves.

understanding of what its demand function looks like. In their book on Power Pricing, Robert Dolan and Hermann Simon identify four approaches to estimating demand functions.[13] These approaches are summarized in Figure 9.10. A more comprehensive treatment of this topic is beyond the scope of this book, and we encourage the interested reader to look at Chapter 3 of the Power Pricing book.

The second set of caveats has to do with conditions under which this approach is a good bedrock for making pricing decisions. It works when products are purchased independently (i.e., when any one product has no bearing on the likelihood of purchasing another product), and when the organization is evaluating products that are purchased as a one-shot transaction. Given that the main thrust in this book is about looking at how we could move customers up the value ladder, it is easy to see why this simple approach to pricing is not very central to our framework. However, in a later section, we will look at how this approach could be extended to study products that are purchased frequently over a period of time.

---

[13]Dolan, R. J. & Simon, H. (1996). *Power Pricing: How Managing Price Transforms the Bottom Line*. New York: The Free Press.

9.5 Price Discrimination, Fairness, and the Cost of Price Changes

We start our discussion on price discrimination with an intriguing example that received a fair bit of media attention back in 1999.[14] These articles reported that the Coca-Cola Company was testing a vending machine that detected the ambient temperature, and automatically increased the price of a can of Coke if the temperature reached a value that could be deemed as "hot." While the articles also announced that Coke had no plans to introduce these vending machines, the concept of a smart vending machine makes for some excellent classroom discussions.

When posed with the question of whether they would actually consider introducing the Coke vending machine if the decision was theirs, students come up with very interesting viewpoints. Many of these viewpoints have to do with the specific context presented in the article, but some have to do with the general concept of changing prices as a function of the ambient temperature. Those in favor of the machine typically come up with statements like the following:

(1) The utility of the product does increase on a hot day, so it makes sense to charge a different price. The machine simply makes this process automatic.
(2) Customers face other situations in which they pay different prices for the same product — prices of flight tickets vary with time, prices of cinema admission are different for adults and children, and the prices of souvenirs are different for a down-town store versus a convenience store at the airport.

---

[14]Hays, C. L. (1999, October 28). Variable-Price Coke Machine Being Tested. *The New York Times*. Retrieved November 19, 2021, from https://www.nytimes.com/1999/10/28/business/variable-price-coke-machine-being-tested.html

(3) Customers already pay different amounts for Coke as a function of whether they buy a can from a vending machine, a 12-pack at the supermarket, or at dinner in a fancy restaurant.

Those opposed to the machine have a simple and resounding argument — this price discrimination is unfair, it is beyond the customer's control. and it will therefore dilute the equity of the brand.

As we mentioned before, there are no right or wrong answers in a class on Managing Customer Value. The interesting questions to answer are the following: (a) Why do people believe that these price differences are unfair, and (b) What could the organization do to make the price discrimination more palatable if indeed there is an economic reason to justify it?

9.5.1 *The Economics of Price Discrimination*

We answer these questions by first addressing two issues. The first issue relates to the economics of price discrimination and is summarized in Figure 9.11. In a downward sloping linear demand curve context, let us assume that an organization charges p^* and ends up with a demand of D^*. If v is the variable cost of producing each unit, the total contribution is represented by the shaded rectangle marked "B."

We now think about two sets of customers on the demand curve. First, we look at customers located in what we label as Zone 1. These are customers who were willing to pay more than p^* — but since the organization charged less than their willingness to pay, they will pay p^*. The shaded triangle "C" then represents additional contributions that could have been from customers in this zone. Second, customers who lie in Zone 2 are those that were willing to pay more than the variable cost and hence those from whom the organization could have made positive contribution. However, the organization

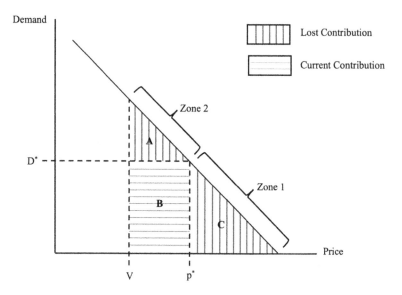

Figure 9.11 The economics of price discrimination.

charged them p^*, which is greater than their willingness to pay. The shaded triangle "A" represents the lost contributions from these customers.

Figure 9.11 summarizes the economics story of price discrimination — if the organization could charge every customer exactly as much as they are willing to pay, they could increase contributions significantly as compared to having a single fixed price. Specifically, in the language of Figure 9.11, they could increase contributions by a factor of $(A + C)/B$. Why don't organizations do this? There are a number of practical problems. First, the legal systems of most countries forbid this form of price discrimination. Second, this form of price discrimination is impractical and possibly expensive. The only reliable manner in which an organization can estimate the willingness to pay of each of its customers is through a process of market research, or a negotiation. Both these are expensive options, and if the cost of determining the individual willingness to pay exceeds the incremental benefits, then price discrimination is simply not worth it. Further, if customers realize that the goal of the market research is to determine their willingness to pay for a pricing decision, they have every incentive to be untruthful.

What organizations can do, however, is to find a surrogate variable that may predict differences in willingness to pay. For instance, one organization might infer using census data that people living in one part of town are wealthier than others

---

Insight Box 9.6

MCV Insight
Price discrimination of differentiation allows you to extract greater value from the customer base. However, it is not always legal and not always easy to do.

---

and hence be willing to pay more. This organization might practice price discrimination by then sending coupons to the lower-willingness-to-pay group. A second organization may infer that students have lower incomes — and hence a lower willingness to pay for business books — than company executives, and thus offer lower prices to students. A third organization, an airline might infer that people who plan ahead are on a tighter budget and hence might increase fares as the flight date approaches. In a similar vein, some students believe that people who want to consume Coke during warm weather should value it more than those that want to consume it in cold weather.

9.5.2 *The Cost of Changing Prices*

In a classroom session on price discrimination, we posed the following situation to students. Suppose that a grocery supermarket knows that most people who shop in the early evening hours are convenience shoppers — people who just need to pick up a few items on their way home and people who are not very price sensitive. Consistent with the discussion above, it would appear that the time of the day is a good surrogate for willingness to pay. The question then is, why doesn't the supermarket increase the prices on some of the most popular items during the early evening hours?

It is easy to see that the biggest deterrent to this policy — aside from behavioral considerations like fairness, which we discuss later — is a practical one. If the supermarket were to change prices, say at 5:30 pm, they would need to send out a posse of employees to change the price labels on the respective shelves (and, in some cases depending on the laws of the land, they would need to change labels on every unit of product for sale), to change any promotional materials and to update the prices on the store's checkout registers. The last is relatively easy and costless to do, but the first two items impose a significant cost on the supermarket. Economists refer to this cost of changing prices as the menu cost. In particular, menu costs are the costs to organizations of updating menus, price lists, brochures, and other materials when prices change.[15] Because of this transaction cost, organizations do not change their prices even when it makes economic sense to do so, leading to price stickiness.[16]

The one thing that organizations can then do to better benefit from customers' changes in willingness to pay is to work toward reducing menu costs. Organizations that sell using electronic channels of communication stand at a natural advantage on this dimension. What about organizations that sell in the physical world? The example of Coke's vending machine is one example of how an organization could use technology to reduce its menu costs. A second example is provided by Dutta and colleagues in their 1999

---

[15]Zbaracki, M. J., Ritson, M., Levy, D., Dutta, S., & Bergen, M. (2004). Managerial and Customer Costs of Price Adjustment: Direct Evidence from Industrial Markets. *Review of Economics and Statistics, 86*(2), 514–533. https://doi.org/10.1162/003465304323031085; Dutta, S., Bergen, M., Levy, D., & Venable, R. (1999). Menu Costs, Posted Prices, and Multiproduct Retailers. *Journal of Money, Credit and Banking, 31*(4), 683. https://doi.org/10.2307/2601217

[16]Levy, D., Dutta, S., & Bergen, M. (2002). Heterogeneity in Price Rigidity: Evidence from a Case Study Using Microlevel Data. *Journal of Money, Credit, and Banking, 34*(1), 197–220. https://doi.org/10.1353/mcb.2002.0031

article.[17] They write about an electronic shelf label systems used by a U.S. drugstore. In describing the system, these authors write:

> These systems allow retailers to manage the pricing in real time by displaying the shelf prices on a small calculator-like digital display attached to the shelves. The system consists of a PC-based system controller, wireless communication network, and electronic shelf labels and rails. Obtaining information from the in store item and the database, the system broadcasts this information to the shelf labels through a controller at each gondola. The system also maintains a continuous surveillance of the electronic shelf labels to ensure that they are present and that they are displaying the correct information. In addition, this label polling process creates data on the physical location of the label within the store. The system is controlled wirelessly from a central computer where price changes are actually done. Because of this setup, the electronic shelf label systems can be used by drugstore chains to greatly reduce the physical costs, lead times, and the frequency of mistake occurrences currently associated with changing paper-tag-based shelf prices. In order to sell the product, the electronic shelf label company had to quantify the measurable benefits of its electronic shelf label systems (pp. 686–687).

With such a price display system, the retailer will have the ability to change prices as a function of various drivers of willingness to pay.[18] In the domain of pricing and value creation, we believe that an organization's ability to cut

---

Insight Box 9.7

MCV Insight

Organizations often do not take advantage of the laws of supply and demand because of menu costs — the costs of changing prices. Reducing the menu costs offers a strategic advantage to the organization.

---

[17]Dutta, S., Bergen, M., Levy, D., & Venable, R. (1999). Menu Costs, Posted Prices, and Multiproduct Retailers. *Journal of Money, Credit and Banking, 31*(4), 683. https://doi.org/10.2307/2601217

[18]See also Dutta, S., Zbaracki, M. J., & Bergen, M. (2003). Pricing Process as a Capability: A Resource-Based Perspective. *Strategic Management Journal, 24*(7), 615–630. https://doi.org/10.1002/smj.323

down their menu costs provides them with a key strategic advantage in creating customer value.

9.5.3 *Pricing Psychology*

While we — and many other writers in marketing — have written a lot about the economics, accounting, and analytics of pricing, it is equally — if not more — important to understand how customers perceive pricing information and react to the manner in which prices are presented. A large and growing number of researchers in the area of behavioral decision research have documented a number of interesting psychological phenomena that relate to the effect of pricing on customer decision-making. This research suggests that the manner in which the price is presented matters — and in some cases, might matter more than the dollar amount of the actual price itself. In particular, a review chapter by Liu and Soman presented the following examples in which price presentation seems to influence consumers in ways which cannot be explained by traditional economic and choice theories.[19]

When credit cards were first introduced, consumers had to pay a surcharge to cover the costs of the transactions. This surcharge was strongly resisted by consumers. However, when retailers increased prices across the board and offered cash users a discount, the same differential between cash and credit purchases suddenly became a lot more acceptable to consumers.

In her charity television appearances, Sally Struthers said that "Only 72 cents a day" we can feed a starving child, and a furniture retailer claimed that "if you can afford yogurt for [\$2/day], you can afford a living room set for [\$1.69 a day]." Both Sally and the furniture retailer elicited a greater compliance than similar requests for

---

[19]Liu, M. & Soman, D. (2008). Behavioral Pricing. In *Handbook of Consumer Psychology* (pp. 659–682). London, U.K.: Routledge/Psychology Press.

an equivalent lump sum, even though they were really also asking for a lump sum.

Flat-rate phone plans are more popular amongst customers than paying by the call, even though flat-rate plans may cost the consumer more overall.

A survey of prices in supermarkets and in department stores reveals that prices with odd endings (e.g., either $9 rather than $10, or $14.95 rather than $15) are significantly more prevalent than chance would suggest.

A comprehensive overview of the research in this area is beyond the scope of this chapter and we refer the reader to Liu and Soman's chapter for a comprehensive treatment, but we would like to highlight a few findings that are particularly relevant to the preceding discussion and present some of the key pricing phenomena that we will not be able to discuss in detail here in Figure 9.12. One theory that has drawn considerable interest and attention amongst both academics and managers is prospect theory, whose essential claim is that customers are psychologically more sensitive to changes in dollar amounts than to absolute levels of dollar amounts.[20] Prospect theory distinguishes two phases in the choice process: an early phase of editing information and a subsequent phase of evaluating it. The theory gives us three principles about how customers react to prices. First, customers always evaluate prices in relationship to a reference price and not in isolation. For instance, John's evaluation of the price of gasoline today might depend on what he paid last week; and Jack's evaluation of a discounted price he got on a new pair of shoes might depend on how it compares to the price that his friend Klaus got for the same pair of shoes. This reference point divides the world into losses and gains. If Radhika goes to the store expecting to pay $100 for a product but gets it for $120, she experiences a loss. If Anshu goes in expecting to pay $100 but only pays $80, she

---

[20]Kahneman D. & Tversky, A. (1979). Prospect Theory: An Analysis of Decision under Risk. *Econometrica, 47*(2), 363–391.

Pricing Phenomena	Description
1) Loss Aversion	Customers are more sensitive to increases in price, not as sensitive to decreases
2) The Silver Lining principle	When presenting the customer with a big loss (high priced product) and a small gain (a few dollars off), segregation works better than integration. It is better to present the dollars off separately as a cash back rebate rather than as a price reduction
3) Partitioned Pricing	Breaking down a price into components - base price, surcharge, shipping and tax - increases likelihood of purchase
4) Multiple Discounts	Multiple price decreases are evaluated more favorably than a single price decrease and multiple price increases are evaluated more unfavorably than a single price increase.
5) Temporal Price Reframing	Changing the time frame over which the price is expressed. For instance, a pennies-a-day strategy might take a lump sum $350 price and express it as "For less than $1 a day..."
6) Currency Effects	When prices are expressed in different currencies, decisions change. American consumers tend to under spend in India because of sticker shock, however if their income change is made salient, they overspend
7) Anchoring and Adjustment	Evaluation of prices is driven by other, unrelated prices seen by the customer. When customers see high-ticket products and the low-ticket items, they overspend relative to not having seen the high-ticket items.
8) Price Image	The price image of a store is influenced not only by price, but also by appearance, size, levels of service and marketing materials. Often, actual prices may not play a role in price image.
9) Tensile Pricing	When prices are advertised as a range (say, $1 - $5, or 10%-80% off), customers tend to be optimistic when the probability of getting a discount is low, pessimistic otherwise.
10) Right Digit Pricing	Prices that are just short of major round figures ($0.99, $99.9 etc.) result in greater sales than the corresponding round number.

Figure 9.12 Pricing and customer psychology.

experiences a gain. The second principle is the principle of diminishing sensitivity and talks about how objective gains and losses map onto their subjective values. For both losses and gains, this principle of diminishing sensitivity says that as the objective value of the gain (loss) increases, its subjective value also increases. However, it does so at a slower rate. A gain of $10 makes Anshu happy; a gain of $20 makes her happier, but less than twice her happiness at gaining $10, and so on.

Insight Box 9.8

Most managers believe that setting a price is the fundamental challenge in value management. They ignore the psychology of pricing, which shows that the manner in which the price is presented matters — and often matters more than the actual price.

The third principle of prospect theory refers to the relative valuation of losses versus gains and it says the following — the value of a loss of $X is greater than the value of the gain from the same $X. This principle has also been called loss aversion, and it has interesting consequences for pricing. It suggests that prices are hard to increase but discounts are easier to reduce. Suppose retailer A has been selling a product for $80 while retailer B has posted a $100 regular price and a 20% discount.

Due to market conditions, both retailers need to increase prices by $10; therefore retailer A revises the price to $90 while retailer B reduces the discount to 10%. Customers of retailer A will see this increase as a loss, while those of retailer B will see it more as a reduced gain and hence prospect theory would predict that retailer B's customers will be more accepting of the price increase. Indeed, empirical evidence collected by us and others suggest that this is true.[21]

Another interesting phenomenon has to do with the effect of the availability of choice on perceptions of fairness. When prices of gasoline rise at the petrol pump, there is a lot of hue and cry amongst end users and the media.[22] However, when the price of bottled water or a bag of chips goes up by the same amount, not too many people seem to care. There are two reasons that drive this difference in outrage. First, petrol is bought in isolation and prices are displayed prominently at the entrance to gas stations. As a result, price increases are bound to get noticed. Bottled water or chips, however, are purchased in a different context. The purchase price gets bundled in with a large number of other purchases, and hence the shopper is not as sensitive to the price changes. Second, petrol is seen by many to be a necessity and customers feel like they have no choice but to pay increased prices. Chips and bottled water are different — if the customer does not like the price increase, they can vote with their wallets and choose other options.

A related phenomenon is called downsizing.[23] Suppose that a packaged foods manufacturer experiences an increase in the price

---

[21] Liu, M. & Soman, D. (2008). Behavioral Pricing. In *Handbook of Consumer Psychology* (pp. 659–682). London, U.K.: Routledge/Psychology Press.
[22] Armstrong, J. (2008, August 14). Pump Complaints Rise with Gas Prices: Up 65 Percent from Last Year. *Onlineathens.com*. Retrieved January 22, 2009, from http://www.onlineathens.com/stories/081508/new_318747647.shtml
[23] Gourville, J. & Koehler, J. (2004, June). Downsizing Price Increases: A Greater Sensitivity to Price Than Quantity in Consumer Markets. *Harvard Business School Marketing Research Papers*. Retrieved January 21, 2009, from http://ssrn.com/abstract_id=xxxxxx

of raw materials, increasing its cost of goods sold and decreasing its contribution margins. The organization decides it must respond by a price increase but realizes that it could deliver the increase in one of two ways. First, it could increase the sticker price of its products. Alternately, it could maintain the price but reduce the content contained in each unit of packaging.

While the second approach is a less obvious form of price increase, the net effect should be quite similar. However, researchers John Gourville and Jonathan Koehler find that there are systematic differences between the two options — increasing the per package price evokes a negative reaction but decreasing the per package content does not. As an example, they discuss PepsiCo, the parent brand for Pepsi soft drinks and Frito-Lay snacks. In announcing its 2001 first quarter earnings, PepsiCo reported its "sixth consecutive quarter of double digit earnings growth," apparently due to its recently introduced "weight out" strategy within its Frito-Lay division.[24] As captured by *The New York Times*, "Net income grew to $498 million, or 34 cents per share, as the company continued to reap benefits from its 'weight out' strategy — in which it cut costs by putting fewer chips in bags of Lays, Doritos, and other Frito-Lay products."[25] There are many other examples, as Gourville and Koehler point out. Chock Full o' Nuts was one of the first and most visible companies to employ this tactic back in 1988 when it reduced its 1-pound tin of ground coffee to 13 ounces (it is down to 11.5 ounces in 2004). More recently, Dannon trimmed the amount of yogurt contained in its single servings from 8 to 6 ounces, Poland Springs reduced the quantity of water in its large bottles from 6 gallons to 5 gallons, and Pampers reduced the number of diapers contained in a typical package from, say, 44 diapers to 38 diapers. The net result in each of

---

[24]Winter, G. (2001, April 24). Pepsi Earnings Increase 18%, Continuing Growth Streak. *The New York Times*. Retrieved November 19, 2021, from https://www.nytimes.com/2001/04/24/business/pepsi-earnings-increase-18-continuing-growth-streak.html

[25] *Ibid.*

these cases is the same — a per unit price increase. Rather than increase the price of a product by raising the sticker price, organizations increased price through a content reduction.

We do not in any way endorse the downsizing approach. Like Gourville and Koehler, we believe that the practice needs to be more transparent and consumers need to be better sensitized to the changes in quantity. Indeed, extracting a greater price by downsizing is completely antithetic to our notion of value creation. However, we are intrigued by the underlying consumer psychology. It appears that customers' sensitivity to changes in prices is significantly greater than their sensitivity to changes in weights and measures.

This takes us back to the question that we raised earlier in this chapter: What constitutes a fair price increase? One of the first set of researchers to study fairness in the domain of prices was Kahneman *et al.*[26] These authors set up a series of scenarios in which it was economically correct to increase prices, and then asked customers whether they thought the price increases were fair. For instance, in one scenario respondents were told about a hardware store that was selling snow shovels for $15. After a large snowstorm, however, the store increased their price to $20. While this price increase would be consistent with the laws of demand and supply would, most respondents reported that the price increase was unfair. Their research, as well as the work of others suggests that price increases are seen as fair when justified by cost increases, but not otherwise.[27] Moreover, they also find that perceived fairness is moderated by the manner in which the price outcomes were framed. Consider the following example from their research:

[26]Kahneman, D., Knetsch, J. L., & Thaler, R. H. (1986). Fairness and the Assumptions of Economics. *The Journal of Business*, *59*(S4). https://doi.org/10.1086/296367; Kahneman, D., Knetsch, J. L., & Thaler, R. H. (2000). Fairness as a Constraint on Profit Seeking: Entitlements in the Market. *Choices, Values, and Frames*, 317–334. https://doi.org/10.1017/cbo9780511803475.019
[27]Okun, A. (1981). *Prices and Quantities. A Macroeconomic Analysis*. Washington, DC: Brookings Institution.

Version 1: A shortage has developed for a popular model of automobile, and customers must now wait two months for delivery. A dealer has been selling these cars at list prices. Now the dealer prices the model at $200 above list price.

Version 2: A shortage has developed for a popular model of automobile, and customers must now wait two months for delivery. A dealer has been selling these cars at a discount of $200 below list prices. Now the dealer prices the model at the list price.

Kahneman and colleagues found that a vast majority of respondents felt that the price increase was unfair under version 1 of the question, but the majority thought that it was acceptable under version 2!

Our own research, as well as some of the examples given above led us to conclude that fairness was a function of three factors, and that a fourth factor moderated customers' annoyance.

(1) A price increase is considered fair if it is justified by an increased cost.
(2) A price increase is considered fair if it is accompanied by an enhancement in quality of services offered.[28]
(3) A price increase is more likely to be seen as fair if the customer has the ability to choose an alternate product.
(4) The palatability of a price increase is greater if it is framed as a reduced loss, or as a discount.

What do each of these implications mean for a smart vending machine like the Coke example we looked at earlier? In a survey, we asked a number of respondents whether a smart vending machine like the one described in the articles would be considered fair.

---

[28]Bolton, L. E., Warlop, L., & Alba, J. W. (2003). Consumer Perceptions of Price (Un)Fairness. *Journal of Consumer Research, 29*(4), 474–491. https://doi.org/10.1086/346244

Most respondents — like some of our students — responded with an emphatic no. However, we asked a separate group of respondents a similar question but changed some of the details of the context. In particular, we (a) included a line which said the costs of keeping a can of soda cold were higher in warm

> **Insight Box 9.9**
>
> **MCV Insight**
> A fair price increase is one in which (a) is justified by increased costs, (b) is justified by greater quality or levels of service, (c) the customer has choices and can easily defect to other products, and (d) the price differential is framed as a reduced gain rather than a pure loss.

weather, (b) framed the price differential as a discount — the regular price was high and customers got a discount if the weather was cold, and (c) we explicitly mentioned that such machines would be located only at locations where vending machines of other brands were available. Under these circumstances, most of our respondents saw no problems with the concept of the smart vending machine.

9.5.4 *Fairness and Customer Management*

In Chapter 2, we introduced the notion of the customer portfolio matrix (see Figure 2.6). We then raised the issue of customer management, and in particular made some suggestions on how dogs — customers who are low in revenue potential and high in cost to serve — should be handled. One specific strategy that we wrote about is a pricing structure that forces the customer to pay for every unit of service consumed. The example we gave was that of many banks who announced that customers who have less than a certain amount of cumulative balances would need to pay a fee for every teller transaction they make.

While this pricing strategy is conceptually grounded in good analytics, we emphasize that an organization — in this case, the bank — should be careful in ensuring that they do not ignore customer psychology and the possible negative effects it might have on the brand. One bank that learnt this the hard way was First Chicago, when — in 1995 — they decided to charge customers who had balances less than $2,500 in their checking accounts a $3 fee for every teller transaction.[29] As this *Wall Street Journal* article reported, "news of the proposed fee ignited a firestorm of reaction." A local radio station also reported, "Fielded nearly an hour of angry calls" before returning to other programming. And comedian Jay Leno made the $3 fee a subject of his jokes on prime-time national television.[30] Competitors capitalized on the negative publicity, with some banks advertising that they offered "free tellers" and others assuring customers that they would not impose similar fees. In addition to losing some of the dog customers that pricing strategies like these hope to lose, banks like First Chicago risk media or public backlash. What were so many customers up in arms against this seemingly unfair treatment? What could the bank have done differently in order to minimize this blaze of negative publicity?

Our analysis — and the results of research suggest that the bank could have done four things differently. First, rather than the media fanfare that was used to announce the "innovative" line of products that "represent the future of banking, the bank could have chosen to inform customers of the fees through a simple direct mailing.[31] Second, this mailing could have attempted to explain that teller services cost money, and hence the bank needed to cover these costs. Third, the bank could have experimented with a plan in which a monthly fee was imposed, and then credits offered if the customer did not use the teller. When framed in this manner, the pricing

---

[29] Gibson, R. (1995, April 27). Some Think the Bank Robbers Are on the Wrong Side of the Window. *The Wall Street Journal*, Eastern ed., B1.
[30] O'Sullivan, O. (1997) Some of Your Customers Are Unprofitable. OK, Now What? *American Banking Journal, 89*(11), 42–47.
[31] Gibson, R. (1995, April 27). Some Think the Bank Robbers Are on the Wrong Side of the Window. *The Wall Street Journal*, Eastern ed., B1.

structure is seemed more as a reward for refraining from an undesired behavior (which therefore will have a strong motivating effect) than as a punishment for that behavior (which causes resentment and rebellion). And finally, the bank could have offered the customers a choice between two pricing schemes — say the $3 per transaction scheme or a fixed $10 monthly fee. The ball is now in the customer's court and they could decide to choose one of the options, or to leave the bank in favor of competition. In contrast, the bank simply foisted the fee onto existing customers and this was not seen as fair.

9.5.5 *Conditions for Differential Pricing to Be Successful*

To summarize the discussions on price discrimination, we identify the following set of conditions that all need to be met for differential pricing to be successful:

(1) The market must be comprised of individuals and segments that vary in their willingness to pay for a product. Needless to say, this is a necessary condition for price differentiation.
(2) The organization should have the ability to identify and reach these segments of different willingness to pay. In line with our earlier discussion, the organization should be able to use some other observable variable that acts as a surrogate.
(3) The cost of segmentation should not exceed the economic benefits of differentiation.
(4) There should be no opportunity for arbitrage. Suppose the pricing scheme is such that the price to Segment A is $20 while the price to Segment B is $50. Arbitrage is said to happen when a member of Segment A buys the product on behalf of a member of Segment B.
(5) Fairness perceptions should not be violated.

9.6 The Effects of Pricing on Consumption

We have thus far identified two effects of pricing. First, as captured by the demand curve, pricing changes the demand for a product. Second, with the examples of PaperPusher, we have made the case that pricing changes customer behavior by creating appropriate incentives. In this section, we highlight research showing that pricing has the potential to change consumption rates, and hence the value of a customer.[32]

But how does pricing impact a customer's decision to consume? The answer lies in a phenomenon called mental accounting.[33] Mental accounting makes the following proposition — people account for their money in much the same way as accountants do, with the difference that while real accountants commit their accounts to paper or a computer, mental accountants practice only a cognitive version. Suppose that a customer Catherine had purchased a $50 ticket to the theater, only to find that the play had received poor reviews. Or perhaps her colleague Amar had advance purchased a $75 ticket to a professional soccer game, only to find his team had fallen to last place by the day of the game. In all likelihood, Catherine and Amar felt pressure to attend the play or the football game to get their money's worth: to not to let the ticket go to waste." When Catherine spends the $50, she sets up an account

[32]Gourville, J. T. & Soman, D. (1998). Payment Depreciation: The Behavioral Effects of Temporally Separating Payments from Consumption. *Journal of Consumer Research, 25*(2), 160–174. https://doi.org/10.1086/209533; Soman, D. & Gourville, J. T. (2001). Transaction Decoupling: How Price Bundling Affects the Decision to Consume. *Journal of Marketing Research, 38*(1), 30–44. https://doi.org/10.1509/jmkr.38.1.30.18828; Gourville, J. & Soman, D. (2002). Pricing and the Psychology of Consumption. *Harvard Business Review, 80,* 90–96, 126.
[33]Thaler, R. H. (1999). Mental Accounting Matters. *Journal of Behavioral Decision Making, 12*(3), 183–206. https://doi.org/10.1002/(sici)1099-0771(199909)12:3<183::aid-bdm318>3.0.co;2-f; Soman, D. (2001). Effects of Payment Mechanism on Spending Behavior: The Role of Rehearsal and Immediacy of Payments. *Journal of Consumer Research, 27*(4), 460–474. https://doi.org/10.1086/319621

called "theater ticket" — much like a cost accountant would create a T-entry — with a net balance of –$50. The only way in which she (and Amar) can close their respective mental accounts without a loss is by consuming what they paid for, even when the product may not really be worth it. This phenomenon in which a prepaid amount creates a pressure to consume is called the sunk cost effect. The greater the dollars prepaid, the bigger is this pressure to consume. Interestingly, if Catherine's friend Ying was given a ticket to the same play for free, she would have been happy to forego the show after reading the negative reviews. In her case, there was no mental account in the red, and hence no pressure to consume.

The sunk cost effect has been documented extensively. In one well-known example provided by Richard Thaler of the University of Chicago, a man joins a tennis club and pays a $300 yearly membership fee. After two weeks of playing,

> **Insight Box 9.10**
>
> **MCV Insight**
> Managers price with the objective to sell. They should also think about the effect of pricing on consumption. Increased consumption results in a greater likelihood of repurchasing.

he develops tennis elbow. He continues to play (in pain) saying, "I don't want to waste the $300." In a similar vein, Hal Arkes of Ohio University ran the following experiment. He asked 61 college students to assume that they had mistakenly purchased tickets for both a $50 ski trip and a $100 ski trip for the very same weekend. These students were further told that they thought they would have more fun on the $50 trip than on the $100 trip. Finally, they were told that they had to choose one of the two trips and let their ticket to the other trip go to waste. Amazingly, more than half of the students reported that they would go on the less-enjoyable $100 trip! Arkes concluded that the greater sunk cost of the $100 trip had a greater impact on student's choices than did the higher expected enjoyment of the $50 trip.

Some of the more recent research in mental accounting results in the realization that consumption is driven not so much by the actual cost of a product, but by the perceived cost of that product, with this perception influenced greatly by the manner in which the product is priced.[34] Certain pricing policies tend to highlight the cost of a product, while other pricing policies tend to mask that cost. Consider something as simple as method of payment — cash versus credit card. A cash payment requires a buyer to physically count out currency and receive change in return, two actions that make the cost of the purchased product very salient. A $10 cash transaction feels fundamentally different than a $100 cash transaction. In contrast, a credit card payment involves the same signing of a slip of paper regardless of the size of the purchase. In many ways, a $10 credit card transaction is virtually indistinguishable from a $100 credit card transaction. As a result, paying by cash highlights the cost of the product while paying by credit masks that very same cost.[35]

9.6.1 *The Timing of Payment*

Given the linkage between perception of costs and pricing, a manager's decision of how and when to charge for goods and services can be a powerful tool to promote consumption. In particular, we believe that two dimensions matter — the "timing of price" and the "bundling of price." Organizations have at their disposal great discretion of when to bill for goods and services. For instance, some organizations require payment at or near the time the purchased product is to be consumed. Such is the case when purchasing a newspaper from the local newsstand, a Big Mac and Coke from McDonald's, or a movie ticket from Loew's Theaters. Other organizations require payment far in advance of consumption. Concert

---

[34]Gourville, J. & Soman, D. (2002). Pricing and the Psychology of Consumption. *Harvard Business Review, 80,* 90–96, 126.

[35]Soman, D. (2001). Effects of Payment Mechanism on Spending Behavior: The Role of Rehearsal and Immediacy of Payments. *Journal of Consumer Research, 27*(4), 460–474. https://doi.org/10.1086/319621.

venues and sports teams have long operated on this principle, with individual tickets to see the Rolling Stones or season tickets to see the Mumbai Indians cricket team sold long in advance of the actual events. Sellers of consumer durables similarly require payment in advance of the bulk of consumption. For instance, Sears bills for its Kenmore washers at the time of purchase even though the benefits from the washers extend long into the future. And health clubs and country clubs often charge a large up-front initiation fee for the privilege of club usage over the course of the year. Lastly, some organizations allow customers to pay long after a product is obtained and consumption has begun.

The following scenario was presented to 80 visitors to the Chicago Science Museum:

Six months ago, you noticed an ad for a theater event that you really wanted to attend. At that time, you reserved a $50 ticket and were told that you could pay for that ticket any time prior to the event. *Yesterday, you went to the box office and paid $50 cash for your ticket,* which is nonrefundable. This morning you woke up with a sore throat and headache and you think you might be coming down with the flu. The event is tonight. Do you go to the theater or do you stay at home?

Consistent with the desire to get one's money's worth, almost 60% of those surveyed reported that they would go to the theater in spite of their illness. Compare this result with that obtained from a second scenario presented to a different set of 80 visitors to the same museum:

Six months ago, you noticed an ad for a theater event that you really wanted to attend. *At that time, you went to the box office and paid $50 cash for your ticket,* which is nonrefundable. This morning you woke up with a sore throat and headache and you think you might be coming down with the flu. The event is tonight. Do you go to the theater or do you stay at home?

Note that this second scenario is identical to the first, except for the timing of the payment — the first group was told that they had paid one day prior to the event, the second group was told that they had paid six months prior to the event. This difference in payment timing was sufficient to reduce predicted consumption by half, to fewer than 30% of those surveyed. The conclusion from this, and many other sets of similar data — payments that occur at or near that time of consumption are vivid and easily linked to the consumption experience; payments that are separated from consumption tend to be masked, decreasing attention to a product's cost and consumption.

9.6.2 *Consumption Behavior at a Health Club*

Data from a prominent Colorado-based health club suggest that the effect of timing of payment mattered a lot. Gourville and Soman analyzed one year's worth of payment and attendance data for almost 200 members whose payment schedules differed in terms of timing. The goal was to see whether payment timing had any impact on club usage. The results were striking. All club members were contractually committed to a one-year membership costing $672. However, this health club's flexible pricing policies allowed members to choose between four payment plans: (1) an Annual Plan, which entailed a single payment of $672 at the start of the membership; (2) a Semi-Annual Plan, which entailed two semi-annual payments of $336 each; (3) a Quarterly Plan, which entailed four quarterly payments of $168 each; and (4) a Monthly Plan, which entailed 12 payments of $56 each at the start of every month. In addition, members were free to join at any time of the year, although most joined in January, perhaps as part of a New Year's resolution. Aside from these differences, all other factors related to membership were identical. Figure 9.13 shows the median attendance in each month from payment as a function of payment plans.

Across the board, attendance closely tracked the timing of payments. For members making a single annual payment, attendance was highest in the several months immediately following payment, reflecting a strong sunk cost effect. As that payment faded into the past and its salience decreased, however, this sunk cost effect disappeared. By the final months of membership, individuals seemed to be treating their memberships as if they were "free," attending at a rate that was less than 25% of what it had been in the first few months of membership. The same pattern holds true for members paying on a semiannual and quarterly basis. Attendance was highest immediately following payment, only to decline steadily until the next payment. In contrast to these attendance patterns, members paying monthly — where the cost of membership was salient each and every month — resulted in a strong attention to sunk costs, as reflected in a steady rate of attendance over the course of the year and an annual attendance that was 20% greater than those making payments annually or semiannually.

What does all of this mean for a health club? Health clubs, magazine publishers, sports teams, and theater companies have long encouraged customers to pay in full at the start of a subscription year, to the point of offering a substantial discount for those paying in advance. Why? Because: (1) organizations would rather have their payments sooner than later and (2) organizations believe that customers would prefer to get payments out of the way. But the research shows that this pricing practice comes at a cost. First, attendance suffers greatly in those few critical months just prior to membership renewal. It is easy to see that this is damaging when the reader asks themselves — who is more likely to renew his or her

Month of Membership													
Payment Plan	1st	2nd	3rd	4th	5th	6th	7th	8th	9th	10th	11th	12th	Total
Annual	13	12	9	9	8	7	7	5	3	3	2	4	82
Semi-Annual	13	10	7	6	4	2	12	9	8	5	2	3	81
Quarterly	10	8	6	11	7	5	9	6	5	9	6	4	86
Monthly	11	8	9	8	8	8	8	6	8	7	7	8	96

Figure 9.13 Median attendance across health club members.

membership — the Annual member who has attended 9 times in the final 3 months of membership or the Monthly member who has attended 22 times? Second, given that almost 50% of members join in January, the more frequent payment schedule of the Monthly Plan serves to smooth demand over the course of the year.

This behavioral analysis showed that rather than encourage members to pay annually, this health club should be encouraging members to pay monthly.

9.6.3 *The Coupling of Payment: Transaction and Price Formats*

In addition to the timing of payment, the other factor that influences the perceived cost is the format of the transaction. Credit card transactions feel like less of a cost than cash transactions; likewise paying one sum for a bundle of benefits dissociates the costs with each unit of consumption. A season ticket holder to the opera, for instance, might pay $400 for tickets to six Saturday evening performances. In Gourville and Soman's language, the transaction format makes it difficult to psychologically assign a cost to each performance: a phenomenon they called "transaction decoupling." Consider a well-known festival of Shakespeare plays that involves the production of four plays in repertory, each performed 16 times, for a total of 64 separate performances. Suppose we have the following data for tickets bought to this festival: (a) the date the order was placed, (b) the number of performances for which tickets were purchased, (c) the number of tickets purchased for each performance, (d) the price paid for each ticket, and (e) whether it was paid for by cash or charge. Suppose further that we have attendance data; that is, we knew whether or not a ticket holder actually attended the performance they had paid for. We would expect the "one-play ticket holder" to feel the greatest sunk cost pressure to attend the paid-for play. In contrast, we expected the "four-play ticket holder" to feel the least pressure to attend the paid-for plays. This is exactly what Gourville and Soman found. And as predicted, they also found that customers who paid cash were the most likely to attend and not let their tickets go to waste!

What about consumption of tangible products rather than intangible services? The underlying mental accounting remains the same. We offer the example of Peter and Roger, who both love a particular brand of snack. Peter tends to buy his snacks infrequently but in bulk packs, and Roger buys smaller units. In Peter's case, not only is there decoupling due to bundled pricing; but the temporal separation between paying and consuming also increases. What does mental accounting say in this case — it suggests that the cost associated with each unit of snack has decreased. Consequently, Peter is likely to need a smaller reason to consume the snack than Roger, and as a result, he will consume more. In a series of clever studies, Pierre Chandon and colleagues show that this is indeed the case.[36]

9.6.4 *Why Does Consumption Matter?*

At this stage, the reader might be tempted to say, "given that revenues are generated upon purchase, why care about consumption?" The answer is obvious. We have claimed throughout this book that for any organization, the goal should be to obtain a customer in year one and retain that customer in year two and beyond. As competitive pressures increase and as the cost of customer acquisition continues to rise, customer retention has become the foundation to long-term profitability. But — as Gourville and Soman point out — when most magazines experience renewal rates of 60% or less and

---

[36]Chandon, P. & Wansink, B. (2002). When Are Stockpiled Products Consumed Faster? A Convenience–Salience Framework of Postpurchase Consumption Incidence and Quantity. *Journal of Marketing Research, 39*(3), 321–335. https://doi.org/10.1509/jmkr.39.3.321.19111

the average health club retains only 50% of its members in a given year, there is clear room for improvement. The most critical step in ensuring renewal is to get customers to consume. Research suggests that the YMCA health club member who works out four times per week is more likely to renew her membership than the member who works out one time per week. Likewise, the Hong Kong Philharmonic season ticket holder who goes to 80% of the performances is more likely to renew his ticket package than the season ticket holder who goes to only 40% of those performances. Retaining customers from period to period is easier if those customers feel as if they have received their money's worth by consuming the purchased product.

Product consumption is no less important for organizations that rely upon a two-part revenue stream — a loss leader type of strategy. For movie theaters, sports arenas, and concert halls, ticket sales provide one source of revenue, with parking, food, and souvenir sales providing a second important source of revenues. In our conversations with managers of sporting events, they estimated that the cost for a family of four to attend a major league baseball game in 2,000 was about $120, half of which went to tickets and half of which went to parking, food, and souvenirs. If these ticket holders fail to use their tickets, these high-margin secondary sales vanish.

Some organizations view consumption as part of their core mission. For health maintenance organizations, the active consumption of periodic preventive care improves both the quality of life for those covered and the bottom line for those providing the coverage. These organizations prefer low-cost preventive care, such as immunizations and checkups, to high-cost restorative care, such as bypass surgery. And finally, consumption is at the core of any business that relies upon satisfaction to generate repeat sales and positive word of mouth. For products as diverse as books, fine wines, and tuna fish, it is unlikely that a person will become a loyal customer or a product evangelist if they purchase a product only to let it sit on the shelf.

Consumption truly matters in building a successful value ladder for the customer, and our point here is simple but powerful — in addition to just thinking about the value extraction functions of price, the manner in which it is presented can have dramatic effects on consumption.

9.7 Changing Prices and Margins from Customers over Time: Flat, Penetration, and Skimming Strategies

Thus far, we have talked about the four elements of pricing, and how managers need to understand and analyze these factors to determine not just the price level, but also the manner in which it is presented. We also looked at some examples of how prices might change with time — in particular, we looked at prices that change because levels of activity might change, as well as two-part pricing in which contracts are written such that the customer pays the organization on the basis of value as it accrues over time.

If we observe market prices for a number of goods over time and smooth out the fluctuation, we see three types of trends. The first one is a flat pricing trend, in which the base price remains constant over time, but fluctuations might occur on a day-by-day basis as a function of economic forces like temporary demand and supply fluctuations. In essence, we could model these multiple decisions as a series of demand curve optimization tasks along the lines of what we showed in Figure 9.9. However, in most real-world situations there is a fundamental difference — retention! Put differently, in each period, the organization has to "work" (say, with its price) to get some new customers, but a number of customers stay loyal to the organization over time. As a result, we can show computationally or with mathematical simulations that the optimal price in this multiple-period task is lower than the optimal price that an analysis like Figure 9.9 would suggest. The reason is intuitively simple — the lower price ensures that the organization can gather a larger number of loyal customers and keep them over a period of time.

Insight Box 9.11

MCV Insight

It is important not only for an organization to determine a price, but also to determine how it should evolve with time. If trial is driven by price and the organization can engineer a degree of loyalty, a penetration pricing strategy (initial low prices that increase with time) works best. If there are segments whose willingness to pay depends on their degree of impatience, a skimming strategy (initial high price that declines with time) works best.

We note that using analytical (formula-based) approaches to determine the optimal price result in incredibly complex analyses. For simplicity, consider a two-period problem in which an organization needs to determine the prices for its product in each of two periods given a demand curve, and a rate of loyalty. For the first period, an economist could write out an equation for profit that is a function of price as well as the square of price. This is exactly what they would do for the one-time model that we discussed earlier. But things now get trickier while thinking about the second period. Now the demand is a function not only of the price in the second period, but also the price in the first period and the loyalty rate. And the profit is a function of the price in period 1, the price in period 2, the squares of each of these as well as their product. And when we add periods 3, 4, 5, and so on, and discount these profits to yield value, the resulting equations are a comprehensive mess that is best left alone. One approach to be analytical about changing prices over time is to use a spreadsheet program to simulate different scenarios, and make some inferences based on these scenarios.

9.7.1 *Penetration Pricing*

We are more interested in two-time varying pricing patterns that organizations could strategically employ to increase value. We will refer to the first of these as penetration pricing.[37] In this strategy, introductory prices are low but increase gradually as a function of time. Prior uses of the term "penetration" have typically referred to the trend of increasing prices for a given product only, but in this discussion we broaden the use of this term in which effective prices (and margins) charged to customers increases with time. For the case of an individual customer building a relationship with a particular organization, a penetration strategy can take several forms as exemplified below. All of these specific forms are contingent on the simple general principle that our research revealed — customers are extremely price sensitive and risk averse at the entry-level stage, but their price sensitivity declines over time as their familiarity, comfort, and knowledge about the organization's products increases. Consider the following examples.

Example 1: Consider the example of the PaperPusher, as discussed earlier in this chapter. At the beginning of a relationship with a customer, they might sell printer paper in bulk at a low introductory price. After a while, they could revert to a normal price. Over time, as the customer gets used to the supplier and the services they receive, they could start offering additional services and charge activity-based prices. Over time, therefore, the effective price per unit of paper would effectively increase — but more importantly, because PaperPusher charges an activity-based fee, the margins also increase with time. The goal of the introductory low price is to acquire customers with the anticipation that they will develop loyalty to the services offered by PaperPusher and hence be willing to pay more over time.

Example 2: Consider a new restaurant that uses a low introductory pricing model but then starts charging full price to patrons after

---

[37]Monroe, K. B. (2003). *Pricing: Making Profitable Decisions*. Boston: McGraw-Hill Irwin.

their first few visits. Over time, the restaurant starts adding more expensive options to the menu. The primary goal of the low introductory price is to get customers to visit (acquisition) with the anticipation that they will learn about the quality of the food and hence are willing to pay higher prices over time.

Example 3: For a multiproduct organization, a variant of this strategy is to use different products at different steps in the value ladder of the customer. One specific example is something known as a "loss leader" strategy, in which a service is offered at a low price (sometimes even below cost) in order to attract customers that will be offered other more profitable and higher-priced services.[38] In a grocery supermarket, for example, milk and bread might be loss leaders as supermarkets aggressively advertise their low prices on these products. However, getting to the aisles which carry these products often involves walking past aisles of higher margin products. In this strategy, the goal of the loss leader is to acquire traffic to the store with the anticipation that these customers get used to shopping in the store and exposed to other product lines that the store carries.

Example 4: Many products require the purchase of a "system" and the ongoing purchases of "supplies." For instance, in the home office environment, people buy inkjet printers once but need to buy and replace ink cartridges frequently. In the domestic water purification category, people buy a pitcher once but need to purchase and replace filters on an ongoing basis. And people buy a razor once but need to purchase blades and cartridges on an ongoing basis. Research done by us — and others — shows that customers' price sensitivity to the system is significantly greater than their price sensitivity to the supplies. In the context of safety razors, Monroe notes that Gillette sold its razors relatively cheaply, knowing that "the higher price for Sensor's cartridges did not appear to scare of

---

[38] Clow, K. E. & Kurtz, D. L. (1998). *Services Marketing*. New York: John Wiley & Sons.

consumers."[39] The goal of pricing a system low — and sometimes below cost — is to create an installed base of users with the anticipation that their prince sensitivity to the supplies will be lower, and hence the organization can create valuable customers through the sale of supplies.

9.7.2 *When Does Penetration Pricing Work?*

These examples of penetration pricing are broader than earlier uses of the term. But it is important to recognize that penetration pricing strategies work only under certain conditions:

(1) These strategies are truly beneficial when price is the primary determinant of trial and acquisition. Research in behavioral economics has shown that people believe they are price sensitive, and are actually price sensitive when they can easily compare the prices of several alternatives. This typically happens at the acquisition step.

(2) Penetration strategies are also valuable when, over time, the customer gains value by learning about a product, by getting comfortable with the level of service, or by appreciating that the service truly adds value to it. In addition, once they start consuming a given product or service, inertia or *status quo* effects kick in — people do not change products unless they are compelled to — and it becomes especially hard to make price comparisons. When this occurs, prices start playing a smaller role in their decision-making and price sensitivity decreases.

(3) The customer can learn about product benefits quickly and unambiguously after trial. If no learning occurs, or if the value

---

[39] Symonds, W. C. (1998, April 27). Would You Spend $1.50 for a Razor Blade?; Gillette Is Betting a Billion That the Answer Is Yes. *Business Week*, 46, 386.

of the product to the customer is not immediately obvious, they may continue to be price sensitive.

(4) This strategy works when the organization is active in identifying and delivering new value-adding products and services over time.

9.7.3 *Skimming Pricing*

A skimming pricing pattern is the opposite of penetration pricing — it starts with a high price, and prices then drop down successively over time.[40] We discussed earlier that due to loss aversion, it is easier to reduce prices than it is to increases prices, so a skimming strategy is more easily embraced by customers. The most common examples of skimming pricing strategies are found in the markets for consumer electronics and technology products like smartphones, tablet computers, game consoles, and other mobile devices. Why does a skimming pricing strategy work?

We note that skimming strategies work particularly well in markets in which there are segments of customers that differ in their willingness to pay for a product. Consider a new innovation and think about three customers, Nina, Min, and Claire. All three of them have a fully functional device but have been caught up in the word of mouth about the new innovation. Nina is what the tabloids call a "maven" — she is one of those customers who queue up to be one of the first ones to own the innovation, and she is not particularly sensitive to the price. She would rather pay the extra price and be a trendsetter, or — in the words of Rogers, an innovator.[41] Min would also like to be one of the early adopters, but is not as

---

[40] Monroe, K. B. (2003). *Pricing: Making Profitable Decisions.* Boston: McGraw-Hill Irwin.

[41] Rogers, E. M. (1976). New Product Adoption and Diffusion. *Journal of Consumer Research, 2*(4), 290–301. https://doi.org/10.1086/208642

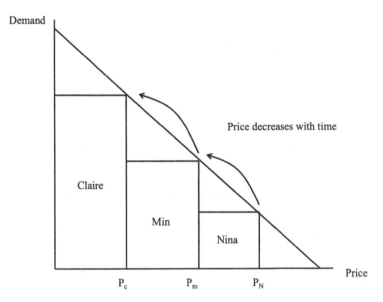

Figure 9.14 Skimming strategies.

enthusiastic as Nina. She would not queue up, and — in fact — would rather wait and make sure that the there are no complaints or concerns about the new product before putting down her hard-earned money to buy one. Her willingness to pay is lower than Nina's. Finally, while Claire has heard a lot about the new product, she is a member of the late majority who would wait and watch, and would probably only make the trip to the closest store only when she has seen enough people around her use the innovation and when she feels that the price is affordable.[42] In some categories, the delay will also allow Claire (and Min) to learn about the utility of the product and therefore increase their desire to purchase it. If Nina, Min, and Claire are each representative of a segment of customers, these three segments can be represented on the demand curve shown in Figure 9.14, where PN, PM, and PC respectively capture the willingness to pay for the three segments.

---

[42] *Ibid.*

In a situation like this, it makes sense for the organization to introduce the product at PN, wait for the whole "Nina" segment to purchase the product and then successively target the "Min" segment with PM and finally the "Claire" segment with PC.

The reader might pause and ask — "Wait, but if customers know that the organization is going to do this, would the 'Nina's' not wait till the price drops down and then purchase?" The answer is simple — if they do display such behavior, then they are not truly a member of the Nina segment. Recall that Nina is the maven, and gets value from being amongst the first to own the product without as much concern for the price! The reader who looks at Figure 9.14 will also note that what skimming pricing has done is to essentially create a price discrimination mechanism. What is the underlying basis? Impatience! The mechanism price discriminates against impatient customers, and as the figure shows it helps the organization get closer to the total contribution triangle.

What then are the conditions for a skimming strategy to be successful? We identify two, and add in other elements that talk about how best to exploit a skimming strategy. The first condition is the existence of segments within the market that vary in terms of their impatience to possess the product and the willingness to pay for the privilege of owning the product immediately. The second condition has to do with the effect of these early mavens on adoption — because these early innovators adopt the product soon and others start seeing the product being used, it creates a second level of demand through learning and through familiarization of the product. This in turn suggests that skimming might not work as well for products that are not consumed conspicuously, and for products that are not complex enough for any learning effects to occur. In making a skimming strategy successful, the organization needs to keep in mind that they need to create a media buzz in order to identify and shake out the mavens, and price sufficiently high so as to allow noticeably decreases in pricing over time.

9.8 What This All Means

In this chapter, we talked about four elements that feed into the pricing decision in a fair level of detail.

9.8.1 Guideline 1: Understand Each of the Four Elements of Pricing

It is important for the manager making the pricing decision to comprehensively understand and analyze the value of the product to the customer, the costs to serve the customer, the economics of demand, and the psychology of prices. Each of these analyses needs to be comprehensive and relevant. For instance, understanding the nature of the costs is critically important — are all the costs absorbed by the COGS (Cost of Goods Sold)? Are there activity-based costs? Likewise, value to customer may vary by segments and over time.

9.8.2 Guideline 2: Look at Variances

How should the manager determine which of the elements should play the central role in determining prices? We offered a simple heuristic: look at the locus of the variance across your customers. If there is a large variance in the activities you need to do to satisfy the needs of customers, use activity-based pricing. If there is a large variance in the benefit your customers get from the products and services, use value-based pricing. And if the transaction is a single shot, infrequently purchased item, a simple economic analysis of the demand curve will be the best approach to determine the profit maximizing price.

Irrespective of which of these three is chosen as the central driver of prices, it is critically important for the manager to put on the "customer psychology hat" and answer questions such as, "Will this pricing policy be seen as fair?," or "Can I present prices in a different way to increase purchase and therefore value?"

9.8.3 Guideline 3: Remember That the Price Decision = Determining the Price + Setting the Time Course of Prices + Price Presentation + Transaction Formats

We would like to remind the reader that in our opinion, setting a price is only a small part of the pricing decision. Once the manager has decided on a price, s/he will need to make further decisions on how those prices might change with time, how the price is presented (for instance, how price changes are framed, whether unit prices are presented, whether price is presented as a lump-sum or a per-day form), and the specific format of the transaction (e.g., the timing of the payment, the degree of bundling, and payment mechanisms). At this stage, the manager might also want to think about the possibility of price differentiation across groups of customers, keeping in mind that five conditions need to be met for effective price differentiation.

9.8.4 Guideline 4: Identify the Goals of the Pricing Decision

As we noted in the preceding pages, pricing can have three classes of effects. First, it obviously has an effect on demand — both in the present, but also in the future because of customer loyalty. Second, it creates strong incentives for particular customer behaviors. In an activity-based pricing scenario, for instance, undesirable customer behavior can be discouraged by appropriate pricing elements. And finally, the manner in which pricing is done can have significant effects on consumption. It is therefore important for the manager to clearly articulate the goals of the specific pricing decision, so that the different components (as presented in Guideline 3) can be best built to address these goals.

9.8.5 Guideline 5: Use All Four Elements in Tandem If Needed

It is important to realize that while the manager might have decided on one central element that would drive pricing decisions — say, value-based pricing — other elements could also be used in combination. Organizations that we studied and worked with provided us with a number of different examples of ways in which the multiple elements can be combined. As one example, a freight and transportation company offered services ranging from very basic package shipping services, to more complex supply chain solutions and even consulting services. This organization classified its customers into three groups. A small select group of customers had a high level of relationship with the organization — the organization actually almost acted as a part of the customer's organization by completely managing the supply chain side of the business. For these customers, the organization used a value-based pricing approach. They would negotiate with the customer the answer to the question, "If we did not manage your supply chain, what would it cost you to do it yourself," and then evolved a pricing schedule using the responses to these questions. A second set of customers were small to medium enterprises (SMEs) — manufacturing units that used the organizations' services heavily for shipping their end products. There were a large number of requests for extra pickups, just-in-time deliveries, customs support, and other such services. For these customers, the organization used activity-based pricing. And finally, there are a large number of infrequent shippers, people who send the occasional package that is often not very time sensitive. For these customers, the organization uses a demand curve analysis to set the price.

Note that this organization also has flexibility in terms of offering discounts to certain customers in this infrequent customers group — customers who the organization's customer intelligence system suspects could be small business owners and hence a potential source of more substantial value.

A second approach for combining the three approaches was exemplified by a seller of business solutions and related software products. They used different pricing approaches as a function of the customer's location on the value ladder. Entry-level customers are priced using the demand curve — with those exhibiting potential to move to the value ladder receiving additional price discounts. Over time, customers graduate to an activity-based pricing model; and assuming that the relationship matures further, they eventually move on to a value-based pricing model.

9.8.6 Guideline 6: Remember That for Managing Customer Value, Pricing is the Moment of Truth. It Lets You Balance Between VOC and VTC

Pricing is probably one of the most crucial decisions that affect the VTC, the VOC, and the balance between the two. As a walk down this chapter probably signaled to the reader, pricing involves a lot of analytics, but at the end of the day it is a subjective decision. It is a science and it is an art; it is as much about psychology as it is about economics. While the traditional demand curve-based approach is adequate for maximizing profit for a given transaction, the need to maximize a lifetime's worth of customer value adds a lot of complexity to the decisions. However, a series of systematic analysis and a detailed understanding of the relative roles of costs, value, and behavior can help the manager in making an informed and sound decision.

Chapter 10

Aligning the Organization

Alignment: (1) The proper positioning or state of adjustment of parts (as of a mechanical or electronic device) in relation to each other. (2) A forming in line. (3) The ground plan (as of a railroad or highway) in distinction from the profile. (4) An arrangement of groups or forces in relation to one another.[1]

We have deliberately used the term "managing" in the title of our book because we strongly believe that the process of creating customer value is meticulous and systematic: a process which requires a degree of active management. We sought out to answer the question of "What do we want the customer to do?" instead of the answer to the question of "What marketers should do?" In a series of chapters, we presented our framework on how organizations should (a) decompose metrics of success and define value ladders, (b) model the value, (c) manage loyalty programs by harnessing customer intelligence data, and (d) price to manage the tightrope between value to the customer and value of the customer. The focus of this chapter is to address the following question: When an organization decides to adopt the framework of managing customer value and the value ladder, what resources and capabilities does it need?

In the preceding chapters, we identified a number of competencies that an organization needs to possess in order to effectively

---

[1]Alignment. (n.d.). *Merriam-Webster.* Retrieved April 1, 2021, from http://www.merriam-webster.com/dictionary/alignment

manage customer value. For the sake of completeness, we list the following key competencies:

(1) The ability to identify customers by their potential lifetime value.
(2) The skills and tools needed to get a complete understanding of customer behavior using a variety of data sources.
(3) The ability to create and deliver targeted and specific marketing interventions.
(4) The ability — backed up by appropriate modeling skills — to create models of value to the customer and value of the customers.
(5) Deliver products that can be mass customized to customers with different needs and different locations on the ladder.
(6) Lower menu costs in order to enable the delivery of customized prices.
(7) An effective internal communication system that disseminates the results of customer intelligence to customer touchpoints.
(8) A set of marketing programs that are coupled to the customer intelligence — in particular, marketing interventions that can be triggered with relatively low costs in response to a value creating opportunity.
(9) A process for designing optimal yet customized customer experiences.
(10) The ability to be behaviorally informed and to test, learn, and adapt interventions.

How should an organization gear itself up to deliver on capabilities like these? In this chapter, we focus on four specific areas: (1) product development, (2) harnessing information technology, (3) harnessing human capital, and (4) structuring the appropriate environments and organizational structures.

We note that the advent of technology over the past 12 years has resulted in a new business model. In particular, the idea of a platform connecting buyers to sellers (or more generally demand with supply) has resulted in a new type of organization that operate in what are called "two sides markets." Companies like Uber, Airbnb, Foodora, Alibaba, Flipkart; and even Google, Twitter, and Facebook need to develop markets on both the demand and supply side. Without enough people willing to drive, it would be pointless for Uber to generate demand for rides, and likewise without enough demand, not too many drivers will be motivated to drive. Given that this balanced market development is central to the success of these companies, it is relatively easy to see why a relentless focus on customer value management is fundamental to each of these. However, the same might not be true of organizations that themselves manufacture products or services and sell to customers. Therefore, while this chapter applies equally to organizations with one-sided and two-sided markets, we will focus our examples on the more difficult problem of organizations with one-sided markets.

We would like to caution the reader that the length of the material in this chapter (vis-à-vis the rest of this book) should not be taken as a signal of its relative importance. If fact, quite the opposite is true — while organizations need a good customer management framework to serve as the bulwark of their activities, a framework alone does not suffice and the organization needs to be geared up to deliver on the promise of the ladder framework. This is where the rubber meets the road, and the ability to deliver probably differentiates organizations that merely "get it" from those that "get it and do it." The goal of this book was to focus on the framework, which — while it may vary in terms of detail — is fundamentally similar across organizations. Experts in the area of organizational strategy have written extensively about what it takes for organizations to deliver on the promise of customer centricity. In particular, we refer the interested reader to two books that illustrate some of the ideas from this chapter in greater depth.[2]

---

[2]Soman, D. & Yeung, C. (2021). *The Behaviorally Informed Organization*. Toronto, Canada: Rotman-UTP Publishing; Gulati, R. (2009). *Silo Busting: Transcending*

10.1 Customer-Focused Product Development

The focus of this entire book has been on the customer. Very early on we identified our unit of analysis as the collection of customer's multiple behavioral stages. Throughout each chapter, we have asked the readers to start from the customer in trying to understand their implicit needs and wants. In observing customer behavior, managers are not only able to extract the customer stages in the value ladder, but also capture their unspecified product or service compromises — willingness to cope with unsatisfactory products or services. It is these unarticulated compromises that managers should explore further in identifying opportunities for creating customer value. We believe that managers should identify a customer compromise first — or more generally an opportunity to add value — and then create solutions that eliminate those compromises through value creation.

An interesting example of a failed attempt at creating customer value is seen in the launch of Segway, a personal transporter for humans. The product uses electrical motors powered by phosphate-based lithium-ion batteries which can be charged from household currents.[3] The technology inside a Segway consists of an intelligent network of sensors, mechanical assemblies, and control systems that balance and move people on two wheels. The maximum speed of the vehicle is approximately 12.5 mph (20 km per hour). Despite the major publicity and hype surrounding the product prior to its launch in 2002, Segway failed to meet market expectations. Its heavy price tag did not justify the product's "perceived" value. The Segway launch has been viewed as perhaps one of the biggest failed product innovations. The idea behind Segway was first triggered when the CEO came across a young man in a wheelchair struggling to get over a curb. This experience led him to think that the

---

Barriers to Build High Growth Organizations. Cambridge, MA: Harvard Business School Press.
[3]Home page. (n.d.). *Segway.* https://www.segway.com/

problem the young man was facing wasn't due to ineffective wheel-chairs, but rather that the world accommodates for people who are able to balance. Based on our discussion thus far about customer centric, the reader should be quick to point out that perhaps his observation of the young man in the wheelchair should have inspired him to create value for wheelchair customers. Instead, Segway is targeted at "walkers" — post office workers, policemen and women, and simply anyone looking to get from one place to the next at a faster pace. The market struggled with the product's value prop-osition and was not willing to pay the heavy price tag.

What is a good general approach to designing better products and services? Earlier, we proposed the use of deci-sion mapping to design better

---

Insight Box 10.1

MCV Insight

Don't innovate and launch products or services you are capable of innovating and launching. Instead, offer value to customers.

---

interventions, products, and services. In work we have done with organizations, we have often used a simple diagram that describes what happens to our products after they are delivered to customers. Such a flowchart will allow the manager to critically examine every interaction that the customer has with a product or service, and ask if the organization can do anything to add value at any of those inter-actions. In a similar vein, the notion of empathic design[4] advocates that researchers or developers try to get closer to the lives and expe-riences of (putative, potential, or future) end users, and to apply what they learn together with end users in the design process. The goal of empathic design is to ensure that the product or service designed meets end users' needs and is usable.

In the domain of service design, a commonly used technique to identify critical touchpoints is known as service blueprinting.[5]

---

[4]Leonard-Barton, D. & Rayport, J. F. (1997). *Spark Innovation through Empathic Design*. Cambridge, MA: Harvard Business School Press.
[5]Wilson, A. M., Zeithaml, V. A., Bitner, M. J., & Gremler, D. D. (2006). *Services Marketing: Integrating Customer Focus across the Firm*. New York: McGraw-Hill/Irwin.

Service blueprinting is *a tool for simultaneously depicting the service process, the points of customer contact, and the evidence of the service from the customer's point of view.* Figure 10.1 gives the example of a service blueprint for a segment of a business-class airline passenger. Note that the blueprint makes a distinction between different phases of the service delivery process. In particular, it uses three "lines of interface." The first line represents the line of interaction — active customer touchpoints. These may include the passenger checking in their bags at the counter, the lounge attendant directing them to the business center, and the flight attendant greeting them on boarding. We referred to these personnel as front-line agents. The second line represents the line of visibility; and it demarcates the service delivery process into a zone that is visible to the customer and the zone that is not. For instance, the passenger sees and interacts with check-in agents, flight attendants, customer service representatives, and the online booking site but not with catering services, flight maintenance operations, accounting departments, and baggage handling. Within that invisible zone, there is a further line of interaction — the line of internal interaction. This line demarcates service delivery systems into a zone, which includes staff that support the front-line agents (e.g., the janitorial staff at the lounge or the baggage handlers at the airport) and other aspects of support that occur in the background as part of more general operations (e.g., maintenance and computer support).

Service blueprinting is useful for a number of reasons. First, it allows the designer to visually see the linkages between different elements of the delivery process, and therefore to design more appropriate interactions. Second, it allows the manager to identify areas of possible value additions. Third, it allows the organization to determine appropriate success metrics for each part of the interaction. Fourth, as we will discuss in a later section, it allows every employee in the organization to appreciate that they are part of the "customer value" delivery system.

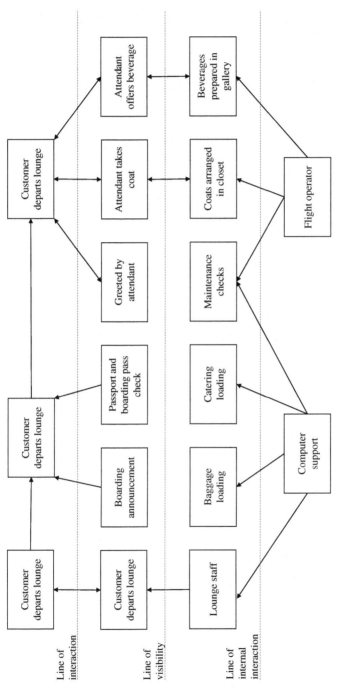

Figure 10.1 A service blueprint

10.2 Align Information Technology

The essence of a well-oiled customer-focused organization is customer data and intelligence that allows the organization to deliver efficient, specific, and targeted interventions. Customer intelligence (CI) solutions must expand across different organizational disciplines in both gathering and producing customer-related information. An effective HCI solution should be capable of standardizing the data entry process, producing insights that are universally understood by various divisions within the organization as follows:

(a) *A standardized system that enables data entry from various departments and units of the organization.* The system should be accessible by every department that comes in direct/indirect contact with the customer; in most organizations that would include just about every department. The IT department should act as an independent third party in controlling the data being inputted and ensuring integrity of the data. In most organizations the marketing and sales teams are the providers and the users of customer data and hence they may need to be incentivized to record accurate information. Hence the role of the IT department is critical in maintaining honest, real time, and relevant customer information.

The Ritz-Carlton hotel chain places a lot of importance on customer service.[6] The hotel chain's data-driven marketing system enables employees to enter unique information on each and every customer into a centrally controlled database system. The information on customers can vary from customer-stimulated requests to employee-gathered data. For example, the system will link a particular customer with various service requests such as preferred newspaper, coffee, and pillow type.

---

[6]Hemp, P. (2002, July). My Week as a Room-Service Waiter at the Ritz. *Harvard Business Review, 80*(6), 50–59.

However what sets Ritz-Carlton apart from its competitors is the non-customer-stimulated requests that exist in the database system. For example, if a cleaning staff notices that a particular guest had to rearrange the furniture in the room to take advantage of the view, they would capture that in the central information system. The next time that particular guest visits any Ritz-Carlton chain, the hotel staff can ensure that the furniture is positioned such that the guest is able to enjoy the view without having to rearrange the furniture themselves. Ritz-Carlton is an excellent example of an organization that has implemented an information technology system that enabled employees from every level and department to feel empowered in capturing the most intimate behavioral actions of their guests.

To pool the entire customer data together across the organization is an onerous task; however, it has significant payoffs. It took Harrah's Entertainment approximately six years to achieve the task.[7] Instead of investing in "must-see" casinos — elaborate structures with high-end entertainment and top restaurants — Harrah invested in its gambling business. They invested in this centralized database to enable the organization to implement some of the most nuanced reward programs in the gambling industry. Competing in an industry notorious for fickle customers — given competitor fragmentation and low switching costs for customers — Harrah's Entertainment has the most devoted clientele in the casino industry.[8]

In many ways, digital first retailers such as Everlane have built their foundation on gathering and harnessing customer insights that help them serve their customers better. Without the initial presence of physical retailer shops, Everlane relied

---

[7]Gulati, R. & Oldroyd, J. B. (2005, April). The Quest for Customer Focus. *Harvard Business Review, 83*(4), 92–101.
[8]Loveman, G. (2003, May). Diamonds in the Data Mine. *Harvard Business Review, 81*(5), 109–113.

on its comprehensive data gathering and analytics to evaluate success of its product launches and to predict the trends of its customer base.

(b) *A system which can effectively standardize the data entered such that it can easily be used in a meaningful way by different groups of individuals within the organization.* It is not enough to have different departments inputting every customer detail. The value in the information is realized only when all the employees are able to analyze the data, draw meaningful conclusions, and act on these insights. In an event where the data is being handed off from one department to another, consistency in data format is of paramount importance, as illustrated by the following example.

When the Royal Bank of Canada (RBC) — Canada's largest financial institution — was deciding the fate of one of its bundled offerings, it resorted to customer data from different departments to assess the true profitability of the bundle.[9] The bundles consisted of checking accounts, credit cards, and a bill payment service via ATMs. Despite the popularity of the bundles among customers, at first glance the analysis found 60% of the bundles unprofitable. Instead of eliminating a product liked by most customers or increasing the package price to compensate for lost profits, RBC decided to investigate each component of the bundle to identify the unprofitable piece. In doing so RBC required coordination across the different divisions (checking, credit, and ATM services) as well as cooperation between marketing strategy, product management, and finance. The marketing strategy team oversaw the project, the product management group reevaluated the bundle content and pricing, and finance provided a scenario analysis and the impact of options on organization

---

[9]Gulati, R. & Oldroyd, J. B. (2005, April). The Quest for Customer Focus. *Harvard Business Review, 83*(4), 92–101.

performance. The undertaking of the different departments to function effectively in solving a common profitability challenge is streamlined with an IT technology that can be interpreted by each group in inferring relevant insights. At the end of the project, RBC was able to allot the problem to the cost of the ATM services. By simply changing the ATM services to lower cost alternatives, RBC was able to maintain the bundle value while increasing the number of profitable bundles to 90%.

(c) *A data-driven system with systematic capabilities that can process both transactional and behavioral customer information in a meaningful manner.* It is not merely enough to expect employees to be able to interpret the data, despite a capable information technology system. For example, at Continental Airlines (now amalgamated into United Airlines), customer analysis activities were extended down to line employees who are given autonomy to focus on the customer in every possible action they undertake.[10] The organization allowed almost all employees to access customer data and to use the data in making customer-focused decisions and judgments. In doing so, Continental also offers its employees access to training and experts who can assist them in utilizing the technology and help them analyze and interpret the results.

Similarly, companies such as Stitch Fix bring personal shoppers to their customer base by assigning fashion stylist experts to each of their members. Upon taking a style quiz, each member is matched with a stylist who spends time learning about their client by sharing trending styles from Pinterest to narrow down their client's preferences. Once the stylist has a sound understanding of the client's likes and don't likes, they put together styles consisting of tops, bottoms, shoes, and accessories. Depending on the subscription model, the customer will

---

[10] *Ibid.*

receive personalized outfits every month and whatever items they don't like, they can simply mail back. Overtime, as the stylist learns more about their client's transactional (items they kept and ones they returned) and behavioral (browsing, clicks, and likes) information, they can increase their hit rate. This business model requires Stitch Fix to rely not only on data related to items that customers ultimately purchase, but also on insights about their preferences gathered through discussions with the stylists.

Insight Box 10.2
MCV Insight
You can empower employees by offering them access to customer information and allowing them to make informed decisions based on their interpretation of the data.

The key capabilities and competencies required for customer intelligence are evident. These include a robust database infrastructure that enables easy, real-time access to all customer data contained within the Customer Records. Likewise, a "single view of the customer" database design that aggregates all key customer data that the organization holds or has access to into a single, master customer record is needed. This is also critical for the development of a successful omnichannel strategy which allows the modern-day customer to have a seamless experience as they interact with the organization using multiple channels. Tools that allow data analysts and marketing personnel to do quick, real-time data queries and data visualization (e.g., charts and tables) will aid the decision-maker to make timely decisions. Integration of the customer database platform with core organization operating and transactional systems enables seamless and accurate data capture into customer records. Data management and quality processes ensure the matching of data to the appropriate customer record and the flagging of suspect records for treatment. Dedicated and skilled data analytic human resources charged with creating and disseminating "real" customer intelligence throughout the organization are also central to this effort.

10.3 Align Human Resources

The path toward a customer-focused organization is not possible without enthusiastic employee participation. In the previous section, we briefly discussed Ritz-Carlton in the context of employee empowerment and Continental Airlines in the context of employee training. In this section, we will expand on each factor through the use of examples and insights. Top executives of successful service-oriented organizations invest heavily in not just their management teams but also the front-line employees. They understand the vital role employees play in achieving gold standards in customer service. In fact, there are two dynamic areas of focus that we find critical in aligning employee motivation with organization goals, employee training, and employee incentives.

10.3.1 *Helping Employees Learn That They Are in a Customer Value Role*

Very early in this book, we made the distinction between the "customer value" function and the marketing department. The former refers to any function that is related to the creation and management of customer value whereas the latter is restricted to a small number of people whose business cards include the word "marketing" in their designation.

While a large part of this shared understanding that every employee is in a customer value role is a function of the corporate culture created and propagated by top management, it is also a function of the mindset that employees have in doing their jobs. When called on to do corporate training programs with people who are not in a traditional customer facing role (e.g., computer support, operations, or accountants), the common refrain we hear is — "Why should I care about customer value — I never interact with a customer in my role."

While we — and presumably the reader by now — know that this is not the right position to take, an employee who is deeply buried in their day-to-day computer maintenance tasks might not see things our way. In workshop sessions with support functions, we have used a simple tool that we call the "customer connection chart." A conversation during one such workshop with the computer support team of a large airline went like the following:

Facilitator (who had drawn a large circle on the whiteboard): If this circle represents your organization with customers on the outside, which employees sit at the skin of the organization?

Participants: Flight attendants, customer service agents at our call centers. …

Facilitator: Let's think about the flight attendants, what do they do to create value for customers?

Participants: They have to ensure outstanding experiences … food and beverage, in business class, they should know the names of passengers and thank them for their past business.

Facilitator: And how will they be able to do that (name of passenger)?

Participants: The onboard computer has the passenger manifest, it includes brief profiles of our best customers.

Facilitator: And who is responsible for ensuring that the data there is accurate and current?

In a similar vein, participants are pushed to develop linkages between other touchpoints to various groups that "never interact with a customer." This results in a chart that may look like Figure 10.2. At the end of a short session like this, employees quickly figure out that they are typically two or three degrees of separation

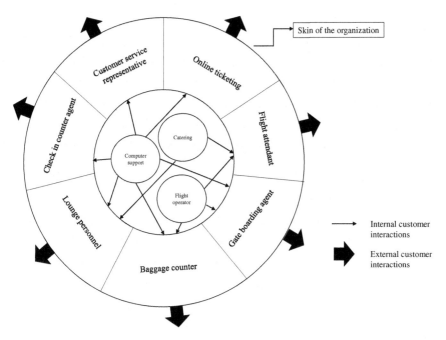

Figure 10.2 The customer connection chart

away from the customer. They are then encouraged to think about the "external customer," the customer that the organization serves and the "internal customer," the group within the organization that they serve in order to let them serve the external customer.

10.3.2 *Employee Training*

As companies become more customer oriented and move away from traditional one-dimensional structures — product/functional structure — they face the challenge of dealing with employees who are used to the traditional one-dimensional model.[11] In transitioning to a solution-based organization, managers must help employees to

---

[11] Gulati, R. (2007, June). Silo Busting: How to Execute on the Promise of Customer Focus. *Harvard Business Review, 85*(5), 98–108.

break out of their "old" habits by ensuring their involvement in the transition process, achieved through formal and informal employee training programs. To understand the relevance and the importance of employee training to customer service levels, we will review three examples of companies known for their exceptional customer service qualities.

The Ritz-Carlton is an excellent example of an organization dedicated to training its employees to walk, talk, and breathe customer focus and experience each and every day, and take pride in doing so.[12] According to Ritz, the key to a successful training is contingent is the type of people who are hired into the organization. The Ritz's look for exceptionally motivated and committed people who are willing to work outside of their realm of their job responsibility. In a similar vein, FedEx's stated recruiting policy is to "hire for attitude, and train for aptitude." Ritz's rigorous two-day job training of each new employee is followed by at least one week of job shadowing a senior employee. As a high-end, luxury hotel, Ritz strives to differentiate itself from its competitors through superior customer service. The organization lives by its motto: that if a customer asks a question, it's already too late. The employees are trained to not only serve the needs and desires of their customers but also to anticipate such needs and desires. In addition to their comprehensive information technology database which tracks each customer irrespective of the Ritz location they had visited in the past, the employees are trained to always stay aware and anticipate customer expectations. For example, when waiters take meals to guest rooms, they often try to anticipate unspecified needs such as additional utensils or cups or even special condiments to complement their meals. The employees are asked to focus on — and are explicitly incentivized for — improving the customer experience instead of focusing on how well they are performing at their jobs. The model follows the notion that by simply focusing on the customer experience first, the employee

---

[12]Hemp, P. (2002, June). My Week as a Room-Service Waiter at the Ritz, 50–59.

job performance will come through after. Ritz has recognized that employee commitment stems from employee job satisfaction and one of the means of fueling employee commitment is through training and reinforcement of its heritage and rituals.

Our second example is the electronics retailer Best Buy. In a strategic shift to a solution-based retailer, Best Buy identified five major profitable customer segments: young tech-savvy adults, busy and affluent professionals, family men, busy suburban moms, and small-business customers.[13] To ensure that each customer group was served according to their varying needs, each store was designed to specifically cater to at least one of its profitable segments. In rolling out its customer-focused strategy, Best Buy conducted extensive and customized training for employees from different stores in helping them understand their store's particular customer base. Through its Customer Centric University, Best Buy provided training at the corporate level for its senior officers who were not involved in the new strategy.

Our third example covers a convenience store chain, QuikTrip (QT), a privately held organization based in Tulsa, Oklahoma. QT has been listed as one of Fortune's 100 best places to work three years in a row.[14] Unlike other retail outlets where on average training lasts seven days, QT invests significant time up front in training new staff. New hires are partnered with "personal trainers" who have previously held the same position. The pairs work the same shift in the same convenience store for two weeks. The personal trainers act as a buddy and a mentor assisting the new hires to adjust to the pace of work and to integrate quickly into the organization's culture. QT's investment in training and employee development has helped

---

[13] Gulati, R. (2009). *Silo Busting: Transcending Barriers to Build High Growth Organizations.* Cambridge, MA: Harvard Business School Press.
[14] Bendapudi, N. & Bendapudi, V. (2005, May). Creating the Living Brand. *Harvard Business Review, 83*(5), 124–132.

the organization distinguish itself from its competitors on customer service and employee loyalty measures.

10.3.3 *Employee Incentives*

Employee incentive is a critical piece of driving any new strategy within an organization. Employee's performance metrics and reward programs must be aligned to the organization's direction and goals. In the two examples that follow, employees continuously demonstrate customer service at the heart of their day-to-day tasks and responsibilities because they are explicitly incentivized to do so.

Harrah's Entertainment increases customer service through two means[15]: (1) Use of database marketing and decision-science-based analytical tools to widen the gap between the organization and casino operator who base their customer incentives more on intuition than evidence and (2) deliver the great service that consumers demand. In many ways, the second factor is the direct result of the first. In addition to their customer intelligence strategy discussed earlier, Harrah's management decided to link employee performance metrics directly to friendliness and speed — features desired by customers. Simply put, the better the experience the guest had, the more money employees were compensated with. On top of the compensations system, employees at all levels are provided with training on how to deliver excellent service. The organization implemented a bonus plan for its employees — employees received extra cash for achieving improved customer satisfaction scores as determined by customer surveys. Harrah's bonus plan rewarded employees based on the collective results of the property's customer service scores. For example, if the casino property's overall rating increased by 3%, each employee could earn $57–$200 more. The reward in fact depended on everyone's performance, hence

---

[15]Loveman, G. (2003). *Diamonds in the Data Mine* (pp. 109–113). Boston, MA: Harvard Business Review Press.

cultivating a culture of collectiveness where employees worked together as one unit in achieving a common goal — improving customer experience.

Cisco is another example of an organization, which excels at rewarding employees on the basis of customer-service performance indicators.[16] Cisco has implemented a web-based survey to measure the pre- and post-sale satisfaction of customer service received. Survey questions focus on a customer's overall experience, perceptions of Cisco, and product-specific issues. All employee bonuses are tied directly to these customer satisfaction data, so employees are encouraged to cooperate across internal boundaries. In order to encourage collective improved performance, Cisco offers stock options to all its part-time and full-time employees.

The service blueprint that we exemplified in Figure 10.1 is a handy tool to determine what the relevant metric for service excellence should be for all employees in the organization. For each activity, the service designer could ask questions such as "What do business class customers value when they board a flight?" Responses could include efficient boarding, quick access to seats, a warm and personalized greeting, and the ability to settle down quickly in their seat. The relevant metrics for the flight attendants who are responsible for this part of the process might then be the time elapsed between boarding and reaching the seat, the tone of the greeting and whether it was personalized, the speed with which they offered to hang up the customer's coat, and the assortment and speed of offered beverages. However, the service designer would then ask

---

Insight Box 10.3

MCV Insight
Just as we're able to influence customer behavior in doing what we want them to do (increase purchase, become loyal) through incentives, we are able to do the same with employees.

---

[16]Gulati, R. & Oldroyd, J. B. (2005). The Quest for Customer Focus, *Harvard Business Review*, *83*, 92–101, 133.

"what resources does the flight attendant need in order for them to deliver on these metrics?" The responses could include the efficiency of the boarding announcements, the availability of beverages supplied by the catering department, access to the most updated passenger manifest, etc. This will allow the manager to further determine the appropriate metrics for these relevant support departments.

Another interesting problem in employee incentives occurs in the domain of multi-location service providers. Consider a hotel chain that has properties in several Asian cities. When a guest, Louis, checks into a hotel in Shanghai — a city that he does not travel to frequently — the hotel has a perfect opportunity to try and deliver an incentive to get the guest to stay at their sister property, say in Mumbai. However, this incentive comes at a cost. The Shanghai property needs to deliver excellent service, and perhaps give this guest a coupon for the Mumbai property. Similarly, a car dealership for Nissan would be better off trying to get a customer to go into another Nissan dealership for their maintenance work rather than lose the customer altogether to a private garage. The problem is this: there is currently no incentive for the Shanghai property manager and the Nissan dealership to spend money on a customer only to have them go to another location because their incentives are tied to the earnings at their location. One business that one of us worked with used an innovative approach to tackle this problem. Their customer database allowed the organization to keep track of every customer as a function of (a) whether they used a coupon while booking a hotel room; and (b) if yes, what the originating property — the location that issued the coupon — was. Using a series of relatively intuitive (but mathematically sophisticated) models, they then calculated what they called the incremental propensity of customers to visit a second location. In the hotel example, for instance, the incremental propensity is defined as "the increase in likelihood that the Shanghai guest would stay at the sister property in Mumbai as a function of being offered an incentive." The organization would then allocate a portion of the profits earned by Mumbai from this customer Louis to the Shanghai property, and create what they called a "shadow profit and loss statement" for each property. Property managers are now compensated on the basis of this shadow profit as opposed to the accounting profit.

Employees are perhaps the most integral component of the endeavor to manage customer value, and great emphasis must be placed on constructing simple yet comprehensive incentive programs which directly align employee performance metrics with customer value goals.

10.4 Align the Organization: Toward a Behaviorally Informed Organization

Having devoted nine chapters to a framework in which a comprehensive view of the customer is the foundation of the organization's activities, it is probably no great surprise that we make the following claim: traditional SBU (strategic business unit)-based organizational structures are not optimal to manage customer value.

Traditional organizational structures typically reflect the different product groups within the organization. For example, an automobile and heavy machinery manufacturer might organize itself by the different types of products they produce — say trucks, cars, and earthmoving machines. Within each business unit, the organization might be structured further along product lines and brand lines. Companies can also structure themselves by functional units, such as marketing, finance, sales, operations, and R&D. The level of efficiency and specialization is certainly evident under this departmental silo model; however, we argue that in order to become truly customer focused, organizations need to structure themselves not by products and/or functions but instead by customers.

The key to a customer-focused structure lies in the organization's ability to integrate the activities of its different product and functional departments to reflect a customer value initiative. For example, Oldroyd and Gulati give the example of the Royal Bank of Canada (RBC), where a data steering committee with representatives from all the banks' lines of businesses (investment, insurance, and banking) establishes priorities and the order in which customer information projects will be funded. This ensures that these projects are aligned with overall strategic objectives and that existing corporate roles and structures do not prohibit learning transfer.[17] RBC has not fully eliminated its departmental silos, however; it has successfully broken the barriers by coordinating across the teams that focus on customer-driven initiatives. It is also worth noting that the steering committee is given the authority to break through existing corporate structures if they impose limitations to learning transfer between the departments. Likewise, major corporations like Procter and Gamble (P&G)[18] and Citibank[19] have recently reorganized themselves in order to create synergies between managers of business units and product lines in managing customer value. While these new structures still do not allow for a perfect 360-degree view of the customer, one of the goals is to increase communication across functional and product groups.

Companies that have attempted to stretch beyond just product offerings to services (e.g., consulting, repair, etc.) have often found it challenging in converting their sales and marketing teams to offer the service solution with the product at hand. This display of reluctance results from departmental barriers which are difficult to eliminate when (a) employees feel threatened by the introduction of

---

[17] *Ibid.*

[18] Hirsch, L. (2018, November 09). P&G to restructure company as maker of Gillette razors simplifies business units. Retrieved November 19, 2021, from https://www.cnbc.com/2018/11/08/pg-to-restructure-company-as-maker-of-gillette-simplifies-units.html

[19] http://www.prdomain.com/companies/C/Citibank/newsreleases/200881960889.htm. Retrieved February 10, 2009.

unfamiliar offerings from other departments and (b) employees have not been incentivized to act in the best interest of the organization and the customer. In 2001, GE Healthcare found itself faced with similar employee conformity challenges.[20] In an attempt to offer customers enhanced solutions, GE coupled its product offering with consulting services and asked its sales team to add consulting services to their sales efforts to offer a comprehensive product to their customers. The program experienced initial success; however, it didn't take long for GE to realize that its salespeople had trouble explaining the value of its consulting services and hence were unable to contribute. Without a full integration of the two product departments or the creation of a new sales team responsible for selling the new product, GE exposed itself to silo boundaries. Customer solutions cannot be achieved by simply trying to layer on a new initiative on top of an existing product silo. GE Healthcare was able to eventually salvage the business by focusing only on the consulting services for both GE product and competitor products. However, not all organizations are willing to reevaluate their core products and to make the tough decisions that may result in the elimination of a core offering. In thinking about customer solutions instead of products, an organization may have to embrace the reality that some of its product offerings are not valued by customers.

More recently, the realization of the centrality of behavioral economics to the success of organizations has led to calls for developing behaviorally informed organizations. These are organizations that (a) recognize that their various stakehold-

Insight Box 10.4
MCV Insight
Don't expect departmental collaborations without sufficient employee involvement and training. Be prepared to actively restructure to eliminate silos.

ers are human (and not econs); (b) understand that human behavior is context dependent; (c) value the fact that there is variability across

---

[20]Gulati, R. & Oldroyd, J. B. (2005). The Quest for Customer Focus, *Harvard Business Review, 83*, 92–101, 133.

humans; (d) rely on sound empirical testing to assess the effectiveness of interventions, products, and services; and (e) believe in the test–learn–adapt approach to developing solutions. Behaviorally informed organizations not only have the ability to conduct quick testing but, importantly, the agility that allows them to change their offerings after learning from the tests. While a comprehensive discussion is beyond the scope of this book, we refer interested readers to a recent book that provides guidelines on how organizations can better embed behavioral science in their operations.[21]

10.5 What This All Means

Our goal in this chapter has been to discuss factors that are key to executing a Managing Customer Value framework. Through the discussion of the three areas of focus — information technology, employee incentives, and organizational alignment, we hope that we've been able to convince the reader of the importance of alignment in encouraging and tactically managing a customer-focused organization. We offer some prescriptive guidelines for managers.

10.5.1 Guideline 1: Offer Customers Value, Not Products

This means start with the customer. Remove yourself from product silos and think about what it is that the customer needs or wants. It is very difficult for companies who have spent decades operating in product silos to change the lens that they view their business from. Too often organizations get pigeonholed by the availability of their current products and resources, inhibiting their desire and willingness to identify customer solutions. Many marketing efforts in

---

[21]Soman, D. & Yeung, C. (2021). *The Behaviorally Informed Organization*, Toronto, Canada: Rotman-UTP Publishing.

sampling, focus groups, and trials and errors can be salvaged if only companies started with the customer in developing a new product idea.

10.5.2 Guideline 2: Think About Employees, Products, Services, and All Organizational Activities as Instruments in Moving the Customer Up the Value Ladder

Each and every critical touchpoint with the customer is an opportunity to move them up the ladder. To think about your business in terms of the service blueprint will allow you to identify the products, services, and activities that are in contact with the customer experience. The service blueprint will help managers control the internal factors that influence the customer purchase decision-making. For example, employee motivation is controlled through the organization's culture in helping employees feel valued and empowered to create value for customers in return. This can also be enhanced through employee incentives and training. Employee satisfaction will have a direct impact on customer satisfaction. Employees are part of an organization's assets that play a critical role in moving customers up the ladder; however, managers can also utilize the organization's products and services as seen in our service blueprint example. The key is to ensure that the customer experience is enhanced at each touchpoint, would it be through improved service, promotions, or products.

10.5.3 Guideline 3: Align the Purpose of Your Information Technology System to Your Organizational Goals

We're certainly not proposing that companies invest in brand new IT systems. We suspect that most companies already have in place sufficient systems; however, we are asking you to realign the purpose of your IT system to match your customer focus goals. This is not to discount the importance of pooling all sorts of customer information under a single system; however, it is more important to focus on how the retrieved data is being analyzed and who is able to analyze the data. As we saw in the case of Harrah's Entertainment, management's actions in mining and dicing the available customer information from the CRM system led to innovative customer solution initiatives around loyalty programs.

10.5.4 Guideline 4: Align Employee Incentives Directly to Organizational Goals

We cannot emphasize the importance of this guideline. Going back to the service-profit chain, a simple missed opportunity in three of the employee-related linkages will break the overall profitability chain. Employees are the organization's means of achieving a customer-focused organization. At every direct or indirect touchpoint that employees have with customers, they are making a fundamental decision about their role in achieving organizational goals. The role of incentives is to guide the employees in making the right decision to support the organization's vision at each decision node.

Chapter 11

A Practitioner's Guide to Managing Customer Value

Guide: Something that provides a person with guiding information.[1]

Over the last 10 chapters, we presented the basic elements of our framework and made the argument that a value-based approach can allow an organization to be more targeted, specific, and scientific in its marketing approach. We discussed the notions of the value ladder, and also made the point that in addition to creating value to the customers (VTC), it is important for organizations to not lose focus on the value created by its customers to the organization (VOC). To this end, we advocated for a value-based approach in making decisions about whom to focus marketing interventions on, how much to spend on different interventions, and the rigorous yet respectful use of data to make decisions about pricing and marketing more generally in the context of a digital and social world. We also presented ways in which the organization can better prepare itself to be value focused.

In this chapter, we present a practitioner's guide — a checklist of ideas, tools, and prescriptive models for how the practitioner can apply the concepts that we have discussed in this book. Several ideas from earlier chapters are discussed briefly, while additional materials

---

[1]Guide. (n.d.). *Merriam-Webster*. Retrieved April 1, 2021, from http://www.merriam-webster.com/dictionary/guide

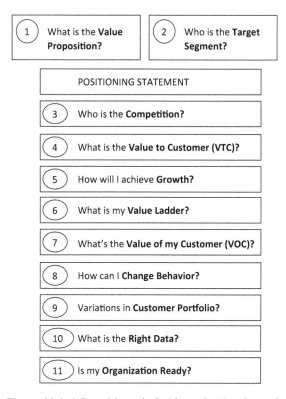

Figure 11.1 A Practitioner's Guide to Getting Started.

from a more traditional treatment of marketing strategy are also introduced. We note that while we present our guide as a linear process, in reality there is a lot of iteration and back and forth between the many steps of the process. Figure 11.1 captures a highly simplified, stylized version of the 11-step framework process.

We describe each of the eleven stages as questions that the manager should ask. Note that the process starts with an analysis of the product and the customer. In theory, an organization could start by identifying a particular group of customers as the group they want to serve, and then proceed to develop products and services for that group. In practice, this rarely happens. New ventures are funded on the basis of a product they have developed and are looking to launch, while more established organizations already have established products. Therefore, in reality, the process usually starts with a product. However, Questions 1 and 2 could be interchanged in sequence without a loss of generality.

11.1 An 11-Step Framework Process to Managing Customer Value

11.1.1 *Question 1. What Is My Value Proposition?*

In thinking through going to market strategies for a particular product or service, the four set of questions that the manager needs to ask are: What are the positive and negative differentiators of my product? A positive differentiator is any dimension on which the product outperforms alternatives, and a negative differentiator is one in which the product is outperformed by competitive options.

Knowing the relative strengths and weaknesses of the product or service will allow the manager to best select the appropriate group of people to serve with that particular product or service. The other question that needs to be answered at this stage is — in the grand scheme of the value-based strategy, what role does the particular product play? For example, is it a product designed to simply acquire a customer without regard for the profitability associated with the product (e.g., a loss leader)? Or, is it a product that is designed to grow and create value for the customer and therefore make them a loyal customer? Knowing the precise role of a product in the strategy will allow the manager to develop appropriate metrics to gauge its success.

11.1.2 *Question 2. What Is My Target Segment?*

The act of segmentation refers to the act of dividing a universe of potential customers into discrete groups or segments, such that the behavior of members of any one group within each segment is similar to each other and across segments is as dissimilar as possible. Note that when we talk about the similarity of behavior, we refer to behavior toward the particular product or service category. Segmentation can be achieved in a number of different ways. It could be done on the basis of demographics (or firmographics), psychographics (attitudes or lifestyles), geographic or behavioral (on the basis of other behaviors that a potential customer displays, types of usage).

Once the universe has been segmented into different groups, the manager must now decide which group or groups they would like to serve with a particular product. Obviously, some logistical constraints might dictate which groups can be served and which ones cannot. For example, exorbitant shipping costs or competitive activity in some geographies may render it impossible or highly difficult to serve those markets. In situations where there are no constraints, the manager should use a product-market fit analysis. In this analysis, the manager lists the key positive and the key negative differentiators of the product along the rows and the various segments along the columns. In each cell, the manager can use research to make a judgement about how important or valuable that particular differentiator is to the target segment. The ideal target segment is one for whom the positive differentiator adds value but the negative differentiator does not detract from the perceived value.

In the 1990s, a flower delivery company called Calyx & Corolla introduced a new distribution model.[2] Unlike the traditional florist where flowers that have been cut and delivered through the supply chain can take about seven or eight days before a customer can

---

[2]Jaworski, B., Kohli, A. K., & Sahay, A. (2000). Market-Driven versus Driving Markets. *Journal of the Academy of Marketing Science, 28*(1), 45–54. https://doi.org/10.1177/0092070300281005; Jaworski B., Kohli A.K., & Sahay A. (2000). Market-Driven Versus Driving Markets. *Journal of the Academy of Marketing Science, 28*(1), 45–54.

choose them, the Calyx model allowed customers to pre-order flowers which would then be cut and shipped by Federal Express. This allowed the recipient to get flowers that were long-lasting — because they had not wasted a few days in the supply chain. On the flip side, the flowers arrived in a courier box and therefore took a bit of effort to make them look aesthetically pleasing. Table 11.1 shows the product-market fit analysis for this offering. Businesses such as hotels and restaurants turn out to be the ideal target for this

Table 11.1 A product-market fit analysis.

	Gifts Segment	Household Purchasing Segment	Businesses Segment (Hotels, Restaurants)	Weddings/ Funerals Segment
Segment characteristics	Small, infrequent individual purchase, high willingness to pay, aesthetics is key	Small, frequent (ongoing) individual purchases Price conscious	Large, frequent purchases, high spends on flowers, housekeeping staff responsible for arrangements	Infrequent but large purchases, additional services important, flowers need to look fresh for one day
Key positive differentiator — longer life of flower	Research shows aesthetics matters more than life	Longer life will add value	Highly beneficial — doubling flower life will halve budget	Long life is irrelevant to this segment
Key negative differentiator — flowers received in a box	Aesthetics very important, hence this is a big negative	Potentially a negative, but flower lovers don't seem to mind the effort	Housekeeping staff can handle arrangements, not a big problem	Need for service is high, this could be a big negative
Product-market fit assessment	Poor fit	Good fit	Excellent fit	Poor fit

Summary: The business segment (hotels and restaurants) offers the best product-market fit. The positive differentiator adds value to it, the negative does not detract value.

offering because the value of the product to these businesses is economical — by doubling the life of the flower, these businesses can halve their flower budget.

11.1.3 *Question 1 and 2. Together Raise a Corollary Question — What Is the Positioning Statement of the Product?*

Positioning statements capture and encapsulate the value of a product to the appropriate target segment. Figure 11.2 provides a template for writing positioning statements and also provides a sample positioning statement for the Calyx & Corolla example that we just discussed.

11.1.4 *Question 3. Who Is My Competition?*

At first blush, it is tempting for an organization to believe that their closest competitors are those organizations that produce a product or service that looks superficially the same as their own. However, we contend that is a very narrow way of looking at competition. A broader look at competition might entail questions such as the following:

- Who else has a big share of the wallet of my target segment? In other words, now that I know who my target segment is, where are they spending their money?
- If people buy my product or service, what will they buy less off?
- What is the highest level of competition for my product? For instance, a theme park like Disney World might think about other theme parks as its competition. Alternatively, they could think about other travel destinations as their competition. At the

POSITIONING STATEMENT: Format	
Target Market:	[Who is the intended target]
Core Benefit:	[The primary positive differentiator]
Other Benefits:	[Other differentiators]
Support:	[Specific actions by organizations that are designed to ensure the delivery of these benefits]
Competitive Advantage:	[General actions by the organization that strengthen its ability to compete]

POSITIONING STATEMENT EXAMPLE: Flower Delivery	
Target Market:	Hotels, restaurants, other hospitality businesses
Core Benefit:	Significantly reduce flower budget by delivering flowers with longer life
Other Benefits:	Wide assortment of flowers, customizable assortments
Support:	Contract with courier company that assures next-morning delivery.
Competitive Advantage:	Strong relationships with growers

Figure 11.2 A template for writing positioning statements.

Source: Adapted from teaching notes prepared by Professor David Dunne, University of Toronto and used with his permission.

highest level, they could think about all other entertainment options as their competition.

The broadest way of conceptualizing competition is often the most useful because it allows the manager to creatively think about what choices the target customer will need to make.

11.1.5 *Question 4. What Is My Value to the Customers (VTC)?*

After articulating the broad value proposition in Question 1, we encourage the manager to now think about the specific properties of the value proposition. Is the value that the product creates economic or is it experiential? What is the locus of the value — is it internal (i.e., is it apparent during consumption of the product) or is it external (i.e., does it show up outside of the consumption experience)? As Chapter 2 indicated, the answers to these questions will have implications for a number of going to market questions. For example, it might be easier to demonstrate economic value *a priori* relative to experiential value. Likewise, certain approaches to pricing can be used for economic value (e.g., value-based pricing) but not for experiential value.

11.1.6 *Question 5. How Can the Organization Achieve Growth?*

Perhaps, the oldest and most simple framework for understanding growth strategies is the Ansoff-matrix framework.[3] This simple framework postulates that organizations can grow in one of two ways — they can either expand their product/service offering, or they can expand to new marketplaces (new geographies, new segments). The combination of these two approaches results in four different strategies that are captured in Figure 11.3.

While the product development, market development, and diversification strategies are fairly intuitive to understand, we would like to dwell on market penetration. This refers to a strategy in which a company can grow without adding new products or services and without moving to new markets. Growth in this quadrant can be achieved in a number of different ways. The first way is simply to

---

[3]Meldrum M. & McDonald M. (1995). The Ansoff Matrix. Concept 24. In *Key Marketing Concepts* (pp. 121–126). Palgrave, London. This is a book written by Meldrum and McDonald, it has a series of short chapters called "Concepts".

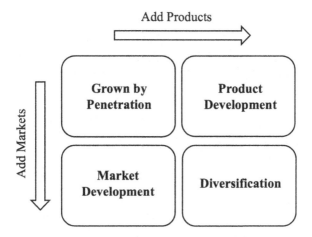

Figure 11.3 The Ansoff matrix — growth strategies.

increase the cumulative volume of purchase. Using the retail metaphor that we discussed earlier in Chapters 3 and 4, this might mean an increase in the frequency of purchasing or the volume of purchasing per frequency. A second approach is to use strategies for increasing the basket size through cross-selling and upselling. It is important for every organization to clearly understand how they would like to grow. There are a lot of gains to be made in a penetration strategy by adding value to existing customers over time.

11.1.7 *Question 6. What Does My Value Ladder Look Like?*

The concept of a value ladder is central to our framework. In building value ladders, we propose that managers first identify what their ideal customer looks like and what behaviors are associated with this ideal customer. For instance, for a retail bank, a good customer might have basic bank accounts, credit cards, a mortgage, as well as wealth management services, and they might prefer to conduct most of their business online or via an app. These customers have high revenue potential and low costs to serve — a "star" customer (see also Table 2.3 "Behaviors of 'Good' and 'Bad' Customers" and Figure 2.5 "Customer Portfolio Matrix").

The manager then needs to think about several discrete steps between a non-customer (a prospect) and this ideal customer. Each step needs to correspond to a different set of behaviors as compared to the immediately previous step. As discussed earlier in Chapter 3, the optimal point for different segments on a particular ladder might vary.

Managers should clearly articulate their value ladders both at the aggregate level (the transition of customers over a longer period of time from a prospect to potentially an ideal customer), as well as a more specific decision-related ladder (e.g., a funnel by which the organization can move people from being non-believers in a product or a service to being loyal users of that product or service).

11.1.8 *Question 7. How Can I Assess the Value of My Customers? What Is the VOC?*

Managers need to be able to categorize their customer as a function of their quality because it allows them to be specific and targeted with marketing interventions. In particular, it allows them to target the right interventions to the right group of people so as to engineer the right behavior change.

In making a determination of how to assess the value of customers, the manager could first ask themselves if they have the data to use discounted cash flow techniques, like the ones discussed in Chapter 5. If not, could revenue be used as a good proxy? Revenue might be a good proxy in situations where the average cost to serve each customer is roughly the same. However, if there is a lot of variability in cost to serve, then the manager might consider using a customer portfolio approach (see Figure 2.5 "Customer Portfolio Matrix"), as a way of assessing customer quality.

11.1.9 *Question 8. How Do I Move Customers Up the Value Ladder? How Do I Change Their Behavior?*

As discussed previously, decisions on whether or not it makes sense to move people up the value ladder are best made through the analysis of the incremental value that such a move would achieve versus the incremental cost of how that move is made. However, it is critically important to understand the psychology of the end user to determine how the move should actually be made.

In Chapter 6, we identified two central principles of engineering behavior change. First, we spoke about approaches to behavior change — restrictions, incentives, information, and choice architecture. Figure 11.4 provides examples of these four approaches. Second, we outlined a process of design interventions to stimulate

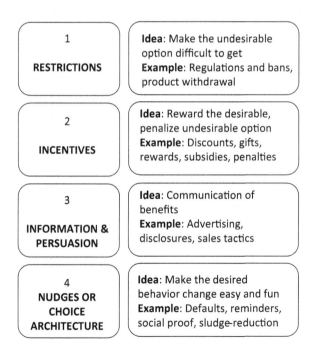

Figure 11.4 Four approaches to behavior change.

behavior change. This process involves the decomposition of the decision-making process into discrete stages and an identification of friction points that might prevent people from making the behavior change.

Prior to mapping out the customer journey, it is also important to audit the decision environment. Table 11.2 provides a list of questions that the manager could ask as part of the auditing process, and Table 11.3 provides a list of important behavioral phenomena and ways to determine why the desired behavior change does not happen.[4]

11.1.10 *Question 9. Where Is the Variation in My Customer Portfolio?*

Understanding the variation in the customer base is critically important because it allows the manager to decide how to deploy various sets of activities across their customer bases. One form of variation across customers might be in the effort required by the organization to satisfy the needs of those customers. If this is the case, the manager needs to: (a) incorporate a model of activities and think through how the activity sets will be different for each segment of customers, and (b) use approaches like activity-based pricing to capture the differential costs across customers.

A second source of variation could be in the value that customers get from the product or service. This variation might happen because of a difference in the cost structure of the customers. If this variability is high, then the manager might need to think about value-based approaches to pricing.

---

[4]Tables 11.2 and 11.3 were part of Appendices 1 and 2, respectively, in Soman, D. (2015). *The Last Mile: Creating Social and Economic Value from Behavioural Insights.* University of Toronto Press. Reprinted with permission of the publisher.

Table 11.2 A checklist for auditing the decision context.

Properties of the Decision

1. Is the decision important to the individual or does it receive little attention?

2. What moments or events motivate an individual to act on the decision?

3. Is this an active or an automatic, passive choice?

4. How many options are available? What is the default option if an individual decides to do nothing?

5. Is feedback available and is it received immediately?

6. What are the incentives? Which ones are most prominent, which ones are not?

7. What are the associated costs (financial, social, and psychological)?

Information Sources

1. What knowledge or expertise is needed to make a decision?

2. How is information or knowledge communicated to the individual (visually, verbally, in text)?

3. Does the information flow sequentially? What information is presented first? Presented last?

Features of the Individual Mindset

1. Are the benefits of making a good decision delayed or experienced immediately?

2. Is the decision usually made when the individual is in an emotional state?

3. Does the decision require exertion of willpower or self-control (such as in the domains of smoking, dieting, exercising)?

Environmental Factors

1. Is the decision made in isolation or in a social environment?

2. Is the decision influenced by what is presented in the media or by expert opinions?

3. Are peers a major source of information?

4. Is there an application process and is it difficult to navigate?

11.1.11 *Question 10. Do I Have the Right Data to Make Appropriate Marketplace Decisions?*

Data is central to managing customer value. Having the right data to assess the value of the product to the customer as well as of the

Table 11.3 Key behavioral phenomena and nudging concepts.

Term	Idea in Brief	Illustrative Examples
Active choice and enhanced active choice[a]	Highlighting the fact that a decision needs to be made increases the attention paid to the decision-making process. This is especially useful for choices which are typically passive (e.g., Getting a flu shot, renewing a health club plan, donating organs). Enhanced active choice refers to the presentation of options that highlight the cost of making a "no" choice.	Rather than waiting for individuals to stop by a clinic to get a flu shot, they could be actively asked whether they intend to get one (active choice). Alternatively, they could be presented with two options: (a) yes, I will get a flu shot and protect me and my family, or (b) no, I am willing to expose myself and my family to the risk of disease. The likelihood of getting a flu shot should increase with active choice, and further increase with enhanced active choice.
Asymmetric dominance/decoy[b]	Consider two options that vary on two attributes. A is better than B on attribute one, but not as good on attribute two. Adding a third option, B*, that is worse than B on both attributes shifts choices toward B. B* can be called a decoy because it is not really preferred, but shifts choices among the other two.	A consumer cannot choose between two headphones. A has a sound quality index of 100 and a comfort rating of 50. B has a sound quality index of 50 and a comfort rating of 100. The addition of a third headphone B* with a 40 sound quality index and a 90 comfort rating will increase his likelihood of choosing B.
Automatic enrolment[c]	Automatically enrolling people in benefit programs or provident funds but giving them the option of withdrawing increases the likelihood that they will continue to participate.	Company A requires all employees who want to participate in their benefits program to sign a form and send it to the human resources department.

		Company B automatically enrolls all employees into an identical benefits program, but allows them to withdraw with no penalties by signing a form and sending it to the human resources department. In the long run, company B has a significantly higher participation rate in its benefits programs.
Choosing versus rejecting[d]	The manner in which people are asked to choose between two options can change the information they use in making the decision. In particular, asking people to choose between A and B results in people focusing on reasons to choose (positive aspects), while asking them to reject A or B results in them focusing on reasons to reject. (Negative aspects.)	A manager is looking to hire one of two job candidates. Mr. A is average on all four relevant attributes, while Ms. B is outstanding on two and weak on the other two. When the manager chooses between the two, B tends to be preferred over A (there are more reasons to choose B). When the manager is rejecting one of the two, B tends to get rejected more often (there are more reasons to reject B).
Compromise effect[e]	When people choose between three options that vary along two dimensions, the option in the middle (which is average on both dimensions) tends to get chosen more often. Conversely, the likelihood of choosing an option can be increased by making it the "compromise" option. This effect is particularly strong for options where it is difficult to evaluate quality.	(1) A gas station sold 89 and 91 octane petrol. The sales of 91 went up after they introduced a 94 octane grade, because 91 now became the "compromise" option. (2) In most coffee shops offering three sizes of beverages, the medium is the most popular size.

(Continued)

Table 11.3 (*Continued*)

Term	Idea in Brief	Illustrative Examples
Decision points[f]	People often start consumption episodes with a decision to consume, but then passively continue consumption 'till they hit a constraint. Inserting an opportunity to pause and think about the consumption in an active manner (a decision point) will increase vigilance and hence, the likelihood that consumption stops. Decision points could take the form of reminders, small transaction costs, or physical partitions.	Mr. X is given a large bucket of popcorn. Mr. Y has the same quantity of popcorn in four equal bags. Assuming that they are both conscious of the need to control consumption, Mr. Y will consume less than Mr. X.
Defaults: opt-in versus opt-out[g]	The default choice in any decision task refers to the outcome that would happen if the individual did not make a choice. If the likelihood that people will choose not to choose is high, making a desired outcome the default will increase the likelihood of it being chosen.	(1) In Canada, citizens wishing to donate organs must follow a procedure to get registered. In France, the assumption is that everybody will donate organs, but citizens wishing to not donate can follow a procedure to get deregistered. Organ donation rates are significantly higher in France than in Canada. (2) In country A, credit card applicants must sign a consent allowing for their mailing address to be shared on a mailing list. In country B, applicants need to sign to prevent their addresses from being on a mailing list. The average citizen in country A receives a lot less junk mail than in country B.

Earmarking[h]	Money that is designated toward a particular cause is more likely to be spent on that cause. Earmarking can be achieved by physically segregating money.	Laborers in India were given a savings target of Rs. 40 per pay period. Some of them were encouraged to earmark Rs. 40 by putting it in a separate envelope. These laborers were more likely to save.
Framing: gain versus loss (loss aversion)[i]	Presenting the same outcome as a loss has a greater psychological effect than presenting it as a gain.	(1) When a 3% credit surcharge was framed as a cash discount, the price difference between paying by credit cards and cash was seen as more acceptable. (2) In one neighborhood, employees of a utility company tried to convince households to purchase energy-efficient appliances saying "If you use these appliances, you will save \$10 per month." In a second neighborhood, this statement was changed to "If you fail to use these appliances, you will lose \$10 per month." The likelihood of purchasing was significantly greater in the second neighborhood.
Peer programs and social comparisons[j]	Making a commitment in the presence of peers increases the likelihood that the commitment will be followed by appropriate action. Also, the presence of peers who have high levels of accomplishment increases the motivation to similarly increase accomplishment.	(1) Members of a self-help group savings program increase their savings rate when their peers routinely meet to discuss progress and outcomes. (2) Households in the UK were sent letters encouraging them to pay taxes on time. When these letters included a statement of peer performance (e.g., "9/10 people in the UK pay their taxes on time") the letters were more effective.

(Continued)

Table 11.3 *(Continued)*

Term	Idea in Brief	Illustrative Examples
Precommitment[k]	When people view events that are in the future, they are more likely to be rational and wise about their choices. When the same events are in the present, people act impulsively and make foolish choices. Therefore, the best way of nudging people to make wise choices is to ask them to commit to making those choices for the future.	Employees in an organization were asked if they would like to increase their savings rate in the future. Most agreed, and committed to setting aside a proportion of their future salary increase into a separate savings account. These people who were asked to save more saved significantly more than people who worked with a traditional financial advisor.

[a] Keller, P. A., Harlam, B., Loewenstein, G., & Volpp, K. G. (2011). Enhanced Active Choice: A New Method to Motivate Behaviour Change. *Journal of Consumer Psychology, 21*(4), 376–383. https://doi.org/10.1016/j.jcps.2011.06.003

[b] Tversky, A. & Kahneman, D. (1974). Judgment under Uncertainty: Heuristics and Biases. *Science, 185*(1124), 1128–1130.

[c] Madrian, B. & Shea, D. (2000). The Power of Suggestion: Inertia in 401(k) Participation and Savings Behaviour. *NBER Working Paper No. 7682.* https://doi.org/10.3386/w7682

[d] Shafir, E. (1993). Choosing versus Rejecting: Why Some Options Are Both Better and Worse than Others. *Memory & Cognition, 21*(4), 546–556. https://doi.org/10.3758/bf03197186

[e] Simonson, I. (1989). Choice Based on Reasons: The Case of Attraction and Compromise Effects. *Journal of Consumer Research, 16*(2), 158. https://doi.org/10.1086/209205

[f] Soman, D., Xu, J., & Cheema, A. (2010). A Theory of Decision Points. *Rotman Magazine, Winter 2010.*

[g] Johnson, E. J., & Goldstein, D. (2003). Do Defaults Save Lives? *Science, 302*(5649), 1338–1339. https://doi.org/10.1126/science.1091721

[h] Soman, D. & Cheema, A. (2011). Earmarking and Partitioning: Increasing Saving by Low-Income Households. *Journal of Marketing Research, 48*(SPL), https://doi.org/10.1509/jmkr.48.spl.s14

[i] Kahneman, D. & Tversky, A. (1979). Prospect Theory: An Analysis of Decision under Risk. *Econometrica, 47*(2), 263. https://doi.org/10.2307/1914185

[j] Kast, F., Meier, S., & Pomeranz, D. (2018). Saving more in groups: Field experimental evidence from Chile. *Journal of Development Economics, 133*(C), 275–294

[k] Thaler, R. H. & Benartzi, S. (2004), Save More Tomorrow: Using Behavioural Economics to Increase Employee Saving. *Journal of Political Economy, 112,* 164–187.

customer to the organization is critical for executing the value-based approach. However, we cautioned the reader from indiscriminately using data without considering the implications that might have for customer privacy. Has that data been collected ethically, fairly, and respectfully? Will it be used in a manner consistent with what the customer has consented to share it for?

We also highlight that simply having data does not mean that the manager has evidence. The applications of data that we discussed in earlier chapters allowed the organization to (a) assess value, and (b) be specific and targeted with its interventions. But the organization often needs to evaluate the effectiveness of its marketing interventions, and needs to go beyond data to collect evidence. Data is descriptive — it allows the manager to see what is happening. But evidence also allows a manager to understand why something is happening. One of the best ways of collecting good evidence to see whether a marketing intervention is working is to conduct an experiment.

In its simplest form, an experiment involves the comparison of outcome variables of interest across two or more "conditions" that might differ on only one dimension. In an A/B test, for instance, an online retailer might be interested in seeing whether a graphic element on a landing page increases the likelihood of clicking through to the purchasing page. This retailer might randomly serve the basic landing page to about half the customers who arrive on the landing page (the "A" condition) and the same landing page with the graphic element to the other half (the "B" condition). The act of randomization should ensure that the two conditions are ideally matched on other dimensions — for example, the distribution of when customers arrived on the landing page, the distribution of gender and other observable factors, etc. — but the retailer should also be able to confirm this by looking at the data. If the retailer now sees that the click through rate in Condition B is greater than in Condition A, they can be assured that the difference could be attributed to the sole factor that was different across them; the presence of the graphic element. A comprehensive discussion of the different types of experiments is beyond the scope of this book, but we refer the interested reader elsewhere.[5]

11.1.12 *Question 11. Is the Organization Ready for a Value-Based Approach?*

As discussed in Chapter 10, much work needs to be done to align the organization to be able to deliver on the promise of the value-based approach. In particular, we alert the manager to address the following questions:

- Is the product development process aligned to create value? Does it leverage insights from design thinking and behavioral science?
- Does the data backbone of the organization ensure that the right data and evidence is available to the right people/departments at the right time? Does it present a full view of the customer?
- Do my employees all understand their role in creating customer value, and therefore creating value to the firm? Are their incentives aligned with a customer value management approach?
- Is my organization as behaviorally informed as it could be? Does it embrace the test-learn-adapt approach?

A final question — and an important one — relates to the central philosophy of our approach: Does the organization see its customers as assets? Is it creating products and services for its most valuable customers, or does it still see customers as mere purchasers of its products? To be truly successful, organizations need to see themselves as having a relationship with customers over time rather than having a simple transaction mentality.

---

[5]Chapter 7 in Soman, D. (2015). *The Last Mile: Creating Social and Economic Value from Behavioural Insights.* Toronto, Canada: University of Toronto Press.

Name Index

Subject Index

Printed in the United States
by Baker & Taylor Publisher Services